A

VOLCANO

BENEATH

THE

SNOW

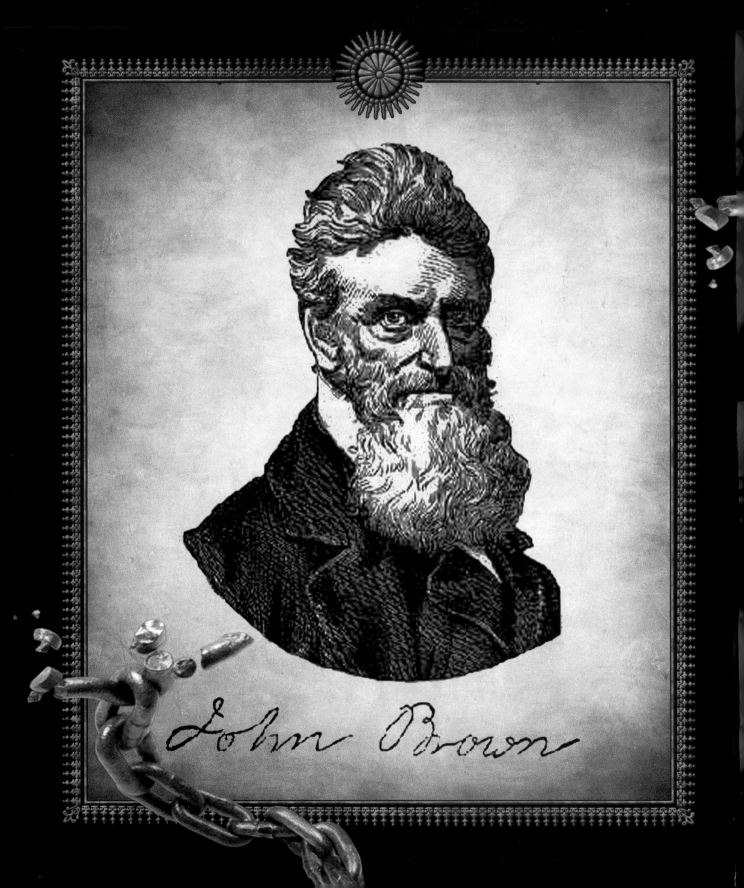

John Brown

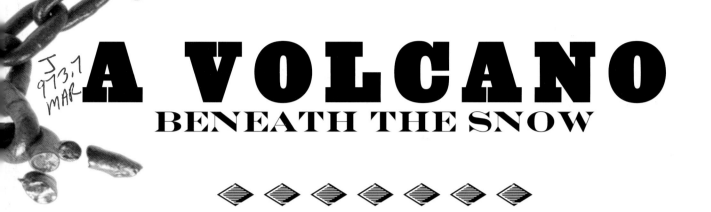

A VOLCANO
BENEATH THE SNOW

◆ ◆ ◆ ◆ ◆ ◆ ◆

JOHN BROWN'S WAR
AGAINST SLAVERY

◆ ◆ ◆ ◆ ◆ ◆ ◆

Albert Marrin

ALFRED A. KNOPF
New York

To the memory of Frederick Douglass, American hero

THIS IS A BORZOI BOOK PUBLISHED BY ALFRED A. KNOPF

Text copyright © 2014 by Albert Marrin

Jacket photographs: shackles © 2014 by the National Civil War Museum, Harrisburg, Pennsylvania; flags and border © 2014 by Shutterstock.com

All rights reserved. Published in the United States by Alfred A. Knopf, an imprint of Random House Children's Books, a division of Random House LLC, a Penguin Random House Company, New York.

Knopf, Borzoi Books, and the colophon are registered trademarks of Random House LLC.

For image credits, please see page 234.

Visit us on the Web! randomhouse.com/teens

Educators and librarians, for a variety of teaching tools, visit us at RHTeachersLibrarians.com

Library of Congress Cataloging-in-Publication Data

Marrin, Albert.

A volcano beneath the snow : John Brown's war against slavery / Albert Marrin. — 1st ed.

p. cm.

Includes bibliographical references and index.

ISBN 978-0-307-98152-3 (trade) — ISBN 978-0-307-98153-0 (lib. bdg.) — ISBN 978-0-385-75340-1 (ebook)

1. Brown, John, 1800–1859—Juvenile literature. 2. Abolitionists—United States—Biography—Juvenile literature. I. Title.

E451.M352 2014

973.7'116092—dc23

[B]

2012043231

The text of this book is set in 11-point Times.

MANUFACTURED IN CHINA

April 2014

10 9 8 7 6 5 4 3 2 1

First Edition

ALSO BY ALBERT MARRIN

Flesh & Blood So Cheap:
The Triangle Fire and Its Legacy

Black Gold:
The Story of Oil in Our Lives

ME.

VT.

N.H.

N.Y.

MASS.

R.I.

CONN.

WIS.

MICH.

PA.

N.J.

ATLANTIC OCEAN

ILL.

IND.

OHIO

MD.

DEL.

VA.

KY.

TENN.

N.C.

S.C.

MISS.

ALA.

GA.

FLA.

GULF OF MEXICO

Free state or territory

Slave state or territory

Territory open to slavery

0   Miles   300

CONTENTS

God give us angry men in every age,
Men with indignant souls at sight of wrong,
Men whose whole being glows with righteous rage,
Men who are strong for those who need the strong.

—Charles M. Sheldon, "God's Angry Man," 1910

Prologue
A House Dividing

On June 16, 1858, a man, by profession a lawyer, stood before a political meeting in Springfield, Illinois. Nobody could call him handsome; indeed, he admitted with a smile, he was downright ugly. Thin as a twig, with big ears, coarse facial features, and sunken cheeks, he was unusually tall. Standing six feet four inches in his socks, he reminded folks of a skeleton, with skin covering the bones and clothes covering the skin.

What captured the audience's attention, however, was not Abraham Lincoln's appearance, but his words. "'A house divided against itself cannot stand,'" he said in a high-pitched voice. "I believe this government cannot endure, permanently half *slave* and half *free*. I do not expect the Union to be *dissolved*—I do not expect the house to *fall*—but I *do* expect it will cease to be divided. It will become *all* one thing, or *all* the other. Either the *opponents* of slavery will arrest the further spread of it . . . or its *advocates* will push it forward, till it shall become alike lawful in *all* the States, *old* as well as *new*—*North* as well as *South*."[1]

The "house" Lincoln meant was the Union—that is, the union of states, or the United States of America, created by the U.S. Constitution. The future sixteenth president said this during a crisis unlike any since July 4, 1776, when representatives of Britain's rebellious colonies issued the Declaration of Independence.

While Americans had finally overthrown British rule, they now faced a greater challenge. By 1858, no foreign power could conquer their country. The threat lay within, from a bitter quarrel over slavery between Northern and Southern states. The issue was as clear as black ink splashed on freshly fallen snow. Americans could no longer dodge *the* moral challenge of the age. They must take a stand on slavery, though whatever stand one person took was bound to infuriate others. That fury, in turn, threatened disunion, a breakup of the country that would lead to civil war.

Yet fear of disunion over slavery was as old as the Union itself. It had haunted the Founding Fathers, and none more than George Washington. One day in the summer of 1798, he met John Bernard, an English actor touring Virginia. The ex-president invited Bernard to visit Mount Vernon, his estate. While they relaxed in a parlor overlooking the Potomac River, a black "servant" set a jug of cool water on the table. As he did, Bernard smiled, seeming to ask a silent question. Washington understood. Yes, he said, he owned slaves, always had. Meanwhile, Bernard recalled, his host's eyes "burned with a steady fire." Finally, Washington said: "I can clearly foresee that nothing but the rooting out of slavery can [save] our union." In short, slavery must die so America could live.[2]

Sixty years later, as Abraham Lincoln spoke in Illinois, Americans worried about what Senator William Henry Seward called the "irrepressible

Abraham Lincoln on October 1, 1858, less than four months after his famous "House Divided" speech.

conflict." A nationwide explosion, they felt, was inevitable, though nobody could tell exactly when or how it would come about, or who might ignite it. Slavery seemed to have the power to drive otherwise sensible people out of their minds. Politics had turned poisonous over it. With few exceptions (Lincoln was one), politicians hurled angry charges, vile insults, and threats of violence at each other. Members of Congress kept loaded pistols in their desks. Respectable folks—community leaders, including clergymen—argued that only they had reason, justice, decency, truth, and God on their side.

Expand slavery, let it spread throughout the Union! No, God forbid—abolish it everywhere, instantly! In the eyes of their opponents, those who disagreed were not merely wrong, but liars, sinners, cursed "little toes of Satan." Growing numbers of Americans said they preferred bullets to ballots to uphold slavery or abolish it. Some stood ready to commit treason for their "noble" cause, and proudly said so. Others, equally sincere, would gladly have used terror against opponents, paralyzing their will to resist. There were also outbursts of real violence, as in Boston, where angry mobs threatened those who would return runaways to bondage in the South.

Into the center of this turmoil charged John Brown. He was not a person you could ignore. It was all or nothing with him; you either loved him or hated him. Deeply religious, he believed God had chosen him to right the wrong of slavery. Slavery was the "crowning evil," the "sin of sins"; that was all Brown knew, or cared to know. It followed, for him, that those who held fellow humans in bondage deserved death and damnation.

Though John Brown never held high office or wrote famous books, he is a key figure in American history. During his lifetime, his words and deeds shaped how Americans thought about him. They still do. To many, he was (and is) a good man, a hero, a freedom fighter, a saint. More, he was a martyr who willingly gave his life, and the lives of three of his sons, to free those in bondage. Yet to many others,

Brown was (and is) "the Father of American Terrorism," a liar, a criminal, a fanatic who would have destroyed a nation to achieve his ends.[3]

In the words of a famous Civil War song about him, "His soul goes marching on." We need to know about John Brown because he raised questions that are as valid today as they were in his lifetime. Is it, for example, ever right to break a "bad" law in a democracy? A simple question, yet without a simple answer.

Democracy is government based on the rule of law. Time and again, history has shown that governments based on the will of individuals become tyrannies ruled by fear, force, and lies. In a democracy, however, the law applies to all alike, rich and poor, wise and stupid. "Nobody is above the law," the saying goes. If people dislike a law, the only way to change it is by legal means. Since people can speak their minds and vote, they can challenge a law in court or elect leaders to replace it. Abraham Lincoln called respect for law America's "political religion," a sacred trust passed down through generations. He asked every American to "pledge his life, his property, and his sacred honor" in an effort "never to violate, in the least particular, the laws of the country; and never to tolerate their violation by others."[4]

Others thought the opposite: there was nothing holy about the law. For Henry David Thoreau, a well-known author of the mid-1800s, people must act according to their own ideas of right and wrong, and disobey laws they think unjust. "Is it not possible," Thoreau asked, "that an individual may be right and a government wrong? Are laws to be enforced simply because they are made? or declared by any number of men to be good, if they are not good? Is there any necessity for a man's being a tool to perform a deed of which his better nature disapproves?"[5]

Now, suppose that changing an unjust law seems impossible due to voter ignorance, apathy, or selfishness. Many Americans had a personal interest in slavery. Enslaved people were property, a source of wealth, work, and social position for their masters. Even for those who had few

John Brown. (photograph c. 1857, memorial frame c. 1897)

slaves, or none at all, slavery seemed to prove that any white person was "better" than any black person. However, others thought differently. Slavery was not about happy, carefree folks dancing to banjo music on summer evenings after days of working in the fields. It was the lifelong abuse of men, women, and children. State laws allowed torture, killing, the breakup of families, and the humiliation of millions.

Slavery raised serious questions. What if no argument could convince voters to correct this outrage? Was it right to disobey laws that allowed such evils to exist? If so, how? Was the safety of slaveholders, their families, and their al-

lies more important than the ongoing torment of innocents? Was violence against such injustice a form of terrorism, or were the terrorists those who denied freedom to others?

John Brown thought he knew the answers. Simply put, he believed in "righteous violence," the willingness to kill and die for a higher good.

Brown acted on his belief at Harpers Ferry, Virginia (now West Virginia), in October 1859 by leading a band of raiders in seizing a federal arsenal to get weapons for a slave rebellion. Brown's action divided the nation further, setting the stage for the Civil War. If not for him, some have said, the war would not have

A field hospital in Virginia after a Civil War battle. (c. June 1862)

happened. Victory for the Union side not only preserved "one nation, indivisible," but also ended slavery, surely America's finest moral achievement.

During four years (1861–1865) of war, Northerners and Southerners fought 2,400 named battles and thousands of skirmishes at places few could find on a map. In what soldiers called a "harvest of death," the Civil War took young, vigorous men and destroyed them with gunfire and disease—measles, malaria, typhoid, smallpox. In all, some 750,000 Americans died. For decades afterward, men with empty sleeves and trouser legs were common sights in the North and South. Others, crushed by heartache, never had

a happy moment for the rest of their lives. As a child, George Norris, a future senator, lost his elder brother. After that, he said, "I never heard a song upon the lips of my mother. I never even heard her hum a tune."[6]

Though he died over 150 years ago, John Brown is still with us. Since 1970, he has been the subject of at least four dozen biographies and scholarly studies. There are also scores of poems, songs, plays, and magazine articles devoted to his legacy. Harpers Ferry has become a national park; Brown's farm in North Elba, New York, is a state landmark.

Brown inspired good and evil. While rejecting violence, Eugene V. Debs, a twentieth-century labor leader and five-time (1900, 1904, 1908, 1912, 1920) presidential candidate, called him "history's greatest hero," one who "set an example of moral courage and of single-hearted devotion to an ideal for all men and for all ages." Mary Harris Jones agreed. A zealous union organizer, she was also kind and gentle, thus her nickname "Mother Jones." She idolized Brown. In the early 1900s, bosses cringed when Mother Jones denounced their greed, calling her "John Brown in petticoats." African American poet Langston Hughes wrote on the hundredth anniversary of the Harpers Ferry raid: "John Brown's name is one of the great martyr names of all history and the men who fought with him rank high on the scrolls of freedom." Still, we cannot ignore Brown's use of violence, and how others later took him as a role model to justify their own violence.[7]

Our task is to place this man within his world and then to see how he helped bring about the most terrible conflict in American history.

I

A Volcano Beneath the Snow

He stands like a solitary rock . . . , [with] a fiery nature,
and a cold temper, and a cool head—a volcano beneath
a covering of snow.

—William Phillips, *The Conquest of Kansas by Missouri and Her Allies,* 1856

Child of a New Century

John Brown was born in Torrington, Connecticut, on May 9, 1800, five months after the death of George Washington. If you could step into a time machine and return to that year, you would hardly recognize the United States. It was very young: only twenty-four years old if we reckon its birth from the Declaration of Independence, eleven if we reckon it by the date the Constitution went into effect. The Union had grown to sixteen states

John Brown's birthplace in Torrington, Connecticut. (date unknown)

from the original thirteen colonies. It had 5,308,483 people, of whom 893,602 were slaves brought from Africa or born to their descendants.[1]

Also in 1800, a slave called "General" Gabriel led a rebellion in Virginia, the first large slave uprising in American history. It failed when another slave revealed the plot, and its leaders were executed. "I have nothing more to offer," one of Gabriel's men told the judge who sentenced them, "than what General Washington would have had to offer, had he been taken by the British and put on trial. I have adventured my life in endeavoring to obtain the liberty of [enslaved people], and am a willing sacrifice in their cause." Meanwhile, Nat Turner, destined to be a more famous rebel leader, was born that same year in Virginia.[2]

Two out of three Americans, white and black, stayed within fifty miles of the Atlantic coast. The vast majority lived in villages or small towns, or on family farms; only 6 percent lived in towns and cities of more than 2,500 people. The nation's largest city, New York, had a population of about 60,500 in 1800. Philadelphia, the capital city, came next with 41,000, and Baltimore was a distant third

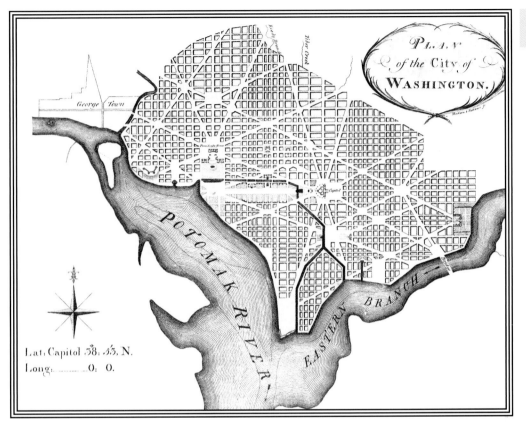

with 26,500 inhabitants. Called "walking cities," these were small enough to allow their inhabitants to reach any place on foot in under an hour. Places like Detroit, Chicago, and Cleveland were still frontier forts surrounded by stockades, walls of pointed logs.[3]

That summer, the federal government moved from Philadelphia to Washington City in the District of Columbia—or Washington, D.C.—at the time a one-hundred-square-mile tract of land along the Potomac River between Maryland and Virginia. It was a leisurely move, because there was not much to do during the hot season. Besides, the Constitution strictly limited the powers of the federal government. It regulated trade between the states, ran the postal system, supported the army and navy, and dealt with foreign countries. There was no income tax, and, unlike today, the federal government had no power in matters of health, education, the environment, safety, local transportation, or labor relations.

Washington City was hardly a city at all. Nearby marshes filled it with the stench of decaying plants. In warm weather, mosquitoes rose from the marshes in clouds, spreading diseases. For want of exact scientific names, residents lumped these together as "fevers." Now-famous landmarks like the U.S. Capitol were still unfinished. Gangs of slave artisans worked on government buildings six days a week. Contractors rented each carpenter, stonemason, plasterer, and painter from his master for between 25 and 50 cents a day. Blacks made nearly all the millions of bricks used for the interior walls of our great public buildings.

Workers rushed to complete the President's House, the original name for what we call the White House. Still, much remained to be done when John Adams arrived early in November. The second president wrote his wife, Abigail, due to come later, that he hoped "none but honest and wise men [shall] ever rule under this roof." Abigail disliked the mansion. Cold and damp in winter, it was bearable only if fires blazed in every room. There were few servants; the First Lady told a friend that she hung the family wash in the elegant but unfinished East Room, the official reception room. The couple lived in the White House for only four months. Soon after they moved in, Thomas Jefferson defeated Adams's bid for reelection.[4]

Frontier Boyhood

John Brown was the third child of the five born to Owen and Ruth Mills Brown. Their oldest was Levi Blakeslee, an orphan adopted after two infant sons died.

The Browns were descended from so-called sound Puritan stock: Peter Brown, a carpenter, began Owen's side of the family in America, arriving on the *Mayflower* at Plymouth, Massachusetts, in 1620. Ruth's ancestors arrived a few years later. Men from both sides of the family served in George Washington's army in the dark days of the American Revolution. Owen's father, Captain John Brown, a farmer, died of disease, probably dysentery, in 1776.[5]

The captain's death left his widow, Hannah, with ten children, and pregnant with yet another. Owen was five years old at the time. "She was one of the best of mothers," he recalled as an old man, "active and sensible. She did all that could be expected of a mother." Still, her best was hardly enough to make ends meet for a large family. Life became such a daily struggle that her children learned early to get by on their own—or do without.[6]

Eventually Owen became a shoemaker. Unlike today, when each pair of shoes has one made to fit the right foot and one the left, back then shoes were called "straights." Each shoe in a pair was the same shape; through use, they molded themselves to the wearer's feet. Later, Owen became a tanner, a person who chemically treated animal hides to turn them into leather. Tanning was a good business. Besides needing a steady supply for shoes, Americans demanded ever more leather for saddles, harnesses, and furniture. Owen prospered and, in 1793, married Ruth Mills, a minister's daughter.

When their son John was five, Owen decided to leave Connecticut for greener pastures. He was not alone. By the early 1800s, Americans were becoming restless. Writers at the time described the "moving, nomadic character of our population"; one marveled that "you will not find one in twenty who lives where his fathers lived or does as his fathers have done." Go west! The frontier meant opportunity, the place to seek a better life! There you would find fertile, cheap land, though you might have to fight Indians to keep it! So, in the spring of 1805, the Browns joined another family. When each family had loaded its belongings into an oxcart, they left for western Ohio.[7]

"Going to Ohio!" was easy to say but hard to do. Before steamboats and railroads, traveling even in settled areas was a challenge. Roads were narrow trails, muddy or dusty depending on the season, and bumpy the year round. A stagecoach, the most common means of road transport, averaged four miles an hour. At that speed, it took two days to go from New York City to Philadelphia. At night, passengers slept six to a bed in cockroach-infested inns, often with strangers. Bridges were rough log affairs, if they existed at all. President Jefferson often traveled the hundred miles between Monticello, his Virginia estate, and the White House. Of the eight rivers he had to cross, five had no bridges.

The trail from Connecticut to Ohio led through a wilderness we can hardly imagine today. Wherever you turned, a traveler wrote in amazement, you saw "woods, woods, woods, as far as the world extends." Overhead, interlaced branches formed a thick canopy, casting gloomy shadows. Forests were so thick that a squirrel could, supposedly, leap through the branches for a thousand miles without touching the ground. Settlers did not see forests as places of beauty to cherish and protect. Forests were enemies. Before you could plant a seed or pasture a cow, you had to clear the trees—backbreaking, dangerous work. "By *clearing America* of Woods," said Benjamin Franklin, settlers were "*Scouring* our Planet," opening the way to progress.[8]

Forests teemed with bears, deer, foxes, possums, squirrels, and raccoons. Flocks of wild turkeys strutted in the clearings. But for sheer numbers, nothing matched the passenger pigeons, which totaled about five billion when Europeans first arrived in North America. These graceful birds, now extinct, flew in flocks a mile wide that blotted out the sun. A farmer recalled: "There would be days and days when the air was alive with them, hardly a break occurring in the flocks for half a day at a time. Flocks stretched as far as a

person could see, one tier above another."
When a flock landed, its combined weight
broke thick branches, even toppled giant
trees. Pigeon droppings covered the
ground in layers four inches deep.[9]

After a seven-week trek through the
wilds, the Browns' caravan reached Hudson, Ohio, a tiny settlement thirty miles
southeast of Cleveland. If they thought the
journey had been hard, they found making
a home an ordeal. Everyone had to work.
Because the children were small, they did
small things: carrying firewood, gathering
berries, pitching in with the chores. Like
other frontier women, their mother prepared the meals, made soap and candles
from animal fat, spun flax and wool into
cloth, and made the family's clothing. In
her spare time, Ruth tended the vegetable
garden.

As the only adult male, Owen did
the heavy work. He cut down trees, built
a log cabin and a tannery, cleared farm-
land, and plowed. Whenever possible, he
hunted in the forest, for game provided
much of the family's food until the first
crop came in. The passenger pigeon was
a blessing. "My father," John recalled,
"caught the pigeons with a large net set
with a spring. He baited this with straw
and wheat spread thin on the ground. . . .
He would catch sixty or seventy with one
swoop of the net." Ruth then baked them
into delicious pies.[10]

We know little about John's child-

John Brown's father, Owen Brown. (date unknown)

hood except what he wrote years later in
a letter to Henry Stearns, the young son
of an ally. At first, John was "rather afraid
of the Indians, & of their Rifles; but this
soon wore off." His parents must have
trusted the local Indians—largely Sen-
ecas, Chippewas, Ottawas, and Oneidas.
Once John got over his fear, they allowed
him to visit their camps alone.[11]

Contrary to popular ideas about
"wild" Indians, the youngster found kind,
unselfish people who welcomed those
who came in peace. John picked up a few
phrases in their language, soon making
friends with a boy who gave him a gor-
geous yellow marble. He prized that marble, but lost it. That hurt. "*It took years to
heal the wound* & I *think* he cried at times

about it." A pet squirrel also died, "& for a year or two John was *in mourning*."[12]

When John was eight, he experienced the first of many family tragedies. His mother died at the age of thirty-six. Torn by grief, his father found it almost impossible to cope with her loss. When trying to express his feelings, he could not get the words out, but stuttered uncontrollably. Owen had to pull himself together— fast. He had to be practical, for by then he had six children to raise and a business to run. So, within a year of Ruth's funeral, he married twenty-year-old Sally Root, a neighbor's daughter.

Owen's sons, especially John, resented their stepmother. Although "a sensible, intelligent" woman, Sally was not his real mother. He simply could not warm up to her, or let her get close to him, try as she did. As he put it, he "never *adopted her in feeling;* but continued to pine after his own Mother for years." John and his adopted brother, Levi Blakeslee, made Sally's life miserable, tormenting her with practical jokes that were hardly funny—to her. Once they tried to blow her up, making a gunpowder bomb that they intended to set off while she sat in the outhouse. Luckily, it was a dud.[13]

John was not what folks call a "model child." By his early teens, he had developed some irritating habits. Unable to take criticism, he admitted telling lies to "screen himself from blame [and] punish-

ment." Bossy and aggressive, he enjoyed the "*hardest & roughest* kinds of plays." He liked "to wrestle & Snow ball & run & jump & knock off old seedy Wool hats." In short, the youngster was a troublemaker.[14]

Such behavior demanded correction. What we might call brutality today was once an accepted part of raising children. In the early 1800s, most parents saw physical punishment as an expression of love. The Bible (Proverbs 23:14) explains a father's duty toward his child this way: "Thou shalt beat him with the rod, and shalt deliver his soul from hell." Americans believed children were naturally willful, easily falling into evil ways. To spare the rod was to spoil the child, earning him or her punishment in the next world for misbehavior. A father who allowed any offense, however small, to go unpunished helped send his child's soul to hell. So, to save John's soul, Owen would cut a slim, flexible branch from a tree and peel off the bark. With a firm hand, he applied this "limber persuader" to the culprit's backside. Though it stung, leaving a red welt, John gritted his teeth, refusing to cry out.[15]

Finding His Way

Like most frontier children, John had little formal education. He preferred his father's tannery to school. The youngster spent countless hours watching Owen and his hired men cure animal skins. Before long, he became expert at making squirrel, raccoon, wolf, and dog skins into soft leather. At night, by candlelight and the blazing fireplace, he learned his "letters" from a few books borrowed from neighbors. History fascinated him, particularly the lives of famous military leaders in ancient and modern times.

For just a few weeks each year, John attended a blab school, where pupils "blabbed," or recited lessons. Each recited in his or her own way and at his or her own speed, for students were not separated into grades. Since there were no public schools in frontier Ohio, several families chipped in to build a one-room log schoolhouse and hire a teacher, paying him in cash and food. John found school boring. It did little to hold his attention or inspire him. Besides, he later admitted, he was "not . . . much of a schollar." He "learned nothing of Grammer; nor did he get at school so much knowledge of common Arithmetic as the Four ground rules"—that is, addition, subtraction, multiplication, and division.[16]

Religion formed the core of John's education. He grew up in a deeply religious home, taught from an early age to " 'fear God and keep His commandments.' " Since colonial times, the Brown family had been strict Puritans, members of a Protestant religious movement that began in England in the mid-1500s. Like his ancestors, Owen Brown believed God con-

stantly tested humans' worthiness to go to heaven when they died. To prove worthy, one had to obey the Ten Commandments, pray, and do good deeds. These deeds included helping those in need, defending the weak, and serving justice. Finally, Puritans believed God sometimes chose individual people as instruments to act for Him in the world.[17]

A friend once called John "a Puritan of the Puritans." It was true. Religion shaped nearly every aspect of his life. He read the Bible daily, took pride in knowing its "entire contents" by heart, and constantly thought about its meaning. Even in normal conversation, John clothed his ideas in Bible verses. Like his Puritan ancestors, he stressed the Almighty's demanding, rather than loving, side. For John, God was stern, harsh, punishing—and warlike. When the Bible said that "the wages of sin *is* death" (Romans 6:23) and "The LORD *is* a man of war" (Exodus 15:3), he agreed.[18]

Lawyers and ministers were the most respected men in frontier communities. Lawyers protected settlers' rights, ministers their souls. At age sixteen, John asked himself questions we all must ask: What path shall I take in life? What career should I follow? He chose the ministry.

With their father's blessing, John and his brother Salmon, fourteen, went east in the autumn of 1816. They rode double on a horse, later sold to pay their tuition and living expenses. In Plainfield, Massachusetts, they enrolled in an academy run by the Reverend Moses Hallock, the brother of a family friend. Things did not go well. John felt out of place among classmates who were far ahead of him in their studies. He knew the Bible well enough, but no Latin, which was required for advanced religious studies. After a few months, the brothers transferred to the Morris Academy in Litchfield, Connecticut. John studied hard, but fell behind. The brothers also ran short of money. John developed an eye infection. When he tried to read, his eyes felt as if they had hot coals in them. Early in the summer of 1817, the brothers returned to Ohio. God had other plans for him, John felt.[19]

On His Own

Back home, John decided to follow his father's trade but not work for him. In 1818, he and Levi Blakeslee built a log cabin and a tannery a mile from Owen's place. However, earning money, though important, was not John's only goal. Every day, in every way, he strove to please God. Local people admired his "invincible honesty." Customers knew he would never cheat them, never sell an inferior piece of leather, though nobody would ever notice the defect. God noticed, and that was enough for John.[20]

The tannery left little time for anything else. "Bachelors' Hall," as John called his and Levi's cabin, grew messy. Unwashed clothes lay scattered about. Beds stayed unmade for weeks, and windows were black with soot from the fireplace. In desperation, John hired the widow Lusk and her nineteen-year-old daughter, Dianthe, as housekeepers. Dianthe was no beauty; John thought her *"remarkably plain."* But she was a "neat, industrious & economical girl; of excellent character . . . & good practical common sense." She also shared his religious beliefs—she even had a secret place in the forest where she went to pray alone. Encouraged by his father, John married Dianthe in June 1820. Just over a year later, she gave birth to John Jr., the first of their seven children, of whom five survived into adulthood.[21]

Dianthe had "a most powerful; & good influence" on her husband. Sadly, though, she suffered spells of "insanity." During an outburst, she threw John Jr. into the fireplace. Fortunately, the infant's father pulled him out safely. Despite his wife's outbursts, John loved her. When Dianthe and a newborn son died in August 1832, he buried them with his own hands. Numb with grief, he often returned to her grave. Once, John Jr. found him sprawled on it, moaning in anguish.[22]

Like his father before him, John needed help with his house and children. He hired a young woman, who often brought her sister, Mary Ann Day, to do the sewing. At sixteen, Mary Ann

John Brown's second wife, Mary Ann Day, and two of their children. (date unknown)

JOHN BROWN'S CHILDREN
Children born to Dianthe Lusk

John Jr., 1821–1895

Jason, 1823–1912

Owen, 1824–1889

Frederick, 1827–1831

Ruth, 1829–1904

Frederick, 1830–1856

Unnamed son, 1832, died at birth

Children born to Mary Ann Day

Sarah, 1834–1843

Watson, 1835–1859

Salmon, 1836–1919

Charles, 1837–1843

Oliver, 1839–1859

Peter, 1840–1843

Austin, 1842–1843

Anne (Annie), 1843–1926

Amelia, 1845–1846

Sarah, 1846–1916

Ellen, 1848–1849

*Unnamed son, 1852,
died twenty-one days after birth*

Ellen, 1854–1916

was "a large silent girl" just half his age. The lonely widower liked her immediately, and decided to marry her. Too shy to propose outright, he handed her a written offer of marriage. Mary Ann "dared not open it but took it to bed that night and slept with it under her pillow. Next morning she found courage to read it," a daughter later said. She accepted the offer gladly, and they married in July 1833, a month before the anniversary of Dianthe's death. Early marriages were normal for women in America at this time. Not to be married by age twenty was thought a misfortune, and not to bear any children a disgrace. Mary Ann would give birth to thirteen children, nine of whom she outlived. She survived her husband by twenty-five years, dying in 1884 at the age of sixty-seven.[23]

What Manner of Man?

John Brown impressed everyone he met, though not always favorably. Physically, a friend noted, he was "built for times of trouble." A rough-looking fellow, he seemed as if "he could lick a yard full of wild cats before breakfast and without taking off his coat." Sensible folks did not provoke him.[24]

Lean and wiry, Brown moved "as quick as a cat." He stood five feet ten inches tall and weighed about 150 pounds. A long "turkey" neck supported a large, squarish head topped with bristly brown hair. His nose, "hawked and thin," looked like that of a flesh-eating bird. Thin lips, pressed tightly together, formed a straight slash under his nose. His voice was "deep and metallic," like a bronze bell.[25]

Brown's strongest feature was his blue-gray eyes. Oh, such eyes! "The flash of his eye, who can describe it?" asked E. C. Leonard, who knew him well. They were full of menace, and even friends compared them to a snake's or demon's. If Brown fixed you with his gaze, his eyes held you as if by a magical spell. The strongest men could not stare into his eyes for more than a few seconds without having to turn away. Animals felt their power, too. Brown, an acquaintance wrote, "said that he could always, without moving, make a dog or cat leave the room if he wished, by his eye." Brown's eyes reflected his moods. Anger made

them blaze, warning of the explosion to come.[26]

Brown once paid a phrenologist to examine his head. Now rejected, phrenology was used in the 1800s as a method of "reading" a person's character from the bumps and bulges on his or her skull. "You have a pretty good opinion of yourself," the phrenologist noted, and "would rather lead than be led. You might be persuaded but to drive you would be impossible. You like your own way, and to think and act for yourself."[27]

The description fit Brown perfectly. He had a *very* high opinion of himself. Brown talked and acted as if he, and he alone, knew what was right. A busybody, he asked strangers about whatever he pleased. Do you go to church regularly? If not, why? The "right" answer brought a nod of approval, and a "wrong" answer a spine-chilling frown. Anyone who disagreed or had the audacity to argue with him got a harsh scolding.[28]

Brown's words stung, giving meaning to the term *tongue-lashing.* For example, a traveling preacher once disagreed with him about the meaning of a Bible verse. Challenged by the preacher to a public debate, Brown snapped that his challenger was "no gentleman, let alone a clergyman." "What did you say, sir?" asked the preacher. "I said, sir," Brown replied with a sneer, "that it would take as many men like you to make a gentleman as it would take wrens to make a cock turkey!" Victims of a Brown tongue-lashing would slink away, feeling battered and small.[29]

Brown also had a more likeable side. Though he had not been a model child, he had become a model citizen who gave the needy money, food, and clothing. He taught Sunday school, built a schoolhouse, and paid a woman to teach in it full-time. That was unusual, because teaching was usually a man's work on the frontier. Sick neighbors often sought his help. No laws regulated medicine in the early 1800s, so anyone could practice. Like any physician, "Doctor Brown" could lance a boil, treat a sprain, or set a broken arm. He had a sense of humor, too, but showed it in an odd way. "When he laughed," said an old friend, "he made not the slightest sound, not even a whisper or an intake of breath; but he shook all over and laughed violently. It was the most curious thing imaginable to see him, in utter silence, rock and quake with mirth."[30]

Brown's family lived with both his harsh and his tender sides. Like an old-time Puritan, he focused their daily life on worship and work. Worship came first. Brown served as household minister and moral guide. Every morning before breakfast, he led the family in Bible reading, prayer, and hymn singing. After the meal, everyone, including the young children, set about their tasks for the day. "There were no drones in the Brown hive," his son

Salmon wrote years later. "Little toddlers unable to help were at least not allowed to hinder; as soon as they had achieved a show of stable control of their uncertain little legs the world of work opened to them. There was no pampering, little petting. The boys could turn a steak or brown a loaf of bread as well as their mother."[31]

Like his father, Brown believed in firm discipline. Usually he reasoned with the smaller children "in the way of the Bible." When, for example, daughter Ruth brought home a piece of cloth she had found at school, he took her aside. Do you know who lost it? No. Fine, but you must follow the Golden Rule: treat others as you would want them to treat you. When you go to school tomorrow, try to find the owner. "It is a trifling thing," he added, "but always remember that if you should lose anything *you* valued, no matter how small, you would want the person that found it to give it back to you."[32]

More serious offenses brought out the "limber persuader." Lying was a mortal sin, a threat to the soul. When son Jason admitted to making up a story about a tame raccoon, his father would hear no excuse, even from a small boy. Jason never forgot his punishment. As an old man, he told how "Father stripped off my trousers—no one wore drawers in those days. He took both my hands in his and held me up in the air and thrashed me. How I danced! How it cut! I was only four. But *Father* had tears in his eyes while he did it, and mother [Dianthe] was crying," too. Both parents cried because it hurt them to hurt their son, though they thought it necessary to prevent further lying.[33]

John Jr. had a different, stranger experience. As a teenager, he worked in the tannery, not his favorite activity. Sometimes he got bored and daydreamed—the sin of idleness. One day, his father showed him a page in a little leather-bound account book. It said:

John, Jr.,

For disobeying mother.......... 8 lashes

" unfaithfulness at work........ 3 "

" telling a lie .... 8 "

Now he had to pay up.[34]

Well-aimed blows fell quickly. John Jr. gritted his teeth and silently took each as it came. But before finishing, Brown stopped. Suddenly he took off his shirt, handing his son the persuader. "Lay it on," he demanded. The boy hesitated. His father insisted. John Jr. obeyed. "Harder!" Brown cried as the blows fell. "Harder, harder!" Blood oozed from the welts on his back. That settled the account. Only later did John Jr. realize that his father shared the punishment because he partly blamed himself for his son's behavior. Had he been more vigilant, the boy would not have "sinned."[35]

Nevertheless, the children loved their father. While not always understanding the reasons for his actions, deep down they felt he loved them. That feeling allowed them to see beyond his harshness. "He showed a great deal of tenderness," daughter Ruth recalled as an adult. "He sometimes seemed very stern and strict with me; yet his tenderness made me forget that he was stern."[36]

Concern for others, the children said, brought out "the woman in him." If Grandfather Owen stayed overnight, Brown tucked him into bed, "always seeming so kind and loving to him that his example was beautiful to see." When the little children were restless, Brown picked them up, cuddled them, and sang them to sleep with a hymn. When the children came down with scarlet fever, named for the bright red skin rash that develops during the illness, Brown cared for them himself. He spent entire nights nursing each in turn while his wife slept.[37]

Brown also showed kindness toward those who fell on hard times through no fault of their own. He once had a man jailed for stealing a cow. But Brown sent the thief's family food until his release, since the innocent should not suffer for the crimes of the guilty.[38]

Years of Sorrow

Brown was most tender in the face of family tragedy. In his day, medical science was primitive, even deadly, since doctors used drugs like calomel, a poisonous mixture of mercury and chlorine, to treat many illnesses. There were no anti-biotics to fight infections. Worse, nobody knew that bacteria cause disease. Rubber gloves did not exist, and doctors washed their hands after treating a patient, not be-fore. Small wonder that out of one hun-dred people born in 1800, only sixty-four reached the age of six. Of the survivors, a mere ten made it to age forty-six. Thus, every family, regardless of wealth and social position, could expect to lose sev-eral loved ones in the "normal" course of events.[39]

So it was with the Browns. In Sep-tember 1843, dysentery, a disease char-acterized by bloody diarrhea, struck the household. Caused by bacteria in im-pure drinking water, the disease sick-ened everyone, including Brown. In less than a month, it killed four of the Brown children, all between the ages of one and nine: Charles, Peter, Sarah, and Austin.

"My punishment is greater than I can bear," Brown cried, but at least his little ones were with God in heaven.[40]

Other tragedies followed. In 1846, daughter Ruth, seventeen, dropped a ket-tle of boiling water as she took it from the fireplace. The water spilled on baby Ame-lia, scalding her to death. Brown got the news while away on a business trip. "One more dear little feeble child I am to meet no more till the dead small & great shall stand before God," he wrote. "This is a bitter cup indeed, but blessed be God." Please do not blame "my dear Ruth," he added; she meant no harm. God knows best.[41]

Two and a half years later, Brown was home when baby Ellen came down with pneumonia. Burning with fever, she died in her father's arms. "He was very calm," Ruth recalled. He "closed her eyes, folded her hands, and laid her in her cradle."

A replica of the Clermont, or North River Steamboat, *the first commercially successful steamboat.* (c. 1909)

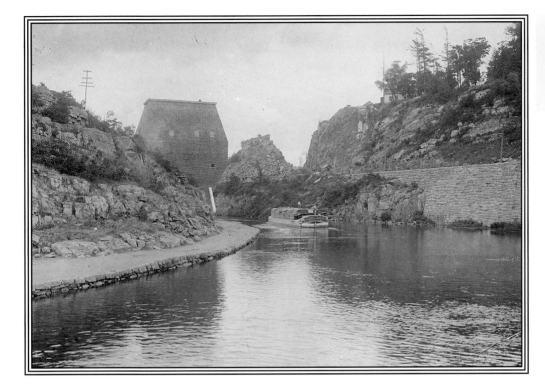

A barge chugs along the Erie Canal, a major boon for commerce in the nineteenth century, at Little Falls, New York. (c. 1880–1897)

God's will be done—but, oh, so hard to bear! At the funeral, "father broke down completely, and sobbed like a child."[42]

Business failures made these deaths yet more painful. In the decades since Brown's birth, the Industrial Revolution had begun to change America. Starting in England in the 1760s, inventors built machinery to manufacture desirable goods: cloth, shoes, pots, pans, pottery, nails, screws, tableware. Originally, *manufacture* meant making an item by hand. That changed with the invention of machines driven by waterwheels and steam engines. By gathering machines at central points, called factories, manufacturers increased production while lowering prices. Gradu-

ally, the Industrial Revolution spread across the Atlantic Ocean. Steamboats and railroads began to carry passengers and cargo. In 1837, an American, Samuel F. B. Morse, invented the telegraph, a device for sending messages by means of wires and electric current.

Rapid progress made it seem that anyone with a good idea and some money could get rich. "We are THE PEOPLE OF THE FUTURE," optimists boasted. "Custom [has] lost its sway, and Time and Change are the Champions."[43]

John Brown caught the get-rich-quick fever. His tanning business had always done well—so well that he employed fifteen men full-time. Yet he needed an ever-growing income to support his ever-growing family. What to do?

Besides the nation's expanding railroad and steamboat routes, a network of canals began to link the interior with coastal seaports. Completed in 1825, the Erie Canal linked the Great Lakes to the Atlantic Ocean, allowing settlers and manufactured goods to flow westward and farm products to move eastward. As a result, New York City, with its splendid seaport, became the nation's wealthiest city.

The Erie Canal's success began a "canal boom," a sudden increase in building activity and profits. In Ohio, rumors of new canal projects set off a frenzy of speculating, as "go-ahead" men rushed to buy land along likely routes. Some hit the jackpot. In one deal, lucky investors bought land for $11 an acre, and then sold ten-acre lots for $7,000. Unlucky investors, John Brown among them, lost their shirts.

Brown had borrowed heavily to buy future canal land. All seemed well, until the Panic of 1837 shattered his dream of wealth. A sharp downturn in the economy caused banks to go bankrupt. Businesses failed. Unemployment soared. Work on canals came to a halt. Land values collapsed, leaving Brown—like thousands of others—crushed by debt. The experience taught him a terrible lesson. "Running into debt includes so much of evil," he told John Jr., "that I hope all my children will shun it as they would a pestilence."[44]

In 1840, a court ordered his property sold to repay creditors. Brown exploded with rage. He had a family to support! He was an honest, God-fearing man who had put his sweat and blood into the land! In despair, he and three sons barricaded themselves in a log cabin, promising to shoot anyone who came near. The local sheriff brought a posse. Outnumbered and outgunned, Brown surrendered without firing a shot. After keeping him in jail a few days to cool off, the sheriff let him go.

Yet that did not solve his money problems. Declaring him bankrupt, the court persisted in its order to have his property sold at auction. However, it allowed the family to keep a few "articles and necessaries" such as pots, pans, dishes, and clothing. "Oh, we were poor!" Brown's son Jason recalled many years later.[45]

Brown tried various ways to earn money. He surveyed land, traded horses, and herded sheep. In time, he became a sheep and wool expert, winning awards for excellence. That impressed Simon Perkins, a wealthy businessman in Akron, Ohio. In 1844, Perkins invited Brown to become his partner. In return for Perkins's financial backing, Brown agreed to do the day-to-day work. The partners decided to rent a warehouse in Springfield, Massachusetts, a major cloth manufacturing center. Brown would collect wool sent by growers throughout Ohio and the Midwest. After sorting it according to quality, he would sell it at fair prices to New England textile mills, keeping part of the profits as the partners' commission.

Things did not work out as planned. The partners soon found that manufacturers offered growers as little as possible for their wool. Mill owners refused to buy the partners' wool because it was too expensive, forcing Brown to find customers in Europe. While overseas, he toured famous battlefields, which made him a military expert—at least in his own eyes. However, he found few customers for wool at the prices he asked. Earnings fell steadily, forcing the firm of Perkins & Brown to close in 1849. After that, whatever else Brown tried seemed doomed to failure. Over the next five years, he had fifteen business failures in four states. Life became a nightmare of court dates, lawyers, and battles over bad debts. What did it all mean?[46]

Nobody could accuse Brown of deliberately harming another person. True, he was a hard man. Yet those who knew him best realized he always did his God-given duty as he saw it. Clearly, for one who constantly read the Bible and books like *Beauties of the Bible,* no raindrop fell to earth without a reason. Through tragedy and failure, he wondered if perhaps God was pointing him toward some sacred mission.[47]

Life's trials deepened John Brown's sympathy for the oppressed. Thus, his story is both private, about an individual's experiences and misfortunes, and part of a chain of events forged centuries before he first saw the light of day. There is no way to understand Brown and his America without pausing to examine the larger issue of human bondage. Slavery's rise in the Old and New Worlds is among history's great terrible stories. We cannot ignore it. For not only has it shaped our past, but its legacy influences how we think and live today.

II

The Foulest Blot

Rise of the African Slave Trade

My ear is pain'd,
My soul is sick with ev'ry day's report
Of wrong and outrage with which earth is fill'd.
. . . .
And worst of all, and most to be deplored
As human nature's broadest, foulest blot,
Chains him, and tasks him, and exacts his sweat
With stripes, that mercy with a bleeding heart
Weeps when she sees inflicted on a beast.
Then what is man? And what man seeing this,
And having human feelings, does not blush
And hang his head, to think himself a man?

—William Cowper, *The Task*, 1785

Beginnings

The most brutal definition of *slavery* is also the briefest and best. More than two thousand years ago, the Greek philosopher Aristotle wrote, "A slave is a living possession." By that, he did not mean a pet or a farm animal, but a person who belongs to another. There is no such thing as "good" and "bad" slavery. Slavery is slavery. Depending on custom and local conditions, it may be harsher or milder than elsewhere. Yet it is always a form of exploitation, and thus the opposite of freedom.[1]

Slavery is older than recorded history. Scientists believe the earliest human ancestors appeared in East Africa about a million years ago, then spread worldwide in search of food. Continually on the move, these nomads lived in small bands, hunting animals, fishing, and gathering edible plants. About ten thousand years ago, people in the Middle East learned how to grow wild grasses like wheat, barley, and rye from seeds. Moreover, they began to domesticate animals—that is, raise animals, like cattle and sheep, in captivity.

These discoveries changed the course of human history. Farming provided more food, more regularly, than hunting and gathering did. Populations grew. As people came to depend on farming, they had to abandon the nomadic lifestyle for permanent settlements. Eventually some settlements grew into the first cities. Over time, cities joined to form organized states ruled by kings, nobles, and priests.

Nomad bands, being small, had a handful of hunters, who also acted as warriors. If bands met, they might fight over a hunting ground, lose a few men, and then move on. Yet as more people took up farming and settled down, fertile land became valuable. To protect what they had, and win more, communities raised armies and fought wars. At first, the victors killed the defeated. Eventually, however, victors found a "better" solution: slavery. Farming demanded strenuous labor. Farmers worked from sunrise to sunset, plowing, planting, watering, harvesting, and storing crops. Enslaving captives, instead of killing them, allowed the victors to lighten their workloads while further increasing food output.

Slavery has existed on all continents except Antarctica, a region of eternal ice and snow that was without people until scientists set up bases there in the twentieth century. There is probably no modern human group without ancestors who were slaves or slave masters. Every advanced society had farming, war, and slavery. Not surprisingly, the earliest written records deal with land ownership, taxes on crops, and slave property. The oldest record, an Egyptian document dating from about 1500 BCE, is about capturing "slaves, male and female" in the land of Punt (modern-day Somalia). In Athens, the chief city of ancient Greece, about one in four adults was a slave. The city of Rome, capital of the Roman Empire, had upwards of four hundred thousand slaves, which was about a third of its population.[2]

Originally, slavery had nothing to do with skin color. The ancients gave no special meaning to a person's color, thinking it depended on a region's climate. "If the country is cold," said an Arab writer in about the year 850, its people "are under-cooked in the womb; if the country is hot, they are burnt in the womb." Slavery was equal opportunity. Anybody, including royalty, could have the bad luck to be enslaved.[3]

Black Africa

While slavery existed throughout the ancient world, historians believe it first began in Africa, where the human race began. Native Africans had a type of slavery different from that which developed elsewhere. Among them, private ownership of land did not exist. Land belonged to the community, which distributed it to families according to the number of workers each had and the number of mouths to feed. Thus, larger families got more land, and their head men gained greater respect in the community.

African slaves might be war captives, or free people fallen on bad times. Suppose a farmer had to borrow seeds for next year's planting. He would go to a better-off neighbor and offer his child, or even himself, as security for the loan. Failure to repay on time meant losing his security and freedom. Male slaves farmed, herded cattle, and practiced crafts such as weaving and metalworking. (Africans were skilled in making objects of iron and bronze, a blend of copper and tin.) In some tribes, male slaves became guards and warriors. Female slaves helped with farmwork, prepared food, and cared for children.

Tribal laws held that a slave was *made,* not *born.* Children born to slaves were free. Masters had to treat slaves humanely, providing for their needs, not overworking them, and avoiding physical punishments except when absolutely "necessary." In the late 1700s, a European traveler wrote that African masters "are remarkably kind to, and careful of their slaves, whom they treat with respect." Africans often counted slaves as family members, calling them "son" and "daughter." Some slaves even married into the master's family.[4]

Olaudah Equiano, born in 1745 in what is today Nigeria, was among the few enslaved native-born Africans to write about his experiences. "With us," he explained, "they do no more work than other members of the community, even their masters; their food, clothing and lodging were nearly the same as theirs (except that they were not permitted to eat with those who were free-born); and there was scarce any other difference between them. . . . Some of these slaves have even slaves under them as their own property, and for their own use."[5]

Arab Slave Traders

While laws all but eliminated slavery in western Europe by the year 1000, the nature of African slavery began to change as blacks met outsiders with stronger militaries. Of these, the Arabs came first.

Around the year 635 CE, Arab armies burst out of the Arabian Peninsula (today's Kingdom of Saudi Arabia) to spread Islam, the faith taught by the Prophet Muhammad. One group of armies moved eastward, crossing Central Asia to conquer what is today Afghanistan, Pakistan, and India. In the years 641–708, other armies swept westward, seizing the North African lands bordering the Mediterranean Sea. Over time, Arabs converted the native peoples to Islam.

After conquering North Africa, the victors looked southward, toward the Sahara, the Arabic word for "desert." Covering about 3.5 million square miles, the Sahara stretches from the Red Sea in the east to the Atlantic Ocean in the west. The world's largest desert, it is roughly equal in size to the United States. The Sahara has rocky plains, towering sand dunes, and "sand seas," seemingly endless flat areas covered by windblown sand ripples, like waves at sea. As the Sahara is almost totally without rainfall, scattered oases and wells formed by underground streams flowing from distant mountain ranges provide the only water and greenery.

Gradually, the Sahara's southern "shore" gives way to a savanna, a rolling grassland with widely scattered trees and shrubs. Arab explorers named the savanna the Bilad as-Sudan—"Land of the Blacks." (Sudan was the name of the entire region, not just the modern nation of Sudan.) The rivers and rain forests of

A thirteenth-century slave market in Yemen. (date unknown)

tropical Africa lie south of the savanna, in the center of the continent.

Since ancient times, North Africans had crossed the Sahara with ox-drawn carts. But the climate is so harsh that crossings were rare until Arabs brought the dromedary, or one-humped camel. Called the "ship of the desert," the dromedary can carry heavy loads yet live on small amounts of water and food, including thornbushes. Upon reaching the desert's southern shore, traders found wealthy kingdoms like Ghana and Mali in the Bilad as-Sudan. As these kingdoms gradually converted to Islam, large-scale trade developed.

Traders offered horses, steel sword blades, glassware, pottery, cloth, and salt. The salt came from mines Arabs worked with slave labor in the western Sahara. Used to preserve and season food, salt was so scarce—and valuable—that some tribes also used it as money. In exchange, traders took gold dust, ostrich feathers, and kola nuts, an ingredient in drinks and medicines. However, traders were most eager for slaves captured by their African partners from pagan tribes.[6]

Arab men took pride in owning slaves. For them, slaves were a measure of achievement and wealth, like a luxury car is in today's America. By having many slaves, a man showed he could afford them, thus winning praise and re-spect from his social equals. Most male slaves did no farmwork, but served in Arab homes as butlers, gardeners, guards, and porters. Women had many more roles, which explains why twice as many women as men were enslaved. Besides performing general household duties as cooks, laundresses, and nursemaids, they became musicians, singers, dancers, and reciters of poetry.[7]

Above all, Arabs valued enslaved women as concubines, who live with men without being married to them. Islamic law allows a man to have four wives at a time, and as many concubines as he can afford to keep. Even humble shopkeepers might have a wife and a concubine. Royalty had more. One Turkish sultan, or king, had fourteen thousand concubines. Not all were African; many were white women captured during raids into Europe or taken from European ships in the Mediterranean Sea.[8]

Among the wealthy, wives, female relatives, and concubines lived in the harem, a part of the house separate from the men's quarters. Eunuchs guarded and managed the harem. These were male slaves who, as boys between the ages of four and twelve, had undergone castration to prevent them from having relations with women as adults. It was a dangerous operation—perhaps nine in ten eunuchs-to-be died of blood loss and infection.[9]

Castration took place soon after the slave caravan left its assembly point on the southern shore of the sand sea. Ahead lay a journey of sixty to seventy days—*if* all went well. At the best of times, everyone faced extremes of heat and cold. Temperatures in the Sahara soar to 136°F in the daytime, falling to 30°F at night. At the worst of times, wells along the way became clogged with sand, caved in, or ran dry, spelling death for both slaves and their captors. For example, in 1805, when John Brown was five, a caravan of two thousand people and eighteen hundred camels died of thirst and exposure.[10]

If its luck held, the caravan reached one of several major North African seaports: Tunis in today's Tunisia, Tripoli in Libya, Algiers in Algeria, Rabat or Ceuta in Morocco. In 1819, British Royal Navy captain G. F. Lyon saw a caravan enter Tripoli with fourteen hundred slaves. It was awful:

> *We rode out to meet the great [caravan], and to see them enter the town—it was indeed a piteous spectacle! These poor oppressed beings were, many of them, so exhausted as to be scarcely able to walk; their legs and feet were much swelled. . . . They were all borne down with loads of firewood; and even poor little children, worn to skeletons by fatigue and hardships, were obliged to bear their [burden], while many of their inhuman masters rode on camels, with the dreaded whip suspended from their wrists, with which they . . . enforced obedience from these wretched captives. . . .*
>
> *. . . No slave dares to be ill or unable to walk; but when the poor sufferer dies, the master suspects there must have been something "wrong inside," and regrets not having liberally applied the usual remedy of burning the belly with a red hot iron.*[11]

Upon arrival, traders drove their living possessions to the "place of display," the slave market. Local men bought many of them. Yet the most prized—beautiful concubines, healthy-looking eunuchs—went on by ship to Egypt and Turkey, where they brought the highest prices at auction.[12]

Another branch of the Arab slave trade operated from towns on the east coast of Africa, along the Indian Ocean. Slave traders set out in well-armed expeditions from Mombasa in modern Kenya and Kilwa in Tanzania. Heading into the interior of Africa, an area of dense forests and vast lakes, they made alliances with tribal kings and chieftains to raid villages for slaves. In 1857, English explorer Sir

Richard Burton saw the frightful result. Wherever the expeditions went, they were like "a flight of locusts over the land," leaving behind "a howling desert" of burned, empty villages.[13]

For the enslaved, the march to the coast was every bit as dreadful as crossing the Sahara. They marched in coffles (long files), often for a thousand miles. Slavers bound men together by the neck with chains or stout forked sticks; each balanced a valuable tusk of elephant ivory on his head. Women usually went unbound; they might carry a small tusk or a bundle of trade goods *and* a baby. In the 1850s, when John Brown had already failed in several business ventures, the Scottish explorer and missionary Dr. David Living-

stone saw the East African slave trade at its worst. "One woman," he wrote, "had her infant's brains knocked out, because she could not carry her load and it; and a man was despatched with an axe, because he had broken down with fatigue."[14]

Upon reaching the coast, captives boarded dhows, traditional Arab sailing craft, for the short trip to Zanzibar, an island off the coast of Tanzania. Sold at auction, many slaves remained in Zanzibar, working on plantations that grew cloves, a costly spice. Most, however, were again loaded aboard dhows to continue their voyage into bondage. Dhows carried them far to the north, into the Red Sea, to Arabia and Egypt. Others went farther, into the Arabian Sea to the Persian Gulf and

Dealers with slaves for sale at a market in Zanzibar, now part of Tanzania, in East Africa. (c. 1873)

Persia (today's Iran). A few hundred men each year made the voyage across the Indian Ocean to the Moluccas (in today's Indonesia), India, and China. As early as 976, an Arab ambassador caused a stir in the court of the Chinese emperor by showing off a "slave with deep-set eyes and black body." Wealthy Chinese kept slaves as tokens of their high social position. At first, Africans seemed so odd that some Chinese people rubbed their skin to see if the black color came off![15]

We will never know the full human cost of the Arab slave trade, for traders did not keep detailed records. Historians estimate that from 650 to 1900, about twelve million made it alive across the Sahara, East Africa, and the sea routes. Historians also believe that for every person sold into slavery, probably another ten died along the way.[16]

Grim as the picture was, enslaved people suffered most during the time between capture and sale. After they were sold, conditions usually improved for slaves, due to the influence of Islam.

The Qur'an (or Koran), Islam's holy book, and Shari'a, its law code, regulate slavery in minute detail. They say, among other things, that

> *slaves must not be overworked or harmed;*
> *slaves must be properly fed, clothed,*
>   *housed, given medical treatment, and*
>   *supported in old age;*
> *slaves may own property, save any money*
>   *they earn, and buy their freedom;*
> *slaves may ask for their freedom and*
>   *repay their cost, in installments, from*
>   *future earnings;*
> *it is a sin to separate a mother from her*
>   *child, and the child of a master and his*
>   *concubine is automatically free;*
> *Allah [God] favors the master who frees*
>   *slaves during his lifetime, or in his will*
>   *after he dies.*[17]

The Prophet Muhammad, who captured and owned slaves, accepted slavery as a fact of life. Slavery was so deeply rooted in Arabia that rather than demand its end, he sought only to curb its abuses and make it more humane. "Do not forget that they [slaves] are your brothers," he cautioned Muslims. "God has given you the right of ownership over them; He could have given them the right of ownership over you." Devout Muslim slave owners heeded the Prophet. As for those who did not, let them beware. Allah sees all, and no sin goes unpunished.[18]

The Meeting of Africa and the New World

New World slavery belongs to the Age of Exploration. In the year 1415, Portugal attacked Ceuta, the Moroccan seaport near the western entrance to the Mediterranean Sea. Among the Portuguese army's leaders was Prince Henry, son of King John I, later famous as Henry the Navigator. While in Ceuta, the prince saw slaves and gold. These, he learned from traders, had come across the Sahara from wealthy kingdoms in the land of the blacks. Since Prince Henry cared more about gold than slaves, he decided to bypass the Arab caravan routes. He would send ships along the coast of West Africa to find the source of the gold, opening sea trade with the black kingdoms.[19]

Year by year, Portuguese ships sailed farther down the West African coast. As they did, merchants set up trading posts called "forts" and "castles." In exchange for cloth, wine, and metal tools, they took gold, ivory, and, starting in 1441, a few slaves each year, as house servants and farm laborers. In 1450, the pope, as head of the Roman Catholic Church, approved the enslavement of Africans to save their souls by getting them to convert to Christianity. By then, Europeans wanted Africans not only as workers but also as curiosities, showing them off as one would a rare butterfly or flower. For centuries, painted family portraits often showed a well-dressed slave-servant as a sign of wealth. In John Brown's America, photographs served the same purpose.

Meanwhile, Portuguese ships rounded the Cape of Good Hope, the southern tip of Africa, and crossed the Indian Ocean. When they opened a profitable trade with China, India, and the Spice Islands (called the Moluccas today), Spain sent Christopher Columbus to find a shorter route to Asia by sailing west rather than east. Instead, in 1492 he stumbled upon what

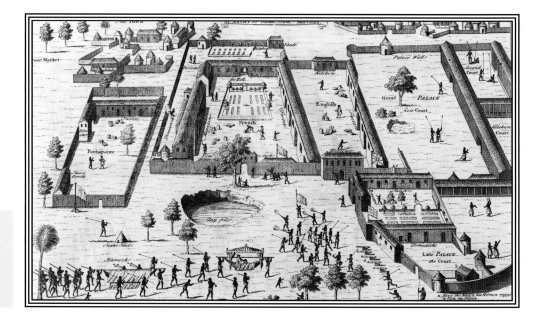

A 1746 drawing of slave "factories," or compounds, maintained by European traders in present-day Nigeria.

Europeans called the New World. Both Spain and Portugal claimed these lands, so in 1494 Pope Alexander VI awarded half to each, along an imaginary north-south line. Lands west of the line, except Brazil, went to Spain; Portugal got the lands to the east. England, France, and Holland called the pope's decision unfair and seized islands in the Caribbean Sea, or the West Indies, and land in North America for themselves.

Europeans said they came to the New World for "gold, glory, and the Gospel." Yes, they wished to spread Christianity, and win glory in doing so. But gold came first. Spain led the way. Its soldiers looted the gold and silver of the Aztec and Inca empires in Mexico and Peru. Yet the real treasure lay in sugar grown in the soil. It is no accident that the West Indies were first called the Sugar Islands.

During their invasion of Asia, Arabs found sugarcane growing. Merchants returned with stem cuttings and refined sugar; farmers planted the cane in Morocco and Tunisia. Christopher Columbus carried cuttings to Hispaniola ("Little Spain") on his second voyage, in 1493. Spanish settlers then introduced the crop to the islands of Cuba, Puerto Rico, and Jamaica. Later, the Portuguese carried it to Brazil, the British to Barbados, and the French to Martinique.

Europeans could not get enough of the sweet stuff, which was a rare delicacy and very expensive. As the French said, "Adding sugar never hurt any food." The wealthy showed off by garnishing every dish with it, including meat and fish. Cake recipes called for "three quarters of a pound of the best moist sugar." In the late 1500s, Queen Elizabeth I of England had black teeth—"a defect the English

Slaves working on a sugar plantation while overseers watch them with whips at the ready, most likely in the West Indies. (c. 1874)

seem subject to," a Dutch visitor wrote, "from their too great use of sugar." Thus, sugar, like ivory, became "white gold," the maker of fortunes.[20]

However, growing sugar required a large workforce. The Spanish colonies were the first to experience a severe labor shortage. There were never enough Europeans to do all the necessary work. To meet the demand for labor, Spaniards at first enslaved Native Americans, people who had never experienced European diseases and had no immunity to them. Epidemics, particularly of smallpox, killed millions. In Hispaniola, for example, the native population fell from over two million in 1493 to zero within forty years. So, around 1505, Spaniards brought the first enslaved Africans across the Atlantic Ocean. Africans were no strangers to smallpox. Centuries before Europeans arrived, many tribes inoculated their members to build immunity to the disease.

Rise of the Atlantic Slave Trade

Sugar made the slave trade big business, and the cause of untold misery. A poem of the time said it best:

> There is a beauteous plant that grows
> In Western India's sultry clime,
> Which makes, alas! the Black man's
> woes
> And also makes the White man's
> crime.[21]

High profits came with high risks. War and pirates took their toll in lost ships, crews, and slave "cargo." In the early 1600s, France, Holland, and England seized control of the slave trade from Spain and Portugal. Historians believe that no fewer than 54,200 separate voyages made up the Atlantic slave trade. Though different in detail, each voyage followed a similar pattern. Let's invite ourselves on a typical English slaving voyage to West Africa in 1793, the year John Brown's parents married.[22]

A voyage began in London, Bristol, or Liverpool, England's chief seaports. There, moneymen—investors, bankers, accountants, insurance agents—met in offices to "undertake" a voyage. These men in elegant clothes, powdered wigs, and silver shoe buckles would not sail in person, for that was not their role. Instead, they kept their hands clean, giving others the means to do the dirty work that enriched them. Undertakers, as they called themselves, followed a business plan designed to take three separate profits, thus the name "triangle trade." First, on the Outward Passage, they sent European goods to Africa to exchange for slaves. Second, on the Middle Passage, they shipped enslaved people across the Atlantic to sell for cash in the West Indies and on the North American mainland. Finally, on the Return Passage, their ships carried New World goods—sugar, tobacco, rice, and indigo, a purple dye—to sell in Europe.

Undertakers pooled their money to buy or rent ships that were specially built for the slave trade. Seamen called such vessels "slavers" or "Guineamen," their version of *Bilad Ghana* ("Land of Wealth"), the Arabic term for the coast of West Africa.

Next, they engaged (hired) a captain, paying him a salary and a share of the profits. They chose carefully, for a captain had to be an experienced seaman and trader. Upon taking command, he enlisted a crew. A Guineaman had thirty to forty crew members. These were mostly "broken-down sailors": debtors, drunks, jailbirds, outlaws on the run. Since such men were hard to control, captains and their officers were hard as nails, having, one said, neither "dainty fingers nor dainty noses."[23]

Meanwhile, the undertakers equipped the ship. In addition to food and water, they stocked it with the tools of the slave trade. Ironware shops lined the cobblestoned streets leading to the docks. Shop windows displayed the "hardware of bondage": locks, chains, handcuffs, leg shackles, "iron necklaces" (collars). A typical manifest, or list of a ship's cargo, included such items as "300 pair of well made Shackles" and "150 Iron Collars . . . in suitable order for the confinement of slaves." Manifests also listed

"instrument[s] of correction," a polite term for the cat-o'-nine-tails, a whip made of nine strands of braided rope, with a series of knots along each "tail."[24]

Besides these supplies, Guineamen carried goods to trade for slaves. These included muskets, gunpowder, lead bars to mold into bullets, knives, swords, axes, iron pots, cloth, tobacco, clay smoking pipes, mirrors, and even "cats to catch their mice." Above all, ships carried barrels of a "hot, hellish and terrible liquor" called rum. Nicknamed "kill-devil," it was so strong—75 percent alcohol—that it could supposedly kill the devil. Rum is fermented molasses, the sticky brown liquid left after boiling sugarcane juice into white crystals. West Indian planters sent molasses to England and its New England colonies to turn into rum. Wildly popular in Europe and Africa, rum made countless people alcoholics. The going prices for slaves were 115 gallons of rum for an adult black man, 95 gallons for a woman, and 80 gallons for a child.[25]

The voyage to West Africa was no pleasure cruise. Food often ran short, and what crewmen had they shared with the ship's rats. The rats, always ravenous, gnawed through wooden food boxes, nibbled on ropes and spare sails, and bit men as they slept. No use complaining! At sea, the captain was the law: judge, jury, and executioner. Complaining, let alone disobeying an order, brought a licking by the "cat." Applied to the bare back, the cat-o'-nine-tails raised lines of bloody welts. One hundred lashes could easily kill a strong man, or cripple him for life. Seeing a man whipped, followed by "pickling" of the raw wounds with salt-and-pepper water, terrified his shipmates. It also hardened them for the work ahead.[26]

After about five weeks at sea, depending on the wind, the ship entered the Gulf of Guinea. This is the large, open arm of the Atlantic that is formed where the great bulge of West Africa bends eastward. The gulf follows the coastline from today's Senegal to Angola, a distance of 3,500 miles. It includes two bights, or large bays formed by the curve of the coastline: the Bight of Benin and the Bight of Biafra. Europeans called the lands bordering the Bight of Benin (now Togo, Benin, and southwest Nigeria) the Slave Coast. However, Africans along the entire coastline took part in the Atlantic slave trade.

For Europeans, the first sight of West Africa seemed like a glimpse of another planet. There were few natural harbors, so ships had to anchor offshore. Atlantic waves rolled onto white sandy beaches broken by small rivers, their mouths often blocked by sandbars. Treacherous riptides flowed away from shore, threatening to overturn longboats, which were large rowboats carried by sailing ships. Land breezes brought the odor of decaying crabs, rain forest mold, and swamp mud. Slave-trade veterans called these odors "the breath of Death himself."[27]

During the rainy season, from July to October, rivers overflowed their banks, flooding the countryside for miles around. Suffocating humidity tortured seamen, rotting the clothes off their bodies. When the rains ended in October, strong winds dried the land. "At this season," a traveler wrote, "the winds blow so very hot from off the land, that I can compare them to nothing but the heat proceeding from the mouth of an oven." People raised in cooler lands wilted in the heat and humidity.[28]

The captain had to get a cargo of slaves and leave the coast as quickly as possible. Every moment his ship rode at anchor increased the risk of disease. Tropical diseases plagued coastal lands, diseases no European doctor had ever seen or knew how to treat. Seamen dreaded guinea worms, creatures that live inside the body and grow up to three feet long. Mosquitoes swarmed. These tiny terrors carried malaria, yellow fever, and threadlike worms that bored into one's eyes. No wonder sailors dubbed the lands bordering the Gulf of Guinea the "White Man's Grave." The worst stretch of coastline lay along the Bight of Benin. A sea chanty gave this advice:

Beware and take care
Of the Bight of Benin;

For the one that comes out,

There are forty go in.

There are records of expeditions on which everyone died before the ship took a single slave aboard.[29]

Nowadays, a popular image of the West African slave trade has fierce, gun-toting Europeans raiding villages to enslave helpless victims. The truth is quite different. Disease and ignorance pinned Europeans to their ships. Rivers were the easiest routes to the interior, but no accurate maps of these existed until the late 1800s, decades after the slave trade ended. Captains knew that going inland by longboat carried the risk not only of contracting more diseases but also of getting lost or stuck in swamps and dying in agony. For that reason, white traders relied on Africans to bring enslaved people to them. The Atlantic slave trade would have been impossible without the help of tribal rulers. African American historian Henry Louis Gates Jr. cites estimates that Africans sold nine out of ten slaves that were brought to the New World.[30]

Frederick Douglass, the leading black opponent of slavery before the Civil War and a friend of John Brown's, despised "the savage chiefs of the western coast of Africa, who for ages have been accustomed to selling their captives into bondage." Nevertheless, two wrongs do not make a right. African guilt cannot cancel European and American guilt. For if there were no buyers, there could have been no sellers. The Atlantic slave trade was tailor-made for the needs of the New World, a major driving force behind its development. Unlike the Arabs, New World buyers wanted people for heavy work in the sun. This explains why two men were enslaved for every woman.[31]

White slave traders acted like modern drug pushers. They coaxed Africans into using their products, in this case

A drawing depicting a slave dealer and his customer in Africa in the eighteenth century. (1919)

European trade goods. Once the Africans became "addicted," they demanded ever more goods and rum. For this reason, African rulers ignored ancient traditions of treating slaves humanely. Rulers used any excuse, such as false charges of anything from theft to witchcraft, to sell their own people into bondage. Making war on other tribes, however, was the preferred way of getting slaves. These "wars" had nothing to do with real disputes; they were merely slave-catching raids, encouraged by white traders.

A slave-catching expedition was a brutal affair. It began with warriors moving inland by canoe or, if horses were available, on horseback, often for five hundred miles or more. Rather than fight a battle, they attacked a village at night, seizing villagers as they tried to escape. Captives were bound and marched to the coast in coffles. Major William Gray, a British army officer, came upon a coffle in 1818, the year John Brown went into the tanning business. Gray wrote:

The men were tied in pairs by the necks, the hands secured behind their backs; the women by the necks only, but their hands were not left free from any sense of feeling for them, but in order to enable them to balance the immense loads of . . . corn or rice, which they were forced to carry on

their heads, and the children . . . on their backs. . . .

. . . Many of the women were old, and by no means able to endure such treatment. One in particular . . . was at least sixty years old . . . and with difficulty dragging her toting limbs along. . . . All this did not prevent her inhuman captor from making her carry a heavy load of water, while, with a rope about her neck, he drove her before his horse, and, whenever she shewed [sic] the least inclination to stop, he beat her in the most unmerciful manner with a stick. . . .

. . . One young woman who had (for the first time) become a mother two days only before she was taken, and whose child, being thought by her captor too young to be worth saving, was thrown by the monster into its burning hut, . . . suffered so much. . . . A few blows with a leathern horse fetter, soon made the wretched creature move again.[32]

Kidnappers took Olaudah Equiano in 1756, when he was eleven. Equiano was lucky to have English masters who treated him well; one taught him to read and write, a rarity at this time. Eventually a slave merchant put him to work in his office. Able to earn money in his spare time, Equiano later bought his freedom,

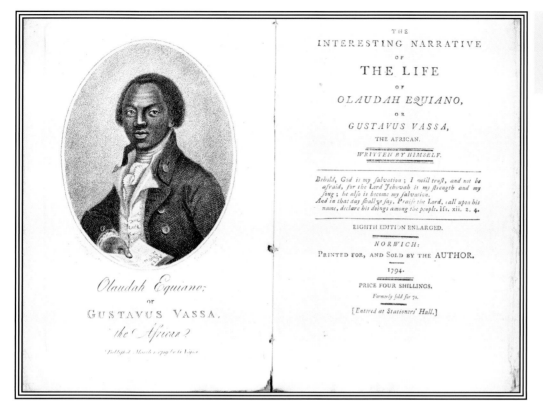

THE
INTERESTING NARRATIVE
OF
THE LIFE
OF
OLAUDAH EQUIANO,
OR
GUSTAVUS VASSA,
THE AFRICAN.

WRITTEN BY HIMSELF.

Behold, God is my salvation; I will trust, and not be
afraid, for the Lord Jehovah is my strength and my
song; he also is become my salvation.
And in that day shall ye say, Praise the Lord, call upon his
name, declare his doings among the people. Isa. xii. 2. 4.

EIGHTH EDITION ENLARGED.

NORWICH:
PRINTED FOR, AND SOLD BY THE AUTHOR.
1794.

PRICE FOUR SHILLINGS.
Formerly sold for 7s.

[*Entered at Stationers' Hall.*]

Olaudah Equiano;
or
GUSTAVUS VASSA,
the African?

The frontispiece and title page from The Interesting Narrative of the Life of Olaudah Equiano. (1794)

converted to Christianity, and became a sailor. In 1789, he published a book, entitled *The Interesting Narrative of the Life of Olaudah Equiano, or Gustavus Vassa, the African.* Probably the only full-length autobiography by a person enslaved in Africa, it became a key work in the early campaign to end the slave trade.

Before he was kidnapped, Equiano, like most people who lived far inland, had never seen the Atlantic. "The first object which saluted my eyes when I arrived on the coast," he recalled, "was the sea, and a slave ship, which was then riding at anchor, and waiting for its cargo. These filled me with astonishment." The great ocean stretched to the horizon, seemingly endless, the bluest of blues. The ship, with its tall masts and billowing sails, seemed magical.[33]

As were most captives, Equiano was terrified at his first sight of white men. Ships' crews had "horrible looks, red faces, and loose hair," he noted. However, he found their skin color most terrifying. Different people, at different times in history, have given different meaning to colors. Certain colors stir strong emotions. White, for Europeans, symbolized God, holiness, purity, beauty, cleanliness, morality; black was the color of Satan, evil, ugliness, dirt, sin, bad luck. Viewed in these terms, Africans were "devilish" and "evil." Seeing blacks this way justified the slaver, removing any sense of guilt he might have had.[34]

Yet Africans gave the opposite meanings to black and white. Black, to them, an English traveler wrote, was "their native beauty," a color they "most delight" in. White, to them, was the color of evil and death. "The devil is white," a saying went. "The white man is an old ape," went another saying. Sea monsters were supposedly white, too. Worse, Equiano and countless others thought whites were "bad spirits," cannibals who bought blacks to eat. Only after crossing the Atlantic did they realize that they would feed an economic machine, not fill whites' stomachs.[35]

The Middle Passage

Known as the Middle Passage, the voyage from Africa to the New World was the longest (3,700 miles), most dreadful leg of the triangle trade. The greatest danger to a ship came while loading captives on the coast. Captives had already been through a shattering ordeal. Even before sailing, most were depressed and in shock. Once aboard the ships, however, they realized they would be torn from everyone and everything they knew and loved. In desperation, many chose "rather to [die], than be ill treated," a sailor recalled.[36]

Occasionally, before sailing, men managed to slip out of their shackles and tried to seize the ship. The sailors usually crushed these uprisings with gunfire, but not without suffering severe losses themselves. Rather than revolt, other captives tried to commit suicide by jumping overboard and drowning, or refusing to eat and dying of starvation. Still others came down with what ships' surgeons called "the sulks"—that is, they died of a "broken heart." Death was not only a way of resisting enslavement. West Africans believed that, in death, their spirits returned

While being transported on the Amistad, slaves took control of the ship and revolted against their captors in an ultimately unsuccessful attempt to return home. (c. 1840)

Death of Capt. Ferrer, the Captain of the Amistad, July, 1839.

Don Jose Ruiz and Don Pedro Montez, of the Island of Cuba, having purchased fifty-three slaves at Havana, recently imported from Africa, put them on board the Amistad, Capt. Ferrer, in order to transport them to Principe, another port on the Island of Cuba. After being out from Havana about four days, the African captives on board, in order to obtain their freedom, and return to Africa, armed themselves with cane knives, and rose upon the Captain and crew of the vessel. Capt. Ferrer and the cook of the vessel were killed; two of the crew escaped; Ruiz and Montez were made prisoners.

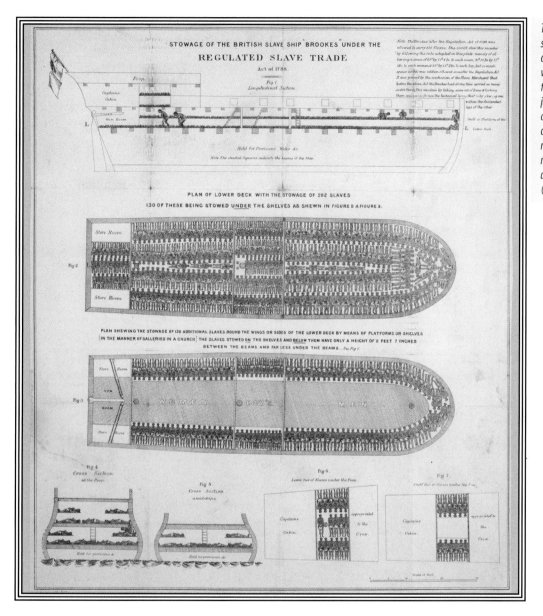

The floor plan of the slave ship Brookes, detailing how slaves were to be packed together during the journey to maximize carrying capacity. The cramped conditions resulted in extreme malnutrition, illness, and even suffocation. (c. 1789)

to their loved ones. In 1788, twelve years before John Brown's birth, Dr. Alexander Falconbridge published his *Account of the Slave Trade on the Coast of Africa*. The veteran slave-ship surgeon found that "Africans . . . have a strong attachment to their native country, together with a just sense of the value of liberty." This realization turned Falconbridge into a fierce opponent of the slave trade.[37]

Ship captains were either "loose packers" or "tight packers," depending on how many captives they crammed below-decks. Most were tight packers. Every

The slave ship
Wildfire, *depicting the
lower part of the main
deck and the women
on the upper deck.*
(c. 1860)

The slave ship Wildfire, depicting the lower part of the main deck and the women on the upper deck. (c. 1860)

space aboard a ship represented money to the captain and the undertakers. For that reason, ships were designed with maximum carrying capacity. The famous plan of the English ship *Brookes,* for example, showed people lying in the hold, or cargo deck, and the exact amount of space allotted to each.

Once aboard, sailors secured the men with leg irons attached to narrow platforms made of raw, splintery boards. They lay so close together that they could hardly turn or change position. Women and children stayed unchained in a separate section. Overcrowding spread diseases, chiefly dysentery and ophthalmia, an eye infection that often led to blindness. When someone died, sailors threw the body to the sharks that always trailed slave ships.

It was impossible to get comfortable or keep clean. The captives' "wretched situation," Olaudah Equiano recalled, was "aggravated by the galling [rubbing] of the chains . . . ; and the filth of the necessary tubs [buckets used as latrines], into which the children often fell, and were almost suffocated. The shrieks of the women, and the groans of the dying, rendered the whole a scene of horror almost inconceivable." Guineamen stank to high heaven—you could smell them five miles away.[38]

Each morning, weather permitting, sailors took captives topside to eat *dabbadabb,* a mixture of yams, salt pork, and palm oil. Alexander Falconbridge described what happened to those who would not eat: "Upon the negroes refusing to take sustenance, I have seen coals of fire, glowing hot, put on a shovel, and placed so near their lips as to scorch and burn them. And this has been accompanied with threats, of forcing them to swallow the coals, if they any longer persisted in refusing to eat." If they still refused, the captain might order them whipped to death as an example to others. After the meal, sailors "danced the slaves," making them move about and sing to ward off the sulks.[39]

In stormy weather, captives had to stay belowdecks. The result was torture by heat, filth, and slow suffocation. For ventilation, each hold had five or six air-ports, openings six by four inches, on either side of the ship. During storms, sailors closed the air-ports. The holds soon became hellish as diarrhea, or "the flux," tormented the captives. "The deck, that is, the floor of their rooms, was so covered with the blood and mucus which had proceeded from them in consequence of the flux, that it resembled a slaughterhouse," Falconbridge recalled. "It is not in the power of the human imagination, to picture to itself a situation more dreadful or disgusting. Numbers of the slaves having fainted, they were carried upon deck, where several of them died, and the rest were, with great difficulty, restored."[40]

After two months at sea, the ship reached the New World with its cargo of misery. To strengthen his "stock" for sale, the captain had them better fed for a few days, and palm oil was rubbed on their skin to hide bruises. Often Guineamen did not dock in port—they smelled too bad. The captain anchored a mile or two offshore, and longboats took his human cargo to auction.

Of the estimated 11.5 million people torn from West Africa, historians believe the Middle Passage killed 20 percent, or one in five. Yet this is not the whole story. For each person put aboard a slave ship, another ten (at least) died during capture, then of disease, exhaustion, or murder on the way to the coast. Thus, the Atlantic and East African slave trades are among history's greatest crimes.

However evil, the Atlantic slave trade helped create the world as we know it. Its profits made English merchants and sugar planters rich as any nobleman. They spent their money, truly "blood money," on vast country estates, valuable paintings, elegant furniture, and high living. They had so much money that they often ran out of ways to spend it, so they invested in factories, mills, mines, and banks. These investments, in turn, earned even larger profits. Those profits financed the early stages of the Industrial Revolution, making England the world's mightiest economic and military power.[41]

Dr. Martin Luther King Jr., the great African American civil rights leader of the 1960s, observed that the slave trade and slavery "scarred the soul and wounded the spirit of the black man." It devastated large parts of Africa, robbing them of generations of vigorous, creative people and starting countless wars. Most captives brought to the New World wound up in the West Indies and Brazil, centers of the sugar industry. Fewer than one in seven went to England's colonies in North America. Nevertheless, slavery shaped the colonies and the future United States in key ways. Before returning to John Brown, we must see what this meant.[42]

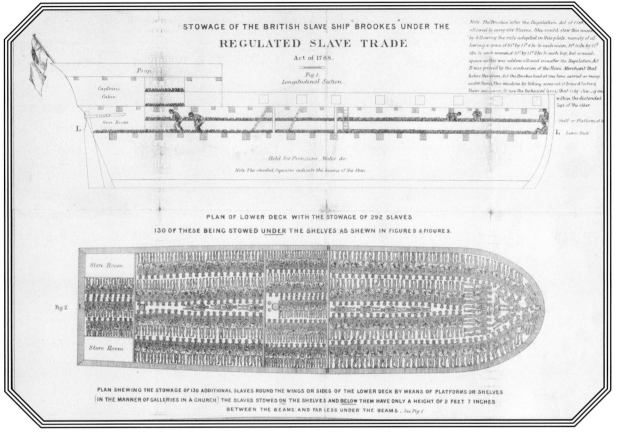

III

An Object Vast in Its Compass

Slavery is the great and foul stain upon the North American Union, and it is
a contemplation worthy of the most exalted soul whether its total abolition is
or is not practicable. . . . This object is vast in its compass [and] awful in its
prospects. . . . A life devoted to it would be nobly spent or sacrificed.
—John Quincy Adams, diary, February 24, 1820

The Rise of American Slavery

In August 1619, an English pirate ship, the *White Lion,* anchored at Jamestown, Virginia, England's first permanent North American settlement. Almost immediately, Colyn Cope, its captain, traded for supplies "20. and Odd Negroes" recently taken from a Portuguese vessel. Since Jamestown needed workers to grow tobacco, its chief moneymaking crop, slavery quickly took hold. Unlike in Arab lands, where slaves were not used in large-scale farming, in the American South they became the engine of economic progress.[1]

We may think of the South as the home of American slavery, the North as the home of American liberty. But the truth is more complicated. Southerners did not need to go to Africa or the West Indies for slaves. Northerners went for them—gladly. In colonial times, all thirteen colonies had slaves. New England, later the center of the antislavery crusade, played a key role in the Atlantic slave trade. Yet the first slaves in New England were not Africans but Native Americans.

New Englanders saw themselves as God's chosen people. The Puritan majority felt the Lord had sent them across the mighty ocean to glorify His name. It seemed to them that Native Americans, with different religious beliefs, were "enemies of the true God." This justified the Puritans' two Indian wars and scores of smaller campaigns. In Connecticut's Pequot War (1637) and Massachusetts's King William's War (1675), they showed no mercy toward those they called "red savages." Puritans boasted that they "Beat them small as the Dust before the Wind, and Cast them out, as the Dirt in the Streets." Villages went up in flames, and the survivors were shot or enslaved and used as farm laborers. Sometimes Puritans sold Native American captives to the West Indies, and they even shipped a few to North Africa as curiosities.[2]

Later, as war and European diseases like smallpox and measles destroyed entire tribes, Puritans turned elsewhere for slaves. They began to trade farm products in the West Indies for Africans, gold, and molasses, which they made into rum. Before long, they sent ships directly to West Africa. Puritan slavers sailed from five main ports: Boston and Salem in Massachusetts, New London in Connecticut, and Providence and Newport in Rhode Island. By the early 1700s, tiny Rhode

A Tennessee slave dealer's business card. (c. 1860)

Island accounted for 60 percent of the American slave trade.

Brought to New England, Africans worked as farm laborers, house servants, and artisans in the towns. But since traders made their highest profits in the Southern colonies, that is where most enslaved people wound up. Few Puritans saw anything wrong with dealing in human flesh or, for that matter, with hanging those convicted of witchcraft. Ministers solemnly preached that black people were "benighted heathens" and "idol worshipers," whom God punished by enslavement.[3]

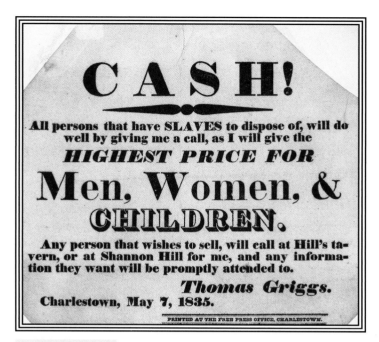

CASH!

All persons that have **SLAVES** to dispose of, will do well by giving me a call, as I will give the

HIGHEST PRICE FOR

Men, Women, & CHILDREN.

Any person that wishes to sell, will call at Hill's tavern, or at Shannon Hill for me, and any information they want will be promptly attended to.

Thomas Griggs.

Charlestown, May 7, 1835.

PRINTED AT THE FREE PRESS OFFICE, CHARLESTOWN.

An advertisement for the sale of slave men, women, and children, described as strictly property rather than as humans. (1835)

Some traders used their wealth to benefit fellow whites. For example, four brothers named Brown, who were leading slavers (and no relation to John Brown), gave generously to the College of Rhode Island, which gratefully changed its name to Brown University. Enslaved Africans built Brown's main building, University Hall. In Massachusetts, the Royall family helped found Harvard University's law school with profits from the slave trade. Boston's Faneuil Hall, called the Cradle of Liberty because of the stirring speeches made there during the American Revolution, was slave trader Peter Faneuil's gift to his beloved city. Slave-trade money also paid for Yale University's early professorships, scholarships, and library fund.[4]

The Peculiar Institution

Still, slavery drove its roots deepest into the soil of the South, becoming what Southerners called their "peculiar institution." (At that time, *peculiar* meant "unique" or "special" rather than "strange" or "odd," as it does today.) Not only was slavery more widespread there than in the North, but it also shaped the South's attitudes and lifestyles in countless ways.

Every Southern colony, and after independence every Southern state, had a set of laws called the slave codes. These laws governed the peculiar institution in every detail. While the wording differed from place to place, they were alike in their aims. All gave rights to the master, none to his human property. These codes defined a slave as "the absolute property of the Owner," and thus *entirely* subject to the will of his master." A slave could not do or say as he or she wished. "All that a slave possesses belongs to his master, he possesses nothing of his own," not even his body. Slaves were simply "chattel," property, with no more rights than a flea, a doorknob, or a speck of dust. The master could sell slaves, trade them, give them as gifts, pawn them, lend them, leave them in wills, wager them in games of chance, and take them in payment of debts. Slaves could not leave their plantations without written permission. If any did, bands of armed whites tracked them down with bloodhounds. Nor could slaves

The storefront of a slave auction site on Whitehall Street in Atlanta, Georgia. (c. 1864)

attend church services without a white person being present, because of the potentially radical nature of what religion could teach. Slave codes also made it a crime to teach enslaved people to read and write—skills likely, a law said, to "excite dissatisfaction in their minds."[5]

While forbidden to improve their minds, the enslaved could think and understand. Lack of education could not hide the injustice of slavery, for people lived it every day. Frederick Douglass quoted a song in black dialect, the form of speech used on plantations in the mid-1800s:

We raise de wheat,
Dey gib us de corn;
We bake de bread,
Dey gib us de cruss;
We sif de meal,
Dey gib us de huss;
We peal de meat,
Dey gib us de skin,

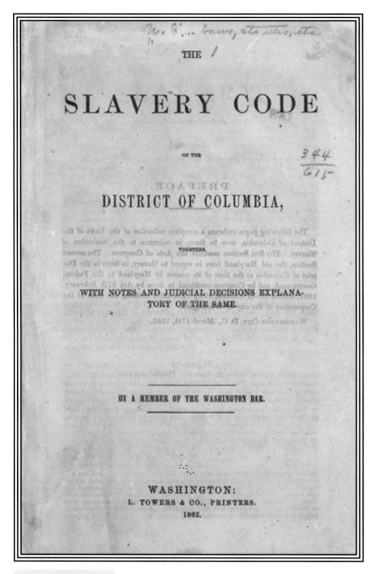

THE

SLAVERY CODE

OF THE

DISTRICT OF COLUMBIA,

TOGETHER

WITH NOTES AND JUDICIAL DECISIONS EXPLANA-
TORY OF THE SAME.

BY A MEMBER OF THE WASHINGTON BAR.

WASHINGTON:
L. TOWERS & CO., PRINTERS.
1862.

The front page of the official slavery code of Washington, D.C., which detailed the rights of the master—and the lack of rights of their human property. (1862)

And dat's de way

Dey takes us in.

We skim de pot,

Dey gib us the liquor,

And say dat's good enough for nigger.

(Whites used *nigger,* from the Spanish word *negro*—"black"—as a coarse insult, a verbal slap in the face.)[6]

Washington, D.C., the nation's capital, had its own slave code. This 122-page pamphlet, printed in small type, covered all aspects of slave life. It had hundreds of don'ts: don't set off firecrackers near a house, don't bathe in the city canal, don't fly kites within the city limits. Should a black person see a white person approaching on the sidewalk, he or she must step into the gutter. Since most streets were unpaved, this meant sinking into ankle-deep mud after a rainstorm.[7]

Washington's slave trade was a thriving business. The Washington slave pen, an open-air market, lay within sight of the U.S. Capitol. Every day—except Sunday, reserved for church services—lines of chained slaves shuffled along the road at the foot of the Capitol's steps. An auction block stood just a hundred yards from the White House.

Enslaved people did all the city's heavy work, including building the Capitol and White House. Slaves cleaned the streets and drove cartloads of human waste, which they dumped in an evil-smelling field ten blocks north of the White House. Slaves also served their masters in the halls of Congress and in the Supreme Court chamber.[8]

As with any group, slaveholders differed from one another in character and temperament. In the 1930s, the Library of Congress interviewed scores of former slaves, then in their eighties and

Slaves passing the U.S. Capitol around 1815.

nineties. Elizabeth Sparks set the tone: "But yer know dey's good an' bad people everywhere. That's the way the white folks wuz. Some had hearts; some had gizzards 'stead o' hearts." Ex-slaves remembered kindly masters who fed them well, did not overwork them, and never beat them. There were monsters, too, who enjoyed making people suffer. Yet the record also shows that both types of master were the exception, not the rule. The truth is, no slave system could ever have existed without brutality or its constant threat.[9]

To survive, the peculiar institution depended upon the threat or actual use of violence to instill fear, and through fear, obedience. Slave codes gave masters a free hand with their human property. Methods of punishment ranged from abusing slaves verbally to kicking them,

branding them with hot irons, and mutilating them—for example, by clipping chunks of flesh from their ears. Some masters made slaves wear iron masks over their faces and iron neck rings with long hooks that prevented them from lying down to sleep. Masters also put runaways to death to discourage others from attempting to escape. Now and then, for example, travelers passed a severed head atop a high pole beside the road.[10]

Whipping, however, was the most common punishment. Masters or overseers (poor white men hired to discipline slaves) used the bullwhip, a length of cowhide for driving oxen. Stripped to the

A depiction of the iron mask, collar, leg shackles, and spurs used to restrict slaves. (c. 1807)

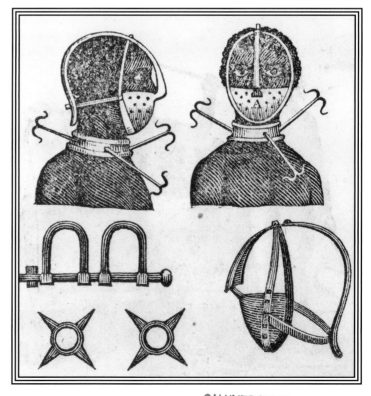

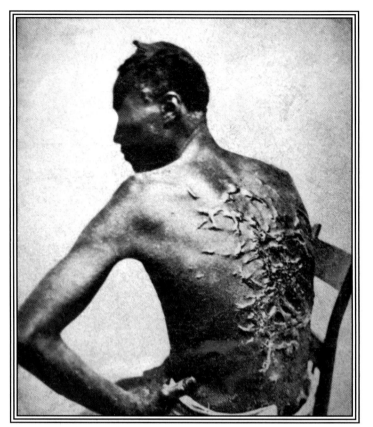

The original caption for this photograph of a slave's scars left by whipping read: "Overseer Artayou Carrier whipped me. I was two months in bed sore from the whipping. My master come after I was whipped; he discharged the overseer. The very words of poor Peter, taken as he sat for his picture." (c. 1863)

whip, *the chain, the gag, the thumb-screw, the pillory, the bowie-knife, the pistol, and the bloodhound. These are the necessary and unvarying accompaniments of the system. Wherever slavery is found, these horrid instruments are also found.*[11]

Whipping left raw, open wounds. Eventually these healed, forming rows of raised scars. Yet the most painful wounds never healed; these lasted a lifetime, buried deep inside the mind and spirit. It was bad enough to feel the lash oneself, worse to watch a loved one whipped and be unable to do anything about it.

Husbands and wives, mothers and children, never forgot how it felt to see the bullwhip tear into a family member. James Curry recalled how, as a child, he saw his mother tied to a tree, blood running down her back, crying. "I must stand there, and did not dare to crook my finger in her defense." Fugitive slave Henry Bibb wrote his former master about how it felt "to be compelled to stand by and see you whip and slash my wife without mercy, when I could afford her no protection, not even by offering myself to suffer the lash in her place. . . . My infant child was also frequently flogged by Mrs. Gatewood [the master's wife], for crying, until its skin was bruised literally purple." Whipping had a double effect. Not only did it punish the offender,

waist, or entirely naked, victims got from twelve to one hundred strokes. Frederick Douglass learned about the bullwhip early in life. He wrote:

To ensure good behavior, the slaveholder relies on the whip; *to induce proper humility, he relies on* the whip; *to rebuke what he is pleased to term insolence, he relies on* the whip; *to supply the place of wages, as an incentive to toil, he relies on* the whip; *to bind down the spirit of the slave, to imbrute [brutalize] and destroy his manhood, he relies on* the it also made onlookers feel powerless, as intended.[12]

Marriage could be a form of abuse, too. When girls became women, masters might order them to become mothers. Sometimes a master allowed a woman to choose her husband. If not, he chose one for her. Since slaves could not legally marry, the master held a mock ceremony in which the couple vowed not the traditional "until death do us part," but "until distance do us part." "Distance" meant the breakup of a family, its members sold to faraway plantations.

Children did not belong to their parents. Masters thought of slaves' children as two-legged farm animals. Louisiana's slave code couched the awful reality in lawyerspeak. It said: "Children born of a mother then in a state of slavery, whether married or not, follow the condition of their mother; they are consequently slaves and belong to the master of their mother." Since slaves were property, masters could legally break up families, a practice forbidden in Arab lands. In America, slaves lived in constant dread of being "sold away," never to see each other again. Historians believe that masters broke up as many as one in three slave marriages.[13]

As in Arab lands, enslaved women had to submit to the master's sexual advances. An American slaveholder could legally force himself on his female "property." As a result, thousands of mulattoes, children of mixed white and black descent, were born each year. "God forgive us," wrote a wealthy South Carolina woman named Mary Chesnut, "but ours is a *monstrous* system. . . . Our men live . . . with their wives and their concubines, and the mulattoes one sees in every family exactly resemble the white children." The master's white children were brothers and sisters to his mulatto children. But there was a difference: masters could (and did) sell their mulatto children, their own flesh and blood. Chesnut wrote on the eve of the Civil War, which shows that some Southern whites, though profiting

Household slaves like this nursemaid often held children for their portraits. (c. 1855)

from the peculiar institution, felt shamed by it.[14]

Slavery and the Founding Fathers

The Quakers, or Religious Society of Friends, were the first Americans to denounce slavery. Members of a small religious group founded in England in the 1640s, Quakers believed God created humans in His image. Harming another person, therefore, injured the divine "spark" within the person who caused the harm. Quakers sought to live by the Bible's Golden Rule: "Do unto others as you would have them do unto you" (Matthew 7:12). True to their belief, they preached against slavery, wrote against slavery, and banned slave traders from their religious services. As Quaker writer Benjamin Lay put it in 1737, slavery was a "Hellish Practice" and a "filthy sin," "the greatest Sin in the World, of the very Nature of Hell itself, and . . . the Belly of Hell."[15]

Quakers had little influence, though, outside their own circles. Yet things began to change in the 1760s, as British lawmakers tried to tax the colonies without their consent. Taxation without representation, Americans cried, was tyranny. Where would it end? George Washington feared the worst. Unless checked in time, the "mother country" would turn freeborn Americans into slaves as oppressed *as the blacks we rule over.*[16]

The American Revolution began in Massachusetts on April 19, 1776, at the Battles of Lexington and Concord. Less than two months later, on June 11, the Second Continental Congress, a gathering of delegates from the colonies in Philadelphia, appointed a committee to prepare a document declaring independence. The committee asked Thomas Jefferson to write the first draft. After making a few changes to Jefferson's draft, Congress issued the Declaration of Independence on July 4, which became the official birthday of the United States. Around this time, Captain John Brown died while serving in the Continental army.[17]

Jefferson gave the most space in the Declaration of Independence to setting out the colonies' grievances against Britain. Americans care little about these today. The part they remember is the first sentence of the second paragraph, among the most eloquent words ever written in the English language. It says: "We hold these Truths to be self-evident, that all Men are created equal, that they are endowed by their Creator with certain unalienable Rights, that among these are Life, Liberty, and the Pursuit of Happiness."

For decades, Americans argued over the meaning of "all Men." Women were not the issue; when Jefferson wrote, the educated called the human race "men" and "mankind." What about black people? Did "all Men" include them? John

Adams and Benjamin Franklin thought so. Blacks, being human, had the God-given right to life, liberty, and happiness. Jefferson agreed that blacks were human, but . . .

Given what we know about Jefferson, "all Men" meant "all free white people." According to scholar Henry Louis Gates Jr., "Thomas Jefferson most certainly was not thinking of black men and women when he wrote the Declaration of Independence, and no amount of romantic historical wishful thinking can alter that fact." But words have power. And whatever Jefferson meant by "all Men," many Americans took the phrase at face value, as a promise of freedom for all people.[18]

The future third president never said God created black people as *his* equals, for that would have meant he was breaking divine law by holding them in bondage. While Jefferson thought slavery was wrong, what made it so was not its abuse of blacks, but its effect on whites. Slavery harmed whites by turning them into brutes and tyrants. He spoke from experience: he had several children with a slave named Sally Hemings. But he did not allow his qualms to interfere with his elegant lifestyle. Jefferson owned 267 slaves, some of whom he sold to pay debts. When a slave named Sandy escaped with a white horse, Jefferson ran newspaper ads offering a reward for the fugitive's return. He

An ad placed in the Virginia Gazette by future president Thomas Jefferson, offering a reward for the return of his runaway slave. (September 14, 1769)

also had slaves whipped and sold away for various offenses.

Called "man's most dangerous myth," racism is the belief that certain groups of people are naturally inferior to others. By this definition, Jefferson was a founder of American racism. While Americans had not studied African history and culture in any serious way, Jefferson felt qualified to insist that he knew all about black people. In his book *Notes on the State of Virginia* (1786), he claimed blacks were "inferior to the whites in . . . body and mind"— lacking any music, poetry, art, or ideas worth discussing. Blackness, he believed, came "from the colour of the blood." Yes, free the slaves, Jefferson said. However, America must then "colonize" them— that is, deport them to Africa; otherwise, they would start a race war.[19]

In the summer of 1787, the Constitutional Convention met in Philadelphia to draw up a plan for a national government.

Besides defining its duties, delegates had to face the problem of slavery. Many issues divided the Northern and Southern states. Yet what divided them most, wrote James Madison, the chief designer of the U.S. Constitution and later the nation's fourth president, was "their having or not having slaves."[20]

The problem was that Georgia and South Carolina delegates claimed their states could not exist without slave labor. South Carolinian Rawlins Lowndes told the convention, "Negroes [are] our wealth, our only natural resource." It was slaves who cleared forests, dug drainage ditches, and did the hundreds of jobs involved in raising crops. Southern delegates demanded that the Constitution make slavery the law of the land, protecting it with all the power of the central government. Without such guarantees, they threatened to leave the convention, ending any chance of a United States of America. For without the Union, the states must go their own ways. Each would tax the others' products, raise armies, and fight over boundaries. Chaos would rule.[21]

In the end, the convention agreed to a constitution. Was the U.S. Constitution for or against slavery? It was both. Neither side got all it wanted. The Constitution was a compromise, in which each side gave up certain things to gain others. To form the Union, antislavery delegates decided to tolerate the peculiar institution

A painting by Jean Leon Gerome Ferris depicting Benjamin Franklin reading a draft of the Declaration of Independence to John Adams, seated, and Thomas Jefferson, standing. (c. 1921)

purely as a state matter, not blessed by America as a whole. As James Madison wrote in his notes, they "thought it wrong to admit in the Constitution the idea that there could be property in men." This explains why the words *slave* and *slavery* do not appear in the document, but *persons, such persons,* and *other persons* do.[22]

Delegates worked out three compromises on slavery. Since the number of people each state sent to the House of Representatives would depend on its population, slaveholders wanted their slaves added to the count. (The House and Senate together form the legislative, or lawmaking, branch of the federal government.) Antislavery delegates did not want slaves counted at all. Slave codes defined slaves as property. Cows and pigs are property. So, antislavery delegates asked, why not count our farm animals, too?

Both sides agreed to count each slave as three-fifths of a person. Opponents of slavery pushed for the rule, intending it to *limit* slaveholders' power. According to historian Don E. Fehrenbacher, "the fraction 'three-fifths' had no racial meaning. It did not represent a perception of blacks as three-fifths human." Yet what people think is true may be more important than the truth itself. The public at large took the three-fifths rule at face value, believing the Constitution viewed slaves as only partially human. Many Americans still believe this of the Constitution, wrongly. What is certain is that the rule gave slaveholders political power greater than their numbers deserved. More Southern congressmen meant increased representation in the Electoral College. (Created by the Constitution, the Electoral College is an institution comprising a body of representatives chosen by each state's voters to elect the president and vice president.) Thomas Jefferson would have lost the election of 1800 if not for the three-fifths rule, which explains why critics called him the "Negro President."[23]

Delegates also compromised on the Atlantic slave trade. Some slaveholders wanted it continued indefinitely. Anti-slavery people wanted it ended immediately. After heated debate, the delegates agreed to allow it for twenty years, ending January 1, 1808. From then on, no slave could be imported. Lastly, the Constitution said the laws of one state could not excuse a person from "Service or Labour" in another state. Translation: States must deliver fugitives to the states they escaped from. In case of trouble, the Constitution guaranteed that federal troops would put down rebellion, understood as slave rebellion.

When the Founders left Philadelphia, they knew they had not solved America's slavery problem, but had done their best to create the Union. Faced with the need to choose between an imperfect Constitution with slavery and no Constitution (and no Union) at all, they chose an imperfect Constitution. The Founders left it to future generations to deal with slavery, hopefully without destroying the country. This meant that generations of innocents paid for national unity with their continued bondage.

Yet the Founders had some reason for optimism. The language of liberty is strong stuff. The Declaration of Independence changed minds in ways its author could not have foreseen when he wrote it. Americans began to ask if a person's color told anything about what Martin Luther King Jr. would call "the content of their character." Slaves were good and bad, smart and stupid, kind and cruel. In short, they were human beings. Abigail Adams, wife of the future second president, spoke for many. It was wrong, she wrote, to "fight ourselfs for what we are daily robbing and plundering from those who have as good a right to freedom as we have."[24]

Northern states had turned against slavery even before the Constitutional Convention. As war raged on, Vermont (1777), New Hampshire (1779), and Pennsylvania (1780) abolished slavery. Massachusetts, Connecticut, New York, and Rhode Island did the same between 1783 and 1786. In 1787, Congress issued the Northwest Ordinance, which banned slavery in the region north of the Ohio River—that is, the future states of Ohio, Indiana, Michigan, Illinois, and Wisconsin. From then on, America had two kinds of states: free states and slave states. This division would last seventy-eight years, until the Civil War made all states free.

But the ideal of liberty was only part of the story. Northerners rejected slavery not simply because they believed "all Men" are created equal. Rejection served their interests. Already, the North had become a magnet for Europeans seeking better lives. Mostly poor and unskilled, they often sought the same jobs done by slaves. This is why the loudest cries for ending slavery came from whites who feared competition from unpaid slaves.

John Adams noted that in Massachusetts, "the real cause" of the abolition of slavery was that whites "would not suffer the labor, by which alone they could obtain [their living], to be done by slaves." Worse, "if the gentlemen had been permitted by law to hold slaves, the common white people would have put the slaves to death, and their masters too perhaps." Thus, ending slavery may have avoided a second American Revolution, this time against the wealthy.[25]

However, ending Northern slavery did not bring liberty and equality. State laws freed few people already held in bondage. Instead, they freed their children, usually after they reached the age of twenty-eight. That way, lawmakers thought, slaves would work off the masters' investments in them and their children. And that was just the beginning. Frederick Douglass explained: "Aliens we are in our native land." He was right. Racism did not respect state borders. It ran as deep in the North as in the South.[26]

Just as slave states had slave codes, free states had black laws, which allowed many forms of discrimination. Black laws banned marriages between blacks and whites; violators faced fines and prison time. Free blacks could vote only in Massachusetts, New Hampshire, Vermont, and Maine. Though they paid taxes, they could not serve on juries or testify against a white person in court. Laws barred them from public transportation, or made them sit separately from whites. Black criminals went to segregated prisons, sick blacks to segregated hospitals, dead blacks to segregated graveyards.

Black children attended segregated schools, if they went to school at all. In 1833, the year John Brown married Mary Ann Day, Prudence Crandall, a white reformer, opened a boarding school for blacks in Canterbury, Connecticut. Pupils sang a song, composed by Crandall, about their treatment by the community:

Prudence Crandall was sent to prison for opening a school for black children in Connecticut. (c. 1897)

> *Sometimes when we have walked the*
> * streets*
> *Saluted we have been,*
> *By guns and drums and cow bells too*
> *And horns of polished tin.*
> *With warnings, threats, and words*
> * severe*
> *They visit us at times,*
> *And gladly would they send us off*
> *To Afric's burning climes.*

Angry whites threw horse manure into the school's well; a mob later tore the building down.[27]

Meanwhile, Southerners took a closer look at their peculiar institution. Some, like some Northerners, felt troubled by slavery and believed "all Men" were entitled to natural rights. So they began to free slaves through manumission, a word derived from the Latin for "hand" and "let

go." In the years 1790–1810, Southerners freed over 100,000 enslaved people. (In contrast, twenty years later, in 1830, about 141,000 blacks lived in the free states, rising to about 225,000 by 1860.)[28]

As in the North, there were also practical reasons for freeing slaves. Until the development of chemical fertilizers in the twentieth century, growing the same crop year after year damaged the soil. This forced growers of tobacco, the South's chief cash crop, to switch to wheat, fruits, and vegetables. Since raising these required fewer workers, plantations became overstocked with slaves. Housing and feeding this surplus became a costly burden. So, as slaves lost value, masters, particularly in Virginia, freed those too old or feeble for farmwork. Moreover, they wished to keep prices for the young and able-bodied high by halting imports from Africa. So it seemed that slavery was on the way out and would, over time, die a natural death in the South. It might have—had cotton not come to revive it.[29]

His Majesty, King Cotton

Since ancient times, people had worn clothing made of wool and linen. Cotton, however, was the ideal fiber: lightweight, cool, and easily dyed in attractive colors. Unfortunately, it was a luxury, affordable only to the rich. England, the world's leading cloth producer, got its cotton from Egypt and India. These countries grew a variety with long fibers and smooth seeds easily picked out by hand. America's Southern states had grown small amounts of this "long-staple" cotton since the 1780s, but soil and climate kept them from growing enough to meet manufacturers' needs. Another variety of cotton, with short fibers, grew well in the South. The only problem was that it had barbed seeds, like tiny fishhooks, which clung to the fibers. That made it unprofitable, for it took a worker half a day to hand-separate a pound of "short-staple" fiber from its seeds.

This changed in 1793, four years after the Constitution took effect. While visiting a Southern friend, a Connecticut inventor named Eli Whitney saw a cat pounce on a chicken. When the cat fin-

ished eating, only the bird's feathers remained in its claws. This gave Whitney the idea for a cotton engine, or *gin* for short. His machine used mechanical claws and could separate a thousand pounds of cotton fiber a day.

Intended to save labor, Whitney's invention brought untold misery. The "new sugar," as some called cotton, gave slavery new life. For it was not enough to remove seeds easily; you needed enough cotton to remove them from. That required land. Cotton did not grow well in Virginia and North Carolina, now specializing in wheat and corn. Worse, before the invention of chemical fertilizers, cotton, like tobacco, drained vital nutrients from the soil, requiring new lands.

Cotton growers looked farther south, toward South Carolina, Georgia, Flor-

Eli Whitney's patent for the cotton gin. (c. 1823)

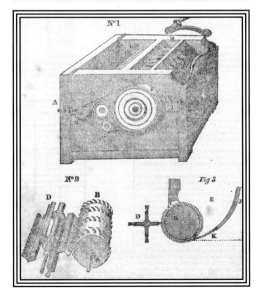

ida, and Alabama; after the Louisiana Purchase (1803) and the Mexican War (1846–1848), they looked toward Mississippi, Arkansas, Louisiana, and Texas. Overstocked states profited, as slave prices shot from $300 for a field worker in 1790 to $1,800 in 1860. Enslaved people called the move to the Deep South the "Second Middle Passage." This time, instead of going by sea as their African ancestors had, they went overland. Men marched in handcuffs and with iron bands fastened around their ankles. Women and children went unbound. Masters rode on horseback or in wagons. In 1856, an English traveler reported:

The hardships the negroes go through
who are attached to one of these
emigrant parties baffle description. . . .
They trudge on foot all day through
mud and thicket without rest. . . .
Thousands of miles are traversed by
these weary wayfarers without their
knowing or caring why, urged on
by the whip. . . . Hard work, coarse
food, merciless floggings, are all that
await them, and all that they can look
[forward] to. I have never passed
them, staggering along in the rear
of the wagons at the close of a long
day's march, the weakest furthest
in the rear, the strongest already
utterly spent, without wondering how

[Christians] . . . can look so calmly . . .
at so foul and monstrous a wrong as
this American slavery.[30]

The age of King Cotton had dawned. The fluffy white stuff became the nation's chief product sold overseas. Cotton, and the slaves that grew it, helped make America a first-class economic power. Less than fifty years after Eli Whitney's invention, Southern short-staple cotton made up three-fourths of the world's supply. In England, cities like Manchester and Leeds turned out an unending supply of cotton goods. Regular shipments of cotton also sped up the Industrial Revolution in New England. Villages in Massachusetts like Lawrence, Lowell, and Andover became thriving cities, with mills to spin the fibers into thread and factories for weaving thread into cloth. Thus, white Southerners were not the only ones to benefit financially from slavery.[31]

Slave-grown cotton saved countless lives. Until its appearance, most people could not afford more than one set of clothes, and often no underwear. Unable to change their clothes, they wore them, unwashed, until they fell apart, and then replaced them. Worse, lice, carriers of disease-causing bacteria, lived in dirty clothes. Most people, however, could now afford cotton garments and a few sets of underwear. By changing to clean clothes while washing dirty clothes, they avoided

Stereographs, like this one of slaves working in a cotton field, place two offset photographs side by side and, viewed through a stereoscope, give an increased element of depth perception. (c. 1860–1870)

dangerous diseases. They also smelled better.

Natural Enemies

A Roman proverb says, "All slaves are enemies." So they are. Slaves may have seemed loyal, peaceful, and obedient— and some really were. But that did not change the reality: slavery is cruelty, and "all Men" crave freedom, at least for themselves. Throughout history, resistance has taken different forms. Some enslaved people resisted passively; that is, they avoided violence but did as little work as they could get away with. Others escaped, murdered masters, or rebelled. America's slaves were no different.[32]

Planters were forever complaining about their "people." Slaves "misunderstood" orders, wasted time, faked illness, broke tools, "accidentally" ruined cotton plants while hoeing, and injured farm ani-

mals. Some fled to avoid punishment or to join relatives who had already escaped. Yet the most common reason, fugitives said, was to protest the very essence of slavery. Slaves fled to assert their humanity. "One and all," recalled Edward Lycurgas, a fugitive, "dey had a good strong notion to see what it was like to own your own body."[33]

Many fugitives "rode" the Underground Railroad, so named in the 1830s when Americans built their first rail lines. This line, however, was a secret (thus "underground") network of volunteers who guided fugitive slaves to safety. It also had "trains," "stations," and "conductors." A train might be a mule, a rowboat, a false-bottomed wagon. A station was any place that offered temporary safety, food, and shelter: a farmhouse, a hayloft, a cellar, or a cubbyhole hidden behind boxes. Conductors were antislavery whites and

African Americans escaping from slavery in wagons and on foot. (c. 1893)

free blacks. Herself a fugitive, Harriet Tubman was the foremost conductor. Known as "the Moses of her people," she carried a pistol and swore to use it on anyone who tried to turn back, for that would endanger the others. Some journeys took weeks or even months. Upon reaching a free state, fugitives hid in communities of free blacks and found jobs. Historians believe over fifty thousand slaves escaped in the years 1830–1860, on their own or by the Underground Railroad.[34]

Slaves could not simply pick up and leave—that would have been suicidal. To succeed, they needed a plan they could keep secret from the master but share with each other. One method of sharing was through quilts made of pieces of cloth stitched together. Women made quilts with cloth from worn-out clothes or scraps discarded by the master's family. In stitching the pieces together, they used patterns that formed a secret code. These patterns showed the best escape routes and how to survive in the wilderness, such as where to cross certain rivers. The symbols' meanings were passed on as part of the slaves' oral tradition of stories and songs. Titles and lyrics of certain spirituals, religious songs originating among blacks, also served as secret traveling instructions. The best known is "Follow the Drinking Gourd." Normally, the term *drinking gourd* refers to the hollowed-out fruit used by many country people as a water dipper. But in this song

Harriet Tubman carried out more than thirteen missions to free slaves, helping over seventy escape. (c. 1860–1875)

it was code for the Big Dipper, a group of seven stars that can be used to point to other parts of the sky. An imaginary line extending from the two stars at the front of the cup points to the North Star. Going north would lead to freedom, or to an Underground Railroad conductor. The song goes, in part:

Follow the Drinking Gourd,

For the old man is a-waiting for to

  carry you to freedom

If you follow the Drinking Gourd.

The riverbank makes a very good road.

The dead trees will show you the way.

Left foot, peg foot, traveling on,

Follow the Drinking Gourd.[35]

When slaves used violence, it took several forms. Often they turned violence inward, against themselves. Masters spoke of people cutting off fingers or gouging out an eye to escape the auction block, "robbing" the owners of the value of their lawful property. Desperate people committed suicide or killed their children for the same reason. Others turned on their masters. Newspapers and court records tell of house servants bewitching masters with obeah, a type of African magic that uses charms to do harm. For example, sticking pins into a doll was supposed to wound the victim it represented. We also read of cooks occasionally mixing ground glass into food and drinks, or poisoning food.

A slaveholder's worst fear has always been rebellion. The Romans, for example, fought three full-scale slave wars, called the Servile Wars. The final war lasted from 73 to 71 BCE. Its leader was the gladiator Spartacus, a slave-warrior trained to fight to the death to amuse an audience. Spartacus led an army of seventy thousand fugitive gladiators and slaves. For two years, he defied Rome's best generals, until he was finally killed in battle. The Romans then crucified six thousand prisoners along the Appian Way, a main road, one every 130 feet or so. For years afterward, travelers passed skeletons on crosses, grisly reminders of what lay in store for rebellious slaves.

New World history is filled with slave revolts. Every European colony that had slaves experienced rebellions. For example, Britain's thirteen North American colonies had no fewer than 250 slave uprisings. These required thoughtful leadership, planning, and organization, testimony to the rebels' intelligence and courage. Yet they failed, defeated by superior forces. In each case, rebel captives died horribly—burned alive, slowly starved, or beaten with iron bars until every bone in their bodies was broken.[36]

The largest slave rebellion took place in Hispaniola, Spain's first colony in the New World. While Spain kept the island's eastern half, renamed Santo Domingo, France seized the western half in 1697, calling it Saint-Domingue. Under French rule, Saint-Domingue grew nearly half the world's sugar and much of its coffee. Its half million slaves outnumbered whites seventeen to one. And its *code noir* (black code) made America's slave laws seem tame, so cruel it was. Planters thought it cheaper to work slaves to death and import fresh ones from Africa than to care for them properly. Their horses and dogs were treated better.

After sundown on August 22, 1791, a massive uprising swept Saint-Domingue. Nearly a thousand plantations burned in

Known as "Black Spartacus," Toussaint L'Ouverture led a slave rebellion that eventually resulted in the independent black state of Haiti. (date unknown)

that night. Meanwhile, slaves killed over two thousand whites, many by torture.[37]

French dictator Napoleon Bonaparte sent an army to crush the rebellion. Instead, his best generals met their match in Toussaint L'Ouverture, described as "small, frail," and "very ugly." This former slave, known to the enemy as "Black Spartacus," was a born leader. Toussaint organized a black army. His forces and yellow fever, a deadly disease carried by mosquitoes, tore the invaders to shreds. (Over the centuries, most Africans exposed to yellow fever developed a natural immunity.) Betrayed, Toussaint was deported to France, where he died in prison.

Yet the struggle continued until Napoleon admitted defeat. In 1804, Saint-Domingue became the Republic of Haiti, from the Indian word for "high country."[38]

France lost more than its prize colony. Upon regaining Haiti, Napoleon planned to use it as a base for building an empire in Louisiana, at the time a vast French-held territory stretching from the Mississippi River to the Rocky Mountains. His empire would block America's westward expansion, limiting it to a narrow strip of land along the Atlantic coast. After his failure in Haiti, however, Napoleon had no use for Louisiana. In 1803, he sold it to President Thomas Jefferson for $15 million. This worked out to four cents an acre for an area of 828,000 square miles.

Not only did the Louisiana Purchase double the nation's size, it also changed attitudes. It was, many Americans believed, their "Manifest Destiny," God's will, that they rule the entire continent. Before long, settlers pushed to create new states out of the purchase. Should these states join the Union as free or slave? Eventually this question would lead to bitter quarrels between North and South—and bloodshed, too. The bloodshed, we will see, made John Brown's name a household word.[39]

Meanwhile, events taking place in Saint-Domingue influenced American attitudes. French refugees brought horrific tales of black vengeance. Southerners feared such tales would inflame their own slaves. Similarly, the language of natural rights might spread the revolutionary "infection" further.

Fifteen years separated the Declaration of Independence from the Saint-Domingue revolt. That document and the war fought to achieve its promise were still living memories. The Fourth of July was *the* national holiday, celebrated with parades, fireworks, and speeches about liberty. Planters toasted the "Glorious Fourth" and read the document aloud at celebrations. Slaves learned its contents, one slave said, "by keepin' still and mindin' things." Then they told others, who told yet others that God created "all Men" equal. Others were able to read copies of the document themselves, for they had learned to read.[40]

The slaves "General" Gabriel in Virginia (1800) and Denmark Vesey in South Carolina (1802) led unsuccessful revolts—and died on the gallows. Toussaint L'Ouverture and the Declaration of Independence had inspired both men. Up north, free blacks paraded on the anniversary of the Haitian revolution. Boston shopkeeper David Walker, the son of a free mother, issued a pamphlet titled *Walker's Appeal, in Four Articles* (1829). Copies circulated widely in Northern black communities. In it, Walker praised "Hayti" as "the glory of the blacks and terror of tyrants." He warned:

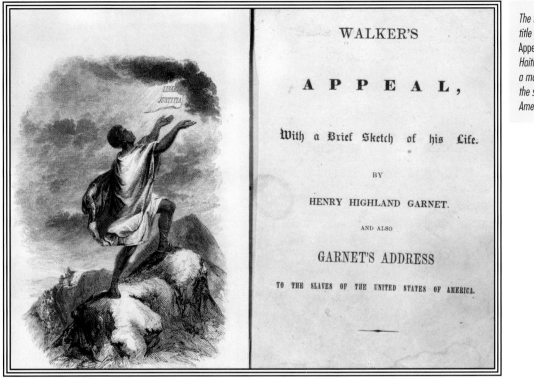

WALKER'S

APPEAL,

With a Brief Sketch of his Life.

BY

HENRY HIGHLAND GARNET.

AND ALSO

GARNET'S ADDRESS

TO THE SLAVES OF THE UNITED STATES OF AMERICA.

The frontispiece and title page of Walker's Appeal, praising the Haitian revolution as a model for freeing the slaves in North America. (c. 1848)

The whites have had us under them for more than three centuries, murdering, and treating us like brutes. . . . [But] get the blacks started, and if you do not have a gang of tigers and lions to deal with, I am a deceiver of the blacks and of the whites. . . . If you [blacks] commence, make sure work—do not trifle . . . kill or be killed. Now, I ask you, had you rather be killed than to be a slave to a tyrant, who takes the life of your mother, wife, and dear little children? . . . Believe this, that there is no more harm for you to kill a man, who is trying to kill you, than it is for you to take a drink of water when thirsty. . . . See your declaration, Americans!! Do you understand your own language? Hear your language, proclaimed to the world, July 4, 1776— WE HOLD THESE TRUTHS TO BE SELF-EVIDENT—THAT ALL MEN ARE CREATED EQUAL!![41]

A year later, America's most lethal slave revolt rocked Southampton County, Virginia. On August 21, 1831, Nat Turner led forty fellow slaves in an uprising that left sixty whites, mostly women and children, dead. On one farm, his men killed a family of five; at another, a mother and her ten children. Somehow Turner had come to believe that God had chosen him

A woodcut illustrating the stages of Nat Turner's Virginia rebellion. (c. 1831)

A woodcut illustrating the stages of Nat Turner's Virginia rebellion. (c. 1831)

to free his fellow slaves. Whites quickly crushed the rebellion, captured Turner, tried him, and sentenced him to death by hanging. After Turner's execution, a surgeon skinned his body "and made grease of the flesh."[42]

News of Nat Turner's revolt struck like a thunderbolt. Ex-slave Fannie Berry, a child then, marveled at the panic. She remembered "my Mistress, Miss Sara Ann, comin' to de window an' hollerin', 'De niggers is arisin'! De niggers is arisin'! De niggers is killin' all de white folks, killin' all de babies in de cradle!'"[43]

Nat Turner's revolt frightened Southerners as nothing had done before. To be sure, there had been many attempted revolts, but those had failed without loss of white lives. Now rebels had drawn blood. On plantations, masters fearing another Saint-Domingue slept with loaded pistols on their night tables, wakening with pounding hearts at any sound. But nothing could restore their sense of security. The rebel's ghost lived on. It would lurk in Southerners' minds for decades, always there, always menacing. Southerners, a traveler wrote, could not shake the idea "that a Nat Turner might be in any family."[44]

Nat Turner's fate, however, taught slaves a lesson. Masters had the law, the guns, and the will to use them with all the cruelty born of fear. America was not Haiti. No rebellion, it seemed, could succeed in America on its own. Only the free states offered any hope of freedom.

The Abolitionists

On New Year's Day of 1831, as Nat Turner prepared to strike, William Lloyd Garrison issued the first edition of a weekly newspaper in Boston. The son of a drunken sailor who had abandoned his family, Garrison, twenty-six, had always felt sympathy for the underdog. Called the *Liberator*, his newspaper became the mouthpiece of the abolitionists, Northerners pledged to the abolition, or ending, of slavery. The peculiar institution, they felt, violated the Golden Rule and the Declaration of Independence. Slavery, as Garrison put it, "turns a man into a thing." Abolitionists demanded freedom for slaves, at once, without regard to cost. Liberty had no dollar price. If planters could not grow cotton without slaves, then let them not grow it. If the Southern economy collapsed, fine. If slaveholders lost their investment in human flesh, valued at billions of dollars, too bad.[45]

These ideas were hardly new; free blacks had been expressing them for years. Garrison's originality lay in his genius for drawing others into the anti-slavery crusade. A religious revival swept America in the 1820s and 1830s. Its aim: to set the country "right with God" by eradicating social evils. Reformers denounced gambling, whiskey drinking, and cruel sports like boxing, in which men fought bare-knuckled until one dropped. They demanded women's rights, particularly the vote, and clothing reform. Wearing long dresses and tight corsets, they said, "imprisoned and crippled" women. Modern women should wear the "Bloomer dress." Named for social

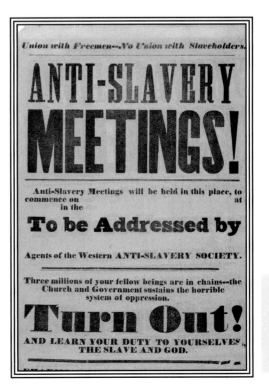

A blank poster to be filled in by local chapters announcing a meeting of the American Anti-Slavery Society. (c. 1850)

reformer Amelia Bloomer, it had full trousers with frills—"bloomers" for short. By championing clothing reform and other worthy causes, Garrison drew reformers to his own cause.[46]

To spread the abolitionist message, in 1833—the year John Brown married his second wife, Mary Ann Day—Garrison formed the American Anti-Slavery Society. Headquartered in Boston, the society became the model for branches in other cities. These caught on quickly, growing in number from 60 (1835) to 1,300 (1838), with about 108,000 members. Local antislavery societies joined others to form networks linked by railroad, telegraph, and the U.S. mail.[47]

Garrison and his followers called themselves "nonresistants," people who did not believe in resisting evil with force. Instead, they hoped to persuade people to abolish slavery by appealing to their conscience, their sense of right and wrong. Abolishing slavery "by the power of love," they thought, was God's way. Though slaves were horribly abused, it would be wrong for them to use violence to gain their freedom, as David Walker threatened. Nothing good, Garrison declared, can come of violence. In the first issue of the *Liberator,* he told blacks:

> *Not by the sword shall your*
> *deliverance be;*

> *Not by the shedding of your master's*
> *blood.*
> *Not by rebellion—or foul*
> *treachery . . . !*

Violence was not only immoral; it always backfired, hardening the opposition. In time, however, as we will see, most abolitionists came to accept violence when it seemed the only way to end slavery.[48]

Garrison's firmest allies were white men, usually well-educated, well-off community leaders and opinion makers: ministers, lawyers, doctors, teachers, writers. Chief among these was Wendell Phillips, a Harvard-educated lawyer who gave up his career to fight slavery full-time. Nicknamed "Abolition's Golden Trumpet," Phillips was a dazzling speaker who used words as weapons. He spoke logically with, a critic said, "concentrated bitterness." When he finished, opponents felt as if they had been physically battered. A master of insults, Phillips called one fellow "a great mass of dough," another "a whining spaniel." He and Garrison were such good friends that the older man named his eldest son Wendell Phillips Garrison.[49]

Another ally, Protestant minister Theodore Parker, was among the most learned people in America. Parker knew sixteen languages and spent a thousand dollars a year on books, a fortune at the time. He owned fifteen thousand volumes, chiefly on religion and history; books overflowed his house from attic to cellar, leaving room for little else. Like Wendell Phillips, Parker fairly hypnotized crowds. "We know that we cannot argue him down," opponents prayed, "but O Lord, put a hook in his jaws so that he may not be able to speak!"[50]

Abolitionists did not have the mass media we take for granted: radio, television, Internet. Speeches, though important, had a local and thus limited reach. How to get their message across quickly, with the greatest impact, to the most people? The English had shown the way. In the 1790s, scholar Thomas Clarkson and politician William Wilberforce began history's first successful effort to change public opinion on a social issue. Through research and the testimony of people like Olaudah Equiano and Alexander Falconbridge, they publicized the evils of the slave trade. Finally, in 1807, Parliament banned English ships from the slave trade. In 1833, Parliament abolished slavery throughout the British Empire, using taxpayer money to buy out the owners.

English methods were easily adapted to American conditions. Abolitionists became expert at collecting money for "information campaigns," another term for propaganda, the organized effort to spread ideas. Campaigns used images and

A print of the British medallion used to spread the abolitionist message. (c. 1837)

slogans embossed on buttons, handkerchiefs, bracelets, banners, cuff links, and lockets—methods all later adopted by political campaigns. A famous medallion, borrowed from England, bore the figure of a kneeling slave above the slogan "Am I not a man and a brother?" Another asked, "Am I not a woman and a sister?" Abolitionist societies also held fairs and "indignation" meetings, featuring fugitive slaves as speakers whenever possible. With their personal knowledge of slavery, fugitives could reach audiences on an emotional level.

Just as Olaudah Equiano was the English abolitionists' star speaker, Frederick Douglass became the Americans'. We have met him before, and we must now get to know him better. Douglass's story has all the drama of a great novel. Six

After escaping from slavery, Frederick Douglass became a major leader of the abolitionist movement. (c. 1847–1852)

feet tall, broad-shouldered, with a ringing voice and piercing eyes, he became *the* black abolitionist of his time. Born in Maryland in 1817, to a slave mother and a white father, he learned to read by coaxing white children into sharing their lessons with him. After savage beatings, he fled at the age of twenty-one to the North, where he met William Lloyd Garrison; friends later bought his freedom. A lecturer and scholar, Douglass ran his own newspaper, the *North Star,* and a magazine, *Douglass' Monthly.* Douglass could speak for hours, without notes, holding the audience spellbound. After one speech, Garrison asked, with deep feeling, "Have we been listening to a man or a thing?"[51]

Above all, abolitionists relied on the printed word. Besides the *Liberator,* scores of newspapers with titles such as *Anti-Slavery Bugle* and *Herald of Freedom* pounded home their message. Journalists skillfully used the Southern press against the peculiar institution. Abolitionists collected ads for fugitive slaves from these newspapers, then reprinted them as evidence of the inhumanity of slavery. Masters usually identified their "property" in ways that made slavery seem all the more horrifying. For example, one ad said: "One hundred dollars reward, for my negrow [*sic*] Glasgow, and Kate, his wife. Glasgow is 24 years old—has marks of the whip on his back. Kate is 26—has a scar on her cheek, and several marks of a whip."[52]

Specialized newspapers like the *Liberty Bell* were aimed at young readers, abolitionists of the future. Societies printed storybooks with titles like *The Child's Anti-Slavery Book: Containing a Few Words About American Slave Children and Stories of Slave-Life.* A popular poem titled "The Anti-Slavery Alphabet" taught the ABCs. It went, in part:

A *is an Abolitionist—*
A man who wants to free
The wretched slave—and give to all
An equal liberty.

B *is a Brother with a skin*
Of somewhat darker hue,
But in our Heavenly Father's sight,
He is as dear as you.

C *is the Cotton-field, to which*
This injured brother's driven,
Where, as the white-man's slave, he
   toils,
From early morn till even.[53]

As children's poetry did, abolition-ist novels focused on noble slaves and wicked masters—there was nothing in between. Harriet Beecher Stowe's *Uncle Tom's Cabin* (1852) was the most famous novel of the age. Stowe's work showed slavery's brutality in highly emotional terms; grown men wept in public while reading it.[54]

Abolitionism also had a hard, nasty side. Its followers were people of their time, as we are of ours. Their time was one in which racism and religious bigotry were widespread, and abolitionists often shared these prejudices. For example, Protestants (the vast majority of abolition-ists) disliked Roman Catholic immigrants from Ireland. Despite his education and books, Theodore Parker was "basically a racialist," as one historian described him. The minister called Irish people "Pad-dies," slang for "Patrick," an insult. Pad-dies had three bad qualities, he said: "*bad habits, bad religion,* and worst of all a *bad nature.*" Parker thought them naturally dirty, dishonest, and lazy, admitting that he could "see an idle Irishwoman *starve and die* with no compunction at all."[55]

While denouncing slavery, many ab-

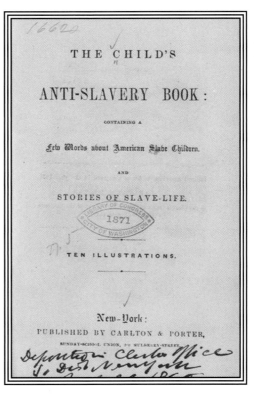

The title page of The Child's Anti-Slavery Book. *(c. 1860)*

olitionists did not view blacks as equals except, perhaps, in the sight of God. Fred-erick Douglass knew this from experi-ence. Fellow abolitionists told him he was too smart, too well spoken, to seem genu-ine. "People don't believe that you were ever a slave, Frederick," they said. "Bet-ter have a little of the plantation speech than not; it is not best that you seem too learned." In other words, Frederick, try not to be yourself.[56]

Others, who should have known bet-ter, went further. Parker, for example, thought black people lower than even the Irish. Blacks, he declared, were born infe-rior to whites, "the superior race," adding, "Negroes, have no general power of mind,

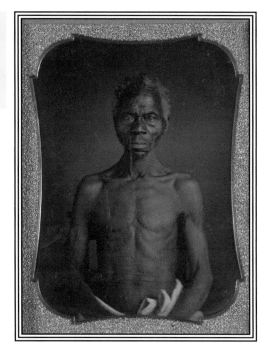

This slave, Renty, was photographed for an 1850 study attempting to show that blacks and whites are two separate species.

or instinctive love of liberty, equal to the whites." Perhaps Parker's most offensive remark came in a letter written on the eve of the Civil War. "What a pity," he wrote, "that the map of our magnificent country should be destined to be so soon torn apart on account of the negro, that poorest of human creatures, satisfied, even in slavery, with sugar cane and a banjo."[57]

Theodore Parker was not alone in demeaning people of African descent. Some abolitionists turned up their noses at blacks' "woolly heads" and "niggerly odor." Female abolitionists debated if it was "proper" to meet blacks socially, "thus putting them on an equality with ourselves." Few thought so. Julia Ward Howe, author of "The Battle Hymn of the Republic," thought the typical black "a

coarse, grinning, flat-footed, thick-skulled creature." Popular preacher Henry Ward Beecher, Harriet Beecher Stowe's brother, insisted, "It is the low animal condition of the African that enslaves him." Even Garrison's *Liberator* declared, "They are branded by the hand of nature" with black skin, "a perpetual mark of disgrace."[58]

Yet none of this made slavery right. Abolitionists judged slavery evil in itself, a crime against God and man. However inferior enslaved people might be in their view, they were human beings. Like "all Men," they were entitled to human rights. "Hence," said Garrison, "I cannot but regard oppression in every form, and most of all, that which turns a man into a thing, with indignation. . . . When I say that freedom is of God and slavery of the devil, I mean just what I say." In that spirit, abolitionists, particularly in Boston, denounced segregated schools and public transportation.[59]

Free blacks praised their allies' work but resented their prejudices, which whites might not even have been aware of. "Our white friends are deceived," noted the *Colored American,* a newspaper aimed at Northern free blacks, "when they imagine they are free from prejudice against color." For the good of all, they should realize how deeply hurtful racism was, and guard against it.[60]

Abolitionists might show prejudice in everyday ways. Those who owned businesses usually hired blacks for menial jobs, if they hired them at all. "A colored boy," according to *Frederick Douglass' Paper* (as the *North Star* was eventually renamed), might make a fine porter or sweeper, but not a clerk or bookkeeper. In both the South and the North, *boy* was an insulting term for black males; it applied both to children and to men with families to support. *Girl* and *auntie* were patronizing terms for black women.[61]

Yet what offended blacks most was the attitude of superiority. Too many abolitionists assumed that whites were more intelligent than blacks. Activist Martin R. Delany charged that whites always "presumed to *think* for, dictate to, and *know* better what suited colored people, than they know for themselves." Not even Frederick Douglass was immune to this form of bigotry. For daring to disagree with him, William Lloyd Garrison slammed Douglass as "destitute of every principle of honor, ungrateful in the last degree, and malevolent in spirit."[62]

Meanwhile, down south, memories of Haiti and Nat Turner kept the fear level high, while abolitionists raised anxiety to hysteria. In reaction, Southern postmasters refused to deliver abolitionist materials. Newspaper ads offered rewards for abolitionists, dead or alive. The mail brought abolitionist Arthur Tappan, of New York, a letter containing a slave's severed ear. Georgia lawmakers offered

William Lloyd Garrison, shown here later in life, began publishing the antislavery newspaper the Liberator *as a young man and had a knack for drawing others to the abolitionist cause.* (date unknown)

$5,000 to anyone who would kidnap Garrison so that the state could try him for inciting rebellion. Had they bothered to read the *Liberator,* they would have found that he cautioned against violence.[63]

Slaveholders also defended themselves with ideas. For decades, they had called the peculiar institution necessary, since their economic existence depended on an unpaid labor force. By the 1830s, it had become a "positive good"—good in itself.

Slavery, declared George Fitzhugh, a well-known Virginia author, came from God. According to Fitzhugh, Almighty God had created blacks to serve their white "betters," thus promoting progress. "Some are born with saddles on their backs," he explained, "and others booted and spurred to ride them—and the riding does them good." By this logic, Africans deserved slavery. It was good for them. It made them happy. It took them, declared Senator John C. Calhoun of South Carolina, from "heathen darkness" to a land lit by "the rays of Christianity." The South must preserve its peculiar institution. No, it must *expand* it into the territories.[64]

Clearly, America was heading for a collision of ideas, morals, and interests. John Brown's moment in history was coming. When it arrived, blood would flow.

IV

Mighty Man of Valor

And the angel of the LORD appeared unto him, and said,
the LORD *is* with thee, thou mighty man of valor.

—Judges 6:12

John Brown, Abolitionist

One of John Brown's favorite Bible stories tells of Gideon, a God-chosen hero who saved the Israelites with a few brave men by striking the enemy at night. Like his Puritan ancestors, Brown believed that God still used special people for special missions. His own mission was to free America's slaves. How? For most of his life, he did not know. The Lord, Brown felt, would tell him in His own good time. Though family and business filled his days, slavery never left his thoughts.

We might say he was born antislavery. Owen Brown, his father, had despised slavery almost from the moment he could remember anything about himself. After his father John's death in the Revolution, a neighbor took pity on Owen's mother, Hannah, sending his African-born slave Sam to plow her fields. A gentle giant, Sam would sweep Owen off the ground and carry him on his shoulders. "I fell in love with him," Owen recalled, and he took Sam as his father replacement. After a few weeks, Sam died, leaving Owen heartbroken.

The title page for the sermon that inspired Owen Brown to become an abolitionist. (1791)

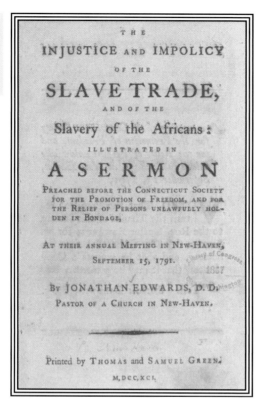

The title page for the sermon that inspired Owen Brown to become an abolitionist. (1791)

Yet a meeting with a stranger, however brief, can change one's entire life, and thus the lives of those one touches.[1]

As a young man, Owen read a sermon by the Reverend Jonathan Edwards Jr. In it, the minister asked Americans a plain question: "Should we be willing that the Africans or any other nation should purchase us, our wives and children, transport us to Africa and there sell us into perpetual and absolute slavery?" Surely not. Clearly, slavery was a sin.[2]

Out of love for Sam, and the force of Edwards's ideas, Owen became an ardent abolitionist. Years later, his own children

constantly heard him call slavery ungodly, wicked, inhuman. It was thus no accident that his son John often said: "I believe in the Golden Rule and the Declaration of Independence. I think they both mean the same thing."[3]

Hudson, Ohio, where his family settled when John was five, was an anti-slavery town. As it was a "station" on the Underground Railroad, fugitives made it a destination. A signpost showed a smiling black man pointing the way and saying, "Dis de road to Hudson." Owen was a "conductor," hiding fugitives until it was safe to send them farther north.[4]

At the age of twelve, John saw the brutality of slavery for himself. A second conflict, the War of 1812, had broken out between the United States and Great Britain. Owen received a contract to supply cattle to army posts in Michigan. His son would drive a few head through the wilderness by himself. Though the Northwest Ordinance banned slavery in the territory, it still existed in many places.

On one trip, the young John Brown stayed in the home of a man who had a slave about his own age. The boys instantly took to each other, becoming friends. While the man welcomed John as a guest, he treated the slave as a dumb beast. The boy wore rags, ate table scraps, and slept in the cold basement. Whenever the master pleased, he beat him, John wrote, "with Iron Shovels or any other things that came first to hand."[5]

Seeing the boy beaten taught Brown something about himself. Though he stood silently as the blows fell, inwardly he cringed. What made him cringe was not fear but empathy, a basic human quality that allows one to identify with another's feelings. "This brought John," he recalled, "to reflect on the wretched, hopeless condition, of *Fatherless & Motherless* slave *children:* for such children have neither Fathers or Mothers to protect & provide for them." From that day on, he so identified with the enslaved that blows to them seemed to fall on his own back. He felt as if slavers were selling *his* family, abusing *his* mother, *his* sister. On that day in Michigan, Brown said, he "declared and swore eternal war with slavery."[6]

What did "eternal war" mean to the twelve-year-old? We cannot say, because the written record is blank on this point. Yet one thing is sure: Brown did no fighting for a long time.

As an adult, he worked, married, and raised a family. Like his father, Brown helped the Underground Railroad. While living in Hudson, he built a secret room in his barn to hide fugitives. These were the first black people his children ever saw. One night, a man and his wife knocked at the cabin door. John Jr., then four or five years old, stared at them, wide-eyed. They were relieved to reach safety, and showed it. "When the woman took me up on her knee and kissed me, I ran away as quick as I could, and rubbed my face 'to get the black off.' " His sister Ruth knew about slavery from the time she could speak— her father taught her about it. When she was around six, the first black person she had ever seen arrived. "I felt such pity for him," she recalled, "that I wanted to ask him if he did not want to come and live in our house." Later, Brown decided to start a school for black children, and even to buy a slave boy to take into his family and educate. But nothing came of these plans.[7]

In 1837, Brown hired two free blacks to work for him. One Sunday, they attended church with his family, but they had to sit in the back. Furious, Brown seated them in the family's front pew the next Sunday, while he led Mary Ann and the children to the back. That did not go over well with the congregation. Church elders told Brown that blacks needed to know their "proper" place. God did not care about color, Brown growled, only about faith and morals. "My brothers," Ruth wrote, "were so disgusted to see such a mockery of religion that they left the church, and have never belonged to another."[8]

Toward the end of 1837, a murder shook the nation. On November 7, a mob in Alton, Illinois, killed Elijah P. Lovejoy,

The proslavery riot in Alton, Illinois, which resulted in the murder of Elijah P. Lovejoy. (c. 1837–1840)

owner of the *Alton Observer,* an abolitionist newspaper. Many free-state whites feared that abolitionists would give their jobs to low-paid blacks or harm business profits by insulting Southern customers. Fear led to violence, as when Boston rioters seized William Lloyd Garrison, vowing to hang him, until the mayor stepped in. Now Lovejoy lay dead. A young Illinois lawyer named Abraham Lincoln called his murder "the most important single event that ever happened in the new world." It had drawn a bloody line between slavery and antislavery, one that others would cross in the future.[9]

John Brown was horrified by the murder. During a memorial service for Lovejoy, he suddenly stood up and raised his right hand. Slowly he said, "Here, before God, in the presence of these witnesses, I consecrate my life to the destruction of slavery." Moreover, he asked his family to pledge themselves to the sacred cause as well. John Jr. remembered how his father "asked *who* of us were willing to make common cause with him, in doing all in our power 'to break the jaws of the wicked.'" Then he asked each in turn, starting with his wife, "Are you, Mary, John, Jason and Owen?" Each said yes. In this way, he "bound us to secrecy and devotion to the purpose of fighting slavery, by force and arms, to the extent of our ability."[10]

Despite this solemn vow, Brown still did nothing. His letters and notebooks show that his chief concern was finding a secure home for his family and saving his failing wool business. Luckily, Gerrit Smith, of Peterboro, New York, gave Brown his chance. Smith owned 750,000 acres of land, more than any other person in America. His holdings brought him a yearly income of $60,000, a fortune in the 1840s, when factory workers earned, at most, $200 a year. Smith gave generously to various social reform causes. An ardent abolitionist, he still urged slaves to endure bondage rather than "sin" by shedding blood to win their freedom.[11]

In 1846, Smith offered free blacks parcels of land, totaling 120,000 acres, in the Adirondack Mountains of northern New York. The idea was to allow three thousand families to leave low-paying city jobs and become self-sufficient farmers. However, those who took Smith's offer found the land undeveloped, rocky, and hard to plow.

Brown saw a chance to help these "poor despised Africans," and his own family, too. In 1848, he visited Smith, described his farming experience, and offered to "show my colored neighbors how such work should be done." In return, Smith sold him a 244-acre farm in North Elba, near Lake Placid, today a famous resort area, for a dollar an acre, a bargain price.[12]

Brown kept his word. Not only did he help his neighbors work their lands, but he treated them as equals. White visitors were amazed to find blacks eating with his family, and him addressing them as "Mister" and "Missus." The farm became his permanent home. Soon after settling in, he brought the tombstone of his grandfather, Captain John Brown, from Connecticut. He placed it in front of the farmhouse, near his own future grave site.[13]

Still, a decade had passed since he had led his family in vowing to fight slavery "by force and arms." During those years, he had done nothing to act on the vow. Yet Brown always felt that slavery was the crime of all crimes. By the 1850s, ideas and events were driving America toward a crisis. That crisis would also spur him to action, to spending his remaining days at war with the peculiar institution.

Deepening Crisis

Northerners saw the new lands of the Louisiana Purchase as places to gain a fresh start in life, a chance to rise as high as ability, work, and luck allowed. Calling themselves "Free-Soilers," whites had a simple formula: "Free Soil = Free Labor = Free Men." Free men, to them, were white men who despised both blacks and slavery. David Wilmot, an influential congressman from Pennsylvania, spoke for many when he claimed the West as white man's country. "I plead the cause of the rights of white freemen," Wilmot said in 1847. "I would preserve for free white labor a free country . . . where the sons of toil, my own race and color, can live without the disgrace which association with negro slavery brings upon free labor."[14]

Slaveholders disagreed. The South had two related problems. First, it needed room to expand, and not just to grow cotton. True, the more land used for cotton, the more land was needed, because cotton drained the soil's fertility faster than tobacco did; planters called it a "soil-killer." But slaves could also raise wheat, mine coal, drive cattle, and cut timber in lands unsuited to cotton. The peculiar institution, then, had to expand or fade away. Second, there was a political problem. Most Southerners owned no slaves at all, and most that did had fewer than ten. Only the South's wealthiest people owned hundreds. Their wealth, in turn, allowed them to control the region's political life. Those they helped elect to Congress strove to protect their backers' interests. In this, they succeeded for decades. Yet nothing stays the same forever.

As more European immigrants arrived, membership in the House of Representatives, based on population size, shifted in favor of the free states, weakening Southern influence. However, each state elects two senators, whatever its population. Since it takes both houses of Congress to pass a law, the Senate can block any measure the House passes. For that reason, Southern leaders wanted the same number of slave and free states.

Better yet, they hoped to bring more slave states into the Union.

By 1820, the Missouri Territory had enough settlers to qualify for statehood. Since most of those settlers were Southerners, they expected it to be a slave state. Free-Soilers wanted no more slave states. Congress settled the dispute with the Missouri Compromise, which admitted Missouri as a slave state and Maine as a free state. The compromise also banned slavery forever from the remainder of the Louisiana Purchase—that is, the western lands north of Missouri's southern border.

In 1836, American settlers in Texas, then Mexican territory, rebelled against "tyranny." The settlers, again mostly Southerners, demanded independence and freedom. Among the "freedoms" Davy Crockett and his friends died for at the Alamo was the right to own slaves, banned by Mexico's constitution. The rebels eventually won and, after nine years of independence, Texas joined the Union as a slave state. After repeated border clashes, the United States declared war on Mexico. The Mexican War (1846–1848) was America's first war fought entirely on foreign soil. Outmatched and defeated, Mexico surrendered territory that included the future states of California, Nevada, and Utah, most of Arizona and New Mexico, and parts of Colorado and Wyoming.

Southern leaders wanted the former

Wendell Phillips, nicknamed Abolition's Golden Trumpet, was one of many antislavery activists to renounce the Constitution. (c. 1853–1860)

Mexican lands to be slave states. Free-Soilers did not. After much debate, congressional leaders made another deal. The Compromise of 1850 admitted California as a free state, balancing the Senate seats held by Texas. To please the North, the compromise abolished the slave trade, but not slavery itself, in the District of Columbia. Finally, Congress passed the strong Fugitive Slave Act, so dear to slaveholders' hearts.

The Fugitive Slave Act enraged abolitionists. Despite all their efforts to change minds, slavery seemed strong as ever. Frustrated, they hurled insults at all Southern people, not just slaveholders.

William Lloyd Garrison, for example, called Southerners "the human hyenas and jackals of America, who delight to listen to negro groans, to revel in negro blood, and to batten upon negro flesh." But name-calling only inflames tempers and closes minds.[15]

Abolitionists began to turn against the Constitution. Here, they felt, lay the root of evil. That document, they knew, resulted from compromises that made the Union possible. Compromise is good if it furthers justice, they said. Compromises that counted a slave as three-fifths of a person were wicked. The Founders, then, had anchored slavery in the highest law of the land. Garrison called their work "a covenant with death and an agreement with hell." "My CURSE be on the Constitution of these United States," stormed Wendell Phillips. "I place it under my feet, where it ought to be."[16]

If the Constitution was evil, it followed that the Union it created was also evil, and must be broken up. The breakup would have two positive results, Garrison and his followers insisted. First, it would weaken slavery by ending the federal government's support. Second, Northerners would no longer share the moral guilt of slavery with Southerners. Garrison thundered:

Accursed be the AMERICAN
  UNION. . . .

Accursed be it, as the most atrocious
compromise ever made to gratify
power and selfishness!

Accursed be it, as stained with human
blood, and supported by human
sacrifices!

Accursed be it, for the terrible evils it
has inflicted on Africa . . . !

Accursed be it, from the foundation to
the roof, and may there soon not be
left one stone upon another, that shall
not be thrown down! . . .

Henceforth, the watchword of every
uncompromising abolitionist, of
every friend of God and liberty,
must be—"NO UNION WITH
SLAVEHOLDERS!"[17]

Frederick Douglass disagreed. The black leader declared that destroying the Union, making a Disunited States of America, made no sense. It was like burning down your house to get rid of the mice. Disunion was immoral, since it abandoned blacks to the brutality of slaveholders. It would leave slaveholders more rather than less secure, free to do as they pleased with their human property.[18]

Despite Douglass, many abolitionists took "NO UNION WITH SLAVE-HOLDERS!" as their motto. They said they would rather have no United States of America at all than one soiled by slavery. Slaveholders answered in kind. "Let

it be, that I am a Traitor," declared South Carolina senator Robert Barnwell Rhett. The hot-tempered Rhett urged secession, Southerners' term for disunion. No union with abolitionists! No union with Free-Soilers! Up with the Fugitive Slave Act![19]

Fighting the Fugitive Slave Act

In 1793, Congress had passed the first nationwide fugitive slave law. It allowed slaveholders to cross state lines to recover their lost "property." All they needed to do was go before a judge and prove ownership of an accused fugitive. Though many Northerners hated black people as strongly as they hated slavery, they also resented strangers meddling in their affairs. So Northern states passed personal liberty laws barring the use of their courts to aid slave catchers.

The Fugitive Slave Act of 1850 put teeth into the 1793 law. Parties of slave catchers invaded the North. Acting as slaveholders' agents, these men were simply kidnappers hiding behind the letter of the law. Armed with forged documents, or only their say-so, they seized *any* black person they chose, fugitive or free. They often grabbed people who were just walking down the street or leaving church after Sunday services. Hauled before a judge, the accused had no right to a trial or to speak in his or her own defense. Furthermore, the law bound every white person to aid the kidnappers. Anyone who re-

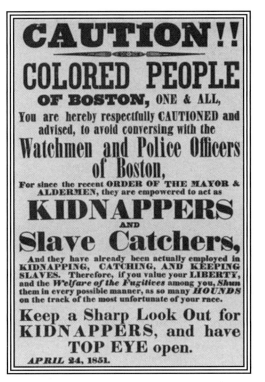

A poster warning free blacks in Boston to beware of kidnappers disguised as police officers. (1851)

noble lawlessness!" the Boston abolitionist declared. "Holy rebellion!" For if we feel a man-made law is wrong, we owe it to God to oppose it by any means.[20]

Critics like Massachusetts senator Daniel Webster saw danger in each person's choosing which laws to obey or disobey. What right have we, Webster asked, to ignore a law made by the people's representatives? How can we avoid social chaos if each person's conscience rules, instead of laws all must obey? "No government can exist," Webster warned the Senate, "where every individual is free to disobey [the laws] whenever they do not happen to square with his private conviction of what is the law of God."[21]

Driven by belief in the higher law, abolitionists disobeyed the Fugitive Slave Act. Throughout the North, vigilance committees sprang up alongside antislavery societies. The Boston Vigilance Committee was the largest, most influential group. Besides Theodore Parker and Wendell Phillips, the Reverend Thomas Wentworth Higginson became a director. A Harvard graduate by the age of thirteen, Higginson saw himself as a "man's man." An avid sportsman, he loved rowing, boxing, swimming, ice-skating, and an especially violent form of touch football. Unlike most abolitionists, who merely talked about lawbreaking, he had no qualms about killing for a just cause.

Vigilance committees made alliances

fused, or interfered with an arrest, faced a fine and a prison term.

Countless Northerners decided they could not abide this "filthy law," as poet Ralph Waldo Emerson called it. Yet disobedience meant defying the voters' will, as expressed by their representatives in Congress. Since repealing the law seemed impossible, opponents justified resistance by looking to a higher law than the Constitution. "God has given us a conscience superior to all law," said Wendell Phillips. The individual's conscience and the Golden Rule top any written law. There is such a thing as righteous lawbreaking. "O with black abolitionists. Together, they helped fugitives escape to Canada; as it was part of the British Empire, slavery no longer existed there. In February 1851, for example, a Boston group freed a slave named Frederick Jackson Shadrach, then smuggled him into Canada. In October, Gerrit Smith secretly funded a group in Utica, New York, that rescued a slave named William Henry, also known as Jerry. "If the rescue of Jerry was not a work of justice and mercy," Smith said in true higher-law fashion, "then there is no justice, no mercy, no God!" Like many of his fellow abolitionists, he had given up on nonresistance.[22]

Boston saw the most sensational rescue attempt. On May 24, 1854, slave catchers seized Anthony Burns, a fugitive from Virginia. While awaiting a judge's decision, Burns remained in a cell in the federal courthouse. In response, Theodore Parker called a protest meeting in Faneuil Hall. Meanwhile, Thomas Wentworth Higginson led a raiding party armed with guns, knives, and clubs to the courthouse. Breaking down the door, they fought the deputies inside, shooting one to death. The deputy's comrades drove the raiders away; Higginson fled with a deep sword cut on his chin. While many Bostonians knew the attackers' identities, nobody stood trial for the deputy's murder.

When a judge ruled against Burns, President Franklin Pierce sent a war-

Runaway slave Anthony Burns, whose arrest and trial under the Fugitive Slave Act of 1850 sparked riots and protests in Boston. (c. 1855)

ship to return him to Virginia. On June 2, troops with rifles, fixed bayonets, and cannons marched Burns to the dock. Over fifty thousand Bostonians lined the route shouting, "Kidnappers! Kidnappers! Shame! Shame!" One window displayed a black coffin and a banner reading, "The Funeral of Liberty." Theodore Parker wrote, using capital letters to drive home his point, "ONE HELD AGAINST HIS WILL AS A SLAVE HAS A NATURAL RIGHT TO KILL EVERY ONE WHO SEEKS TO PREVENT HIS ENJOYMENT OF LIBERTY."[23]

Weeks passed, but Boston still seethed. Abolitionists usually celebrated

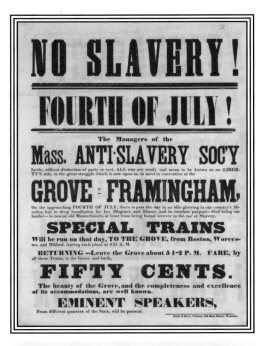

A poster announcing an antislavery rally, during which William Lloyd Garrison set a copy of the Constitution on fire. (1854)

the Fourth of July with a picnic at Harmony Grove, a lovely spot in Framingham, twenty miles west of the city. On this Fourth, a platform stood in the middle of the field, displaying the Stars and Stripes hung upside down. Speaker after speaker denounced the federal government as the tool of slaveholders. William Lloyd Garrison closed with a performance all would remember for the rest of their lives.

The editor of the *Liberator* lit a candle on the table beside him. "To-day, we are called to celebrate the seventy-eighth anniversary of American independence," he said. "In what spirit? With what purpose? To what end? [The Declaration of Independence says] all men are created equal. . . . It is not a declaration of equality of property, bodily strength or beauty, intellectuality or moral development, industrial or inventive powers, but equality of RIGHTS—not of one race, but of all races."

Loud cheers from the crowd.

Suddenly Garrison held up a copy of the Fugitive Slave Act. "Behold!" he said solemnly, touching the paper to the candle. As it caught fire, he urged: "And let all the people say, Amen!"

"Amen!" the crowd roared.

Next, he burned a copy of the judge's decision in the Burns case.

"Amen!" again.

Finally, he held up a copy of the Constitution, that "source and parent of all other atrocities—a covenant with death and an agreement with hell."

Garrison touched it to the candle. Flames rose. As ashes fluttered to the ground, he intoned: "So perish all compromises with tyranny! And let all the people say, Amen!"

"Amen!"

"The only remedy in our case," he said in closing, "is A DISSOLUTION OF THE UNION."[24]

The Firestorm

Garrison was not alone in playing with fire that year. On May 30, 1854, the Kansas-Nebraska Act, brainchild of Illinois senator Stephen A. Douglas, had become law.

At five feet three inches tall, Douglas was a "vulgar little man" with an "immense head," as fellow senators described him. Yet, they admitted, he was also a brilliant deal maker. This time, he outdid himself.[25]

As chair of the Senate Committee on Territories, Douglas hoped to bind the country with a transcontinental railroad running from east to west. But where to locate its eastern terminal? Douglas wanted Chicago, in his home state. Southerners wanted St. Louis, Missouri. To win their backing for Chicago, Douglas proposed a bill to organize the Kansas-Nebraska territory according to what he called "popular sovereignty." That way, he said, settlers would decide for themselves if they wanted a slave or free state.

Nebraska seemed too far north to attract slaveholders, so it would likely join the Union as a free state. Kansas, lying next to Missouri, would probably become a slave state.

The Missouri Compromise had banned slavery in the Louisiana Purchase forever. "Forever" lasted thirty-four years. By repealing the compromise, Douglas's law opened the rest of the Louisiana Purchase to slavery. Now Kansas became a high-stakes game. For Southerners, winning would increase their power in Congress, thus protecting slavery. Losing would keep slavery where it already existed, ensuring its eventual death from soil exhaustion. "If Kansas is not secured," said a New Orleans newspaper, "there

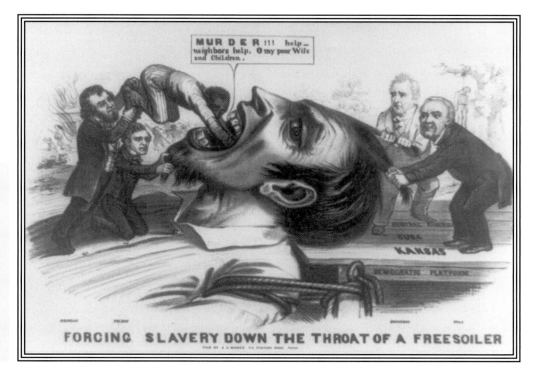

A political cartoon regarding the Kansas-Nebraska Act, showing presidential nominee James Buchanan, Democratic senator Lewis Cass, Democratic senator Stephen A. Douglas, and President Franklin Pierce forcing a black man down the throat of a Free-Soiler. (c. 1856)

will never be another slave state, and the abolitionists will rule the nation." Abolitionists agreed. A slave Kansas would close the West to Free-Soilers, blasting their hopes for better lives. A free Kansas would halt slavery in its tracks.[26]

The Kansas-Nebraska Act raised a firestorm. Even before it went into effect, "Kansas committees" formed in towns and cities throughout the North. Their aim: raise money to provide Kansas settlers with supplies to set up farms. The U.S. Army was forcing Native American tribes off lands they had lived on for centuries. Settlers did not care about Indian rights; "savage" Indians stood in the way of "progress." Free-Soilers were mostly antislavery pioneers, not abolitionists. Kansas, to them, was an opportunity, not a crusade.

The first group left Boston on July 17, 1854, less than two weeks after Garrison burned the Constitution. They left singing:

We cross the prairies as of old
Our fathers crossed the sea,
To make the West as they the East
The homestead of the free!
We go to rear a wall of men
On freedom's southern line,
And plant beside the cotton tree
The rugged Northern pine![27]

These bold Yankees shocked Southerners. Senator David Rice Atchison, of Missouri, saw a wagon train on the move.

"This is a Yankee city going to Kansas," he snarled, "and by God in six months, it will cast a hundred Abolition votes." The wagon train headed for Lawrence, a town twenty-five miles west of the Missouri border. Named for Amos Adams Lawrence, a Massachusetts textile millionaire, it became the free-staters' stronghold.[28]

Before applying for statehood, Kansans had to hold two elections. The first (November 1854) was for a nonvoting delegate who would speak for the territory in Congress. The second (March 1855) was for a legislature to draw up the state constitution. In each case, force decided the outcome. Bands of Missouri thugs called "Border Ruffians" invaded Kansas. Surrounding the polling places, they drove antislavery voters away by force. "Cut his guts out!" they howled. "Cut his throat!" "Tear his heart out!" Senator Atchison urged Border Ruffians "to kill every God damned abolitionist in the Territory."[29]

With proslavery men in control, the legislature passed a slave code as harsh as any Southern state's. Never mind that the Constitution guarantees free speech. In Kansas, anyone who spoke or wrote against slavery faced heavy fines. Worse, helping fugitive slaves brought ten years of hard labor. In reply, free-staters set up their own legislature, whose first meeting left no doubt that "free" meant free of blacks. Racist lawmakers passed a "Negro exclusion clause" banning blacks, slave

Another political cartoon depicting the Democrats as the villains of the Kansas-Nebraska Act. In the center stands Franklin Pierce dressed as a Border Ruffian, with his foot on an American flag draped over Lady Liberty, who kneels at his feet. (c. 1856)

or free, from the territory. Kansas would be lily-white.[30]

The Border Ruffians had stirred up a hornet's nest. News from Kansas enraged Northerners. Abolitionists took up a battle cry: "Guns for free Kansas." They favored the Sharps rifle, the most powerful rifle of its day. Designed for shooting buffalo on the Great Plains, the Sharps could drop a one-ton animal at six hundred yards.

Abolitionist groups set up rifle funds. Individuals gave whatever they could. Theodore Parker cut down on his book buying, using the money saved for guns. After Sunday services, ministers pleaded for rifle money. The Reverend Henry Ward Beecher, of Plymouth Church in Brooklyn, New York, turned his church into a center for the purchase of Sharps rifles. Price: twenty-five dollars each. He

was so successful that it became known as "the Church of the Holy Rifles." Because the rifles were sent to Kansas in boxes marked *Bibles,* abolitionists called them "Beecher's Bibles." Southerners sent guns, too. Kansas became an armed camp. When it seemed that anything might trigger a bloodbath, John Brown arrived.[31]

"Captain Brown"

Last we left him, John Brown was living in the Adirondacks. By the 1850s, Brown's older sons had grown up. They had become farmers in Ohio, married, and started families of their own. The "boys," as their father still called them, were fiery abolitionists; he had seen to *that.*

As settlers poured into Kansas, a drought held Ohio in its grip. Crops withered. Fields turned to dust. Unable to make

The Reverend Henry Ward Beecher turned his Brooklyn, New York, church into a center where abolitionists could purchase rifles, soon known as Beecher's Bibles. (c. 1860–1870)

Missourians rode up and asked if they had seen their stray cattle. No. Oh, by the way, how do you feel about slavery? The boys told them: "We are Free State, and more than that, we are Abolitionists." With that, the Missourians left without another word. The boys knew from their manner that "we were marked for destruction."[33]

In the spring of 1855, John Jr. wrote his father. Kansas was beautiful, a place

a living, farmers hitched up their wagons and headed west. Among them were the Reverend Samuel Adair and his wife, Florella, John Brown's half sister. The boys decided to follow "Uncle Adair." Though they asked their father to join them, he refused, without really explaining why. Naturally, he blessed their going "to help defeat *Satan* and his legions." Beginning in April 1854, John Jr., Jason, Owen, Frederick, and Salmon left in two groups with their families.[32]

Uncle Adair and his wife had settled at Osawatomie, where Pottawatomie Creek joins the Osage River, thirty-five miles southeast of Lawrence. The boys settled nearby, at a place they named Brown's Station. Before long, a band of

John Brown's sons Salmon, John, Owen, and Jason (clockwise from top left). (dates unknown)

SALMON BROWN

JOHN BROWN, JR.

JASON BROWN

OWEN BROWN

FOUR OF JOHN BROWN'S SONS
In later years

where "a poor man can get a start so easy." Come! Come soon! Please! Bring guns, as "we need them more than we do bread."[34]

When Brown first refused to go to Kansas, he wrote, *I feel committed to operate in another part of the field.* What field? He did not say. He could have meant the farm in North Elba, where he still had to settle the rest of his family. Mary had just given birth to Ellen, her thirteenth child. They needed his attention, as did the younger children. Brown may also have meant he was working on a plan to attack slavery. We cannot be sure what he had in mind.[35]

We *do* know that his hatred of slavery had deepened since the Mexican War. With that hatred came disgust and contempt for much of American life. Brown had lost any faith he might have had in the nation's leaders. He despised politicians—all of them. You could never trust a politician, Brown said, because "he was always ready to sacrifice his principles for his advantage." Presidents and members of Congress were, to him, "fiends clothed in human form," for they compromised with evil. Brown thought Congress a moral sewer, where members "pass unjust and wicked enactments and call them laws." He denounced lawyers, judges, sheriffs, and police officers as "the devil's drummers and fifers," enforcers of wickedness.[36]

Brown had equal contempt for abolitionists, or at least most of them. (He liked Frederick Douglass, whom he considered a friend.) The William Lloyd Garrisons and Theodore Parkers talked a good game. That was the trouble. From their writings and newspaper reprints of their speeches, he decided that they were all talk, empty windbags. "Talk! Talk! Talk! That will never free the slaves," he growled. What was needed was not speeches, but "action—action!" Asked about Wendell Phillips, he said, "Well, if it wasn't vulgar, I would say to that as the boys say—'Oh! shit.'" Still, abolitionists had money, or knew how to raise it. He would play along, say the right things, while using them for his own schemes.[37]

Brown's role models came from his boyhood reading and modern history. His heroes were men of action, whose wars against slavery left a legacy for future generations. Spartacus, Rome's gladiator rebel, taught Brown that slaves, properly armed and led, could defeat armies. Haiti's Black Spartacus, Toussaint L'Ouverture, proved that the enslaved could win freedom against heavy odds. Above all, a friend recalled, "he admired Nat Turner, the negro patriot, equally with George Washington, the white deliverer." That Turner had killed innocents seemed not to trouble Brown. Turner had showed that slaveholders were not supermen. Real opposition threw them, like the cowards they were, into a panic.[38]

The Fugitive Slave Act, not Kansas,

finally spurred Brown to violence. While his family lived at the farm in North Elba, New York, he still had to wind down his failed wool business in Springfield, Massachusetts. Yet he could not turn away from those less fortunate. Local blacks, free and fugitive, said they could not sleep for fear of kidnappers stealing their wives and children. Deep down, he felt their fear, and expected his loved ones to feel it, too. "I want all my family to imagine themselves in the same dreadful condition," he wrote Mary.[39]

Brown took his lead from free blacks, who had formed self-defense groups with names like League of Freedom, Liberty League, and American Mysteries. About the year 1851, Brown gathered a group in Springfield. He called it the United States League of Gileadites, from Mount Gilead, where God had commanded Gideon to save the Israelites with a tiny band of warriors. Brown recruited forty-four black men and women, who posted guards and "boiling water brigades" in black neighborhoods to deter kidnappers.[40]

Though Brown did not lead the Gileadites in action, he described how he thought they should act in a document titled "WORDS OF ADVICE." Pick your target carefully, strike boldly, and kill if necessary. Above all, "stand by one another and by your friends, while a drop of blood remains; and be hanged, if you must, but tell no tales out of school. Make

no confession." Brown, we will see, followed this advice to his last breath.[41]

John Jr.'s letter convinced Brown that God wanted him to fulfill his old vow in Kansas. He gave up business, even family duties, to fight slavery full-time. From then on, he wrote Mary, the family would see little of him. It could not be helped. He must devote his every thought and action to the cause. Brown had no choice, he felt, but to obey the Lord's call.

Before leaving North Elba in June 1855, he spoke in Syracuse, New York, at an abolitionist conference called by Gerrit Smith and Frederick Douglass. As yet, he was not an important or well-known figure in abolitionist circles. Now that changed. The conference's sponsors introduced Brown as a friend worth listening to; he did the rest. In appealing for gun money, he quoted Hebrews 9:22, another favorite Bible verse: "Without the shedding of blood there is no remission of sins." In other words, only violence against the wicked could wipe away the sin of slavery. Douglass recalled that "the collection was taken up with much spirit . . . for [when] Brown spoke men believed the man." Like Brown, Douglass and the others had come to believe that "liberty must either cut the throat of slavery or slavery will cut the throat of liberty." Delegates dug deep into their pockets.[42]

In August 1855, Brown set out with his son Oliver, sixteen, and son-in-law

Henry Thompson, his daughter Ruth's husband. Though the family was sad to see them go, Brown asked that they remember how hard it was for slave families bound for sale to part from loved ones.[43]

Brown's wagon carried food and clothing, guns and bullets. At Akron, Ohio, abolitionists raised more money and bought more weapons, including ten broadswords, weapons with short, heavy blades. As the wagon rolled west, Missourians appeared on horseback. "Where are you going?" their leader asked bluntly. "To Kansas," Brown replied softly. "Where from?" "From New York," he replied. "You won't live to get there," the Missourians' leader said. With that, Brown stared into the man's eyes—stared so hard it must have seemed like an eternity. Finally, he said slowly, "We are prepared *not to die alone.*" The Missourians got the message, and rode away.[44]

The party reached Brown's Station in early October. What a mess! With winter coming, the place was merely a few tents and a campfire. Nearly everyone was sick, food was scarce, and the crops were untended. Instantly, Brown took charge. With the boys helping as best they could, he cleaned up, gathered the crops, and built a log cabin.[45]

He finished just in time. Early in December, more than two thousand Border Ruffians massed for an attack on Lawrence. When a rider brought the news, Brown piled the four healthiest boys (John Jr., Owen, Frederick, and Salmon) into the wagon and drove to town. Each man seemed more than a match for ten Ruffians, with a broadsword strapped to his waist, two pistols, and a Sharps rifle. They so impressed the Lawrence defense committee that it put Brown in charge of a twenty-man company called the Liberty Guards. From then on, people knew him as "Captain Brown" or "Old Brown," to distinguish him from his boys.[46]

Lawrence's show of force scared off the Ruffians—this time. Brown became furious. He wanted to fight, and the sooner the better. Rather than let the wicked escape, he offered to attack their camp at night, Gideon-like, butchering them in their sleep. Townspeople refused, for they wanted only to go about their business in peace.[47]

It was not to be. On May 21, 1856, the Border Ruffians returned, stronger than ever. Senator Atchison, their leader, whipped them into a frenzy. "Be brave, be orderly," he shouted, "and if any man or woman stand in your way, blow them to hell with a chunk of cold lead." This time, townspeople gave in rather than risk a bloodbath. Ruffians went on a rampage, looting, burning, and blowing apart the massive stone Free State Hotel with cannon fire. Yet only one person died, a Ruffian brained by a stone falling from the hotel.[48]

Meanwhile, a messenger reached Brown's Station with news that the Ruffians were heading for Lawrence. As captain of the Pottawatomie Rifles, a local defense unit, John Jr. called it to arms. His father went along for inspiration and support.

Hours later, as the Rifles rode toward Lawrence, another messenger brought news that the town lay in ruins. John Jr. decided to camp for the night and await reinforcements. Next morning, May 22, the Rifles continued on their way. Though the timing is unclear, later that day a third messenger brought word of an assault in the very halls of Congress. The victim was Massachusetts senator Charles Sumner, a fiery abolitionist.

Senator Sumner was easy to dislike. Colleagues, even those who agreed with him, thought him a smug, pompous snob

The ruins of Lawrence, Kansas, sketched by a correspondent for Harper's Weekly. (c. 1863)

who could not control his tongue. "Sumner, you're a damned fool," New York senator William Henry Seward said to his face. Like John Brown, the senator could not tolerate anyone who disagreed with him. In the clash of ideas, only one side, Sumner's, could be right. "There is no other side," he declared.[49]

On May 19 and 20, Sumner gave a three-hour speech titled "The Crime Against Kansas." Not only did he criticize the Kansas-Nebraska Act, he ripped apart its supporters, particularly South Carolina senator Andrew P. Butler, absent due to a stroke. Sumner insulted Butler's character

and mocked the way he spoke; because of the stroke, he drooled. Sumner's speech infuriated fellow senators, Southerners and Northerners alike. The Senate had never seen such an outburst of "gross insults." How cowardly to attack an ailing man who could not defend himself![50]

Payback came quickly. On May 22, Sumner sat at his desk doing paperwork. The Senate was not in session, so the chamber was nearly empty. Suddenly Senator Butler's nephew, South Carolina representative Preston Brooks, walked up to Sumner with a raised walking stick. Down it came, again and again, until Sumner lay unconscious in a pool of blood. Had Sumner been a gentleman, Brooks said, he would have challenged him to a duel with pistols. Instead, he beat him as he would a lowly slave.[51]

It serves Sumner right, Southerners said. Hundreds of well-wishers sent Brooks canes as symbols of support. Yet most Southern newspapers thought the beating would make matters worse, for "an unwise friend is more terrible than a score of enemies." Brooks had been unwise, to say the least. He had given ammunition to the South's critics. The Northern press, smelling blood and high sales, branded him a typical Southerner—a whip-wielding brute: "Bully Brooks." Bold headlines declared, "A Border Ruffian in the Senate," "Barbarism in the Capitol," and "Shame! Shame!"[52]

Abolitionists had a field day. Sumner's beating, they said, proved the need to break up the Union. Wendell Phillips could not praise Sumner enough, calling him a hero; true Americans should "be ready to kiss his very footsteps." For weeks after the beating, Congress was a dangerous place. "Every man in both Houses," a senator wrote, "is armed with a revolver—some with two and a bowie

A political cartoon mocking the "Southern chivalry" Preston Brooks displayed while beating Charles Sumner. (c. 1856)

SOUTHERN CHIVALRY — ARGUMENT versus CLUB'S.

knife," a fearsome weapon with a long, wide blade curved to a needle point.[53]

Murders Along the Pottawatomie

For John Brown, Senator Sumner's beating was the last straw. When the news came, John Jr. recalled that his father "went crazy—*crazy*." Something must be done to put fear into slaveholders! An eyewitness later reported that the old man planned "to sweep [Pottawatomie Creek] of all the proslavery men living on it."[54]

Old Brown called for volunteers, but John Jr. said he could not go; he must stay with his command. Jason would not go. A big man, strong as an ox, Jason was gentle as a lamb and never raised a hand to anyone. Brothers Salmon, Frederick, Owen, Watson, and Oliver, and brother-in-law Henry Thompson, were made of sterner stuff. So were Theodore Weiner and James Townsley, neighbors who agreed to join the "sweep." Townsley later wrote the only firsthand account of the event. It showed that Brown was in charge from the outset, and thus responsible for the result.

In the early hours of May 25, the party came to three cabins along Pottawatomie Creek. Waking those inside, they announced themselves as "the Northern army." From the first cabin, they hustled James P. Doyle and his sons William, twenty-one, and Drury, twenty, into the

darkness. Brown would also have taken the youngest Doyle, fourteen-year-old John, had his mother, Mahala, not begged for his life. "Not him," she cried. "Oh, God, not him." Later, the party barged into two other cabins, seizing Allen Wilkinson and William Sherman. None of the captives were armed or put up any resistance. Each time, the "soldiers" took the captives a little way from their homes, then hacked them to pieces with broadswords. Brown shot Mr. Doyle in the forehead.[55]

Why had he marked these five for such a horrible end? They had two things in common. First, although they favored slavery—to Brown an unforgivable sin—they owned no slaves. Second, they had done nothing for which the law required the death penalty. At worst, they had spoken harshly to Free-Soilers, reportedly even threatened some. That was not unusual. In Kansas at this time, proslavery and antislavery men constantly threatened each other, but seldom carried through. Nobody ever proved that Brown's victims had harmed, let alone killed, anyone. Nor had they taken part in the sacking of Lawrence.

This suggests that Brown chose his victims not to punish actual crimes, but to shock and horrify others. Slaveholders enforced their will by violence against individual slaves on their plantations. Brown went further. His own words show that he used violence to influence an en-

John Brown, around 1850.

tire class of people, nearly all of whom he never saw or knew. In short, he became a terrorist.

Salmon Brown said his father ordered proslavery men killed "to strike terror through their wicked ranks." James Townsley heard almost the same words. Before leaving John Jr.'s camp, Brown said he aimed "to strike terror into the hearts of the proslavery people." That aim fits a modern U.S. government definition of terrorism: "The unlawful use of threat of violence against persons or property to further political or social objectives . . . to intimidate or coerce a government, individuals or groups, or to modify their behavior or politics." This explains why Brown biographer David S. Reynolds calls him our first "homegrown terrorist."[56]

By the time the killers returned to camp next day, news of their actions had spread. John Jr., shocked, asked his father if he had had anything to do with the killings. "I did not," Brown replied, lying, "but I stood by and saw it." The killings, Jason recalled years later, sickened him. "I think it was an uncalled for, wicked act," he scolded his father. Frederick burst into tears. Though he had gone with the party, he could not bring himself to kill helpless men. Owen could. "Liberty can only live or survive by the shedding of blood," he told the Adairs, echoing the Bible passage his father liked to quote. Calling Owen "a vile murderer," his aunt and uncle sent him away when he asked to hide in their home.[57]

John Brown had no regrets. By then, he believed it better that ten proslavery men die than one free-stater be driven from Kansas. "I never shed the blood of a fellow-man," he insisted, "except in self-defense, or in promotion of a righteous cause." In self-defense? He attacked his victims; they did not attack him. A righteous cause? Who decided *that*? Not any human judge or written law, but Brown, sure of his God-given mission.[58]

Brown sincerely believed God spoke to him and approved his actions. To speak with God, in his day, did not mean you were odd or insane. Religion was an intimate part of everyday life, and many people "conversed," as they said, with the Lord. So did Brown. Several times, he claimed to act under God's direct orders. A Kansas friend, James Legate, recalled that he "religiously believed that God had sent him as a special messenger to win freedom for the downtrodden slaves in this land." James Hanway, another friend, noted, "Brown firmly believed he was an instrument in the hands of Providence to smite the slave-power."[59]

Nothing shows his state of mind better than a talk he had with E. A. Coleman, a longtime Kansas resident. Brown stopped at the Coleman farm a few weeks after the killings. He came alone and seemed nervous. As he paced back and forth, Coleman asked if he had killed those men on the Pottawatomie. Brown admitted to ordering the killings, but "in doing so I believe I was doing God's service." With that, Mrs. Coleman asked, "Then, Captain, you think that God uses you as an instrument in his hands to kill men?" Brown replied, firmly, "I think he has used me as an instrument to kill men; and if I live, I think he will use me as an instrument to kill a good many more." Another time, he claimed to hold "a commission direct from God Almighty to act against slavery."[60]

Bleeding Kansas

The Pottawatomie killings served their purpose. Calling Old Brown the "old terrifier," scores of proslavery families fled to Missouri. In Kansas, as in Virginia after Nat Turner's uprising, those who stayed feared what each night might bring. "I never lie down," a proslavery man said, "without taking the precaution to fasten my door. . . . I have my rifle, revolver, and pistol where I can lay my hand on them in an instant, besides a hatchet & axe." Before long, however, fear turned to rage, and rage to the violence of "Bleeding Kansas."[61]

The struggle brought out the worst in both sides. Anger and hatred are poisons, infecting minds as bacteria infect bodies. In Kansas, opponents were no longer seen as human beings, but as "evil forces" in human form, with no right to exist.

Each side formed mounted bands of fighters. Bands of Kansans and Missourians hunted free-staters and abolitionists. Robert S. Kelley, editor of a proslavery newspaper, captured their spirit in an article. "If I can't kill a man," Kelley wrote, "I'll kill a woman; and if I can't kill a woman, I'll kill a child!" Free-staters and abolitionists said much the same. Like the enemy, their bands prowled the countryside, raiding, burning, shooting, hacking.[62]

Old Brown did his share. On June 22, 1856, at a place called Black Jack, he led twenty-six volunteers against a band of about equal size. Thinking his band surrounded, the enemy leader, Henry Clay Pate, a wild-eyed gunman, decided to call off the fight if he could. Brown agreed to a meeting, and Pate left his position carrying a white truce flag. When he arrived, however, Brown put a pistol to his head. "You must surrender unconditionally," he snapped. "Give the order!" Clearly Brown meant business, so Pate ordered his men to drop their guns. A few days later, a U.S. Cavalry patrol rode into Brown's camp. Although the commander, Colonel Edwin Sumner (no relation to the senator), knew about the Pottawatomie killings, he decided to talk rather than shoot. In return for releasing the prisoners, he let Brown go free.[63]

On August 30, some three hundred Border Ruffians swept into Osawatomie and Brown's Station. The Reverend Martin White, their leader, was an abolitionist-hating fanatic. Frederick Brown came out to meet the raiders, unarmed and alone. When he asked what they wanted, a silly question, White shot him dead in cold blood. Frederick's father was camped on a hillside nearby with his band, eating breakfast. Hearing the shots, he sprang into action, crying, "Men come on! . . . Take more care to end life well than to live long." Overwhelmed, the small band eventually scattered, leaving the Ruffians free to torch every building and farm in the area. Nevertheless, Brown had fought so bravely that he earned another nickname. From then on, Captain Brown and Old Brown would also be called John Brown of Osawatomie.[64]

Soon after the Battle of Osawatomie, a new governor took over the territory. A no-nonsense official, John W. Geary ordered both sides to stand down. End the raids! Dismiss the bands! Go home—or else! The U.S. Cavalry had orders to keep the peace, and the governor would see that it did so. The fighting stopped. Kansas joined the Union as a free state in 1861.[65]

How bloody was Bleeding Kansas? Surprisingly—thankfully—the terrorism claimed fewer lives than we might expect. Recent studies show 157 violent deaths during the Bleeding Kansas period. The quarrel over slavery claimed 56 of these. Arguments over land and personal feuds account for the other 101 killings, which occurred over many months. Taken together, these were far fewer than the lives lost in a few seconds of a Civil War battle.[66]

Meanwhile, the Browns had had their fill of Kansas. The boys had lost everything they had worked so hard for there, along with a brother. They saw no future in the territory. In October 1856, they hitched up their wagons and headed back to Ohio. John Brown, racked by fever, lay on a cot inside a wagon. We do not know what thoughts went through his mind. Whatever they were, they were surely not about abandoning his mission.

Brown hinted at his intentions after the Battle of Osawatomie. From a hilltop, he looked down at the burning village. His peaceful son, Jason, stood nearby, the only witness to what happened. Old Brown spoke as if in a trance. "God sees it," he said, tears rolling down his cheeks. "I have only a short time to live—only one death to die, and I will die fighting for this cause. There will be no more peace in this land until slavery is done for. I will give them something else to do than to extend slave territory. I will carry the war into Africa."[67]

"Africa" was another term for the South.

V

Into "Africa"

We've had enough talk about "bleeding Kansas."
I will make a bloody spot at another point to be talked about.
—John Brown, 1857

Useful Friends

January 1857 found John Brown in Boston, the capital of American abolitionism. Federal marshals sought him, now a wanted man for the Kansas killings. He had come to Boston seeking allies and weapons for his holy war against slavery in "Africa." Above all, he needed money. Nothing was possible without large sums of cash, which he, a failed businessman with a large family, did not have.

On the day after New Year's, Brown visited the office of the Massachusetts Kansas Aid Committee, the free-state settlers' chief aid organization. Entering the musty room, he introduced himself to Franklin B. Sanborn, the committee's secretary. Sanborn, twenty-five, taught in a small private school he headed. The moment they met, Brown's magnetic personality drew the younger man to him. His first impression of Brown was as vivid a half century later as the moment they met. "He had a purpose, knew what it was, and meant to achieve it," Sanborn wrote. The teacher hero-worshipped Brown as God's "instrument" to destroy slavery.[1]

Sanborn was the right man to see. Though not influential himself, he knew every Boston abolitionist worth knowing. Within days, he arranged for Brown to meet Theodore Parker and Thomas Wentworth Higginson. After long talks with them, Brown met Dr. Samuel Gridley Howe, husband of poet Julia Ward Howe and director of the Perkins School for the Blind. A pioneering physician, Howe specialized in helping the disabled lead fuller lives. His methods enabled Laura Bridgman, stricken in childhood by scarlet fever, to become the first blind and deaf person ever to learn language, and would later help Helen Keller overcome the same disabilities. Finally, Sanborn took Brown to the mansion of George Luther Stearns, a wealthy merchant and generous donor to abolitionist causes.[2]

Brown made as deep an impression on these men as he had on Sanborn. Kansas was quiet, he told them, but the Border Ruffians might easily return to their evil ways. Settlers needed more weapons

Poet, essayist, and abolitionist Ralph Waldo Emerson. (c. 1850–1870)

to defend freedom. Brown's new friends agreed. Within a week of his arrival, they turned over two hundred Sharps rifles stored in Tabor, Iowa, and pledged money to aid his work in Kansas. *In Kansas!* Brown did not say he meant to use their gifts in "Africa." Before leaving Boston to raise more money, he visited Charles Sumner, still recovering from his beating by Preston Brooks. Brown asked to see the coat he had worn that day. The senator never forgot how his visitor stared at the garment, stiff with dried blood, with tightly closed lips and eyes that "shone like polished steel."[3]

Writer and abolitionist Henry David Thoreau. (c. 1880)

In the following weeks, Brown stopped in North Elba. After an absence of a year and a half, he could stay with the family for only a night. From North Elba, he went to New York City, Syracuse, and several towns in Connecticut. At each place the fugitive spoke at abolitionist meetings, urging aid for Kansas. He returned to Boston in April, only to learn that the marshals were hot on his trail. To evade capture, he stayed with friendly abolitionists, who found him an "interesting" guest. One told her children to lock their doors at night, as "that man carries bowie knives in his boots." While staying with Judge Thomas B. Russell,

Brown warned Mrs. Russell that should those "US Hounds" come, he would go down fighting. He added, "I should hate to spoil your carpet."[4]

When it seemed safe to move about, Sanborn took him to nearby Concord to meet Ralph Waldo Emerson and Henry David Thoreau, famous writers and fervent abolitionists. Brown impressed them deeply. He seemed so genuine, so honest, a man who spoke his mind plainly and without any intention to deceive. They praised this "true idealist," this "rarest of heroes," this man of "rare common sense." This gentle soul, they noted, loved God's humblest creatures, and "knew the secret signals by which animals communicate."[5]

Brown revealed another quality, too. During a visit to Emerson's home, he opened a window into his mind and character. The old man said he believed the Golden Rule and the Declaration of Independence meant all people were equal. That was nothing new; he had often made this remark. So had his listeners. What was new came in the next sentence: "It is better that a whole generation should pass off the face of the earth—men, women, and children—by a violent death, than that one jot of either should fail *in this country*."[6]

Emerson nodded in approval, perhaps thinking he spoke for effect. Yet the old fighter declared he meant every word. Nor, apparently, did he ever change his mind. For he held human life cheap, compared to his mission to destroy slavery. Should it cost the lives of millions to reach that goal, then so be it. This was not a once-only remark, or one quoted in error. Brown repeated it to others, using the exact words. Sanborn heard it several times. George Luther Stearns's son Carl, not yet three years old in 1857, recalled it as a grown man. Clearly, Brown chose his words carefully.[7]

What about Kansas? Did those who admired Brown know what he had done there? Did they *want* to know? Their writings do not mention the Pottawatomie killings. This may be because Brown avoided talking about them. If the subject came up, he told half-truths and outright lies. For example, he wrote to the family in North Elba that his party had captured many proslavery men but let them go. Yet, unfairly, "we were accused of murdering five men at Pottawatomie." *We were accused!* That was all he chose to say! Sanborn recalled Brown assuring him "more than once" that he had been twenty miles away at the time of the killings. Press reports were little help in getting at the truth. Often wrong, some even blamed Comanche Indians for the crime. Other reports accused the victims of various misdeeds, implying they deserved death. The fact that so many chose to deny, defend, or ignore Brown's actions shows how bitter the struggle over Kansas had become. A decision by the U.S. Supreme Court made things worse.[8]

Abolitionists Turn to Violence

On March 6, 1857, the justices handed down what some have called the most important ruling ever issued by an American court. Known as the *Dred Scott* decision, it involved a slave who had lived with his master, an army officer, in a free state for several years. Upon Scott's return to Missouri, antislavery lawyers filed a lawsuit on his behalf, claiming that living on free soil automatically made him free. In time, the high court took up the case.

This image of Dred Scott appeared in Century Magazine *in 1887.*

Of its nine justices, five owned slaves. Yet that did not make them all fiery champions of the peculiar institution. For example, Chief Justice Roger Taney had freed his slaves years earlier, except for two very old people whom he supported for life. The justices ruled Dred Scott could not sue in a federal court, as slaves were not American citizens. Taney, writing for the majority, noted that under the Constitution, slaves "had no rights which the white man was bound to respect." Moreover, since slaves were property, masters could take them anywhere, as they could farm animals. Congress had no power to ban slavery in the territories. Thus, the justices overturned every compromise that had limited its spread. Not only did the ruling open the West to slavery, it legalized it in *free* America.[9]

The decision thrilled slaveholders. There, you see, we were right all along: slavery is legal, and we may take our property wherever we please! Georgia senator Robert Toombs spoke for many. "Before long," he boasted, "the master will sit down with his slaves at the foot of the Bunker Hill Monument." This was more than an arrogant outburst; it was a challenge and an insult. Bostonians regarded Bunker Hill as holy ground, blessed by the blood of patriots.[10]

Cooler heads foresaw danger. There is such a thing as victory costing too much. The Supreme Court's decision,

these Southerners warned, was bound to infuriate the North. Already, noted the *Enquirer,* of Richmond, Virginia, "the abolitionists are leaping and weeping, kneeling and swearing, foaming and fuming, yelling and gesticulating, like so many bedlamites." (Bedlam was a London hospital for the mentally ill.)[11]

The *Dred Scott* decision convinced many Northern whites that nothing could stop the march of the "Slave Power." Not Congress. Not the law. Not the courts. Not federal, state, or local government. "Where will the aggressions of slavery cease?" a newspaper editorial asked. "Freedom and white men are no longer safe." Slavery would become *national*. When that happened, masters would use slaves to beat down the wages of free workers and dictate working conditions. Such fears aroused nightmare images of unemployed whites and gangs of chained blacks driven by whips. Noted a Chicago newspaper, "Chicago might become a slave market and men, women, and children may be sold off the [auction] block in our streets."[12]

History shows that as tensions rise and people feel threatened, some will demand drastic solutions. So it was in the toxic atmosphere of the late 1850s. The cry "No union with slaveholders" no longer satisfied William Lloyd Garrison and his followers. With their hopes for a peaceful solution dashed, they decided only violence could end the slavery horror. Respected leaders spoke of treason, defined as a citizen's making war against the nation or aiding its enemies. Garrison, that hater of violence, now declared treason "a mark of high honor." Theodore Parker smiled when Garrison introduced him at a meeting as "a first-rate traitor." Thomas Wentworth Higginson boasted he was "always ready to invest money in treason."[13]

Some hoped for a repeat of Nat Turner's uprising, but on a vaster scale, involving the entire South. Like Theodore Parker, they wanted "the Fire of Vengeance" to annihilate slaveholders. The learned minister told an audience, the *Liberator* reported, that "he was glad that every five minutes gave birth to a black baby, for in its infant wail he recognized the voice which should yet shout the war cry of insurrection; its baby hand would one day hold the dagger which should reach the master's heart."[14]

Short steps lay between slave rebellion, disunion, and civil war. Abolitionist leaders reveled in the idea of a violent breakup of the Union. Theodore Parker prayed disunion would ignite civil war. "I don't care how it comes," he declared. "I want the Federal Government divided; I want State sovereignty assumed. Success to the strongest arm. Might makes right today." For Parker, the end justi-

fied the means, because slavery must die, whatever the cost! Henry David Thoreau agreed. Normally a gentle man, he had been struck by the *Dred Scott* decision in ways he had perhaps not thought possible. "My thoughts are murder to the state," he wrote. Murder, that is, of the Union.[15]

Gerrit Smith went still further, adding terrorism to slave revolt and civil war. In an open letter to the black community of Syracuse, John Brown's patron declared terrorism a proper tool in fighting slavery. Fear of "fire and rape and slaughter," he wrote, would force Southerners to do the right thing. Smith continued:

What portions are there of the South that will cling to slavery after two or three considerable insurrections shall have filled the whole South with horror? . . . Remember too that many, who would be glad to face the insurgents, would be busy in transporting their wives and daughters to places where they would be safe from that worse fate which husbands and fathers can imagine for their wives and daughters. . . . Trembling as they would for their loved ones, I know no part of the world where, so much as in the South, men would be [likely], in a formidable insurrection, to be distracted and panic-stricken.[16]

Given such extremism, North and South, bad days lay ahead for the country. And John Brown would do his best to bring on the crisis.

The Plan

The old man had a plan to carry his war into "Africa." It did not pop into his mind instantly, but developed in stages over a decade at least. The earliest version went back to 1847, when his family lived in Springfield, Massachusetts, and Brown ran his wool business. While visiting there during a lecture tour, Frederick Douglass heard about Brown and decided to meet him. The black leader knocked on Brown's door and introduced himself. Brown invited him to dinner. They bonded immediately, becoming friends. Years later, Douglass described the visit in his autobiography, *Life and Times of Frederick Douglass*. Brown got to the point immediately. Slaveholders had no right to live, he snapped, his eyes "full of light and fire."[17]

Yet he still had limited goals. Brown told his guest that he did not plan a Haiti-style revolt followed by the massacre of slaveholders. Spreading a map on the table, he pointed to the Allegheny Mountains. "These mountains," he said, "are the basis of my plan. God has given the strength of the hills to freedom; they were placed here for the emancipation of the

A stereograph of John Brown and Frederick Douglass. (c. 1890–1900)

negro race; they are full of natural forts, where one man for defense will be equal to a hundred for attack; they are full also of good hiding-places, where large numbers of brave men could be concealed, and baffle and elude pursuit for a long time."[18]

In effect, Brown planned a larger, more aggressive Underground Railroad. He would recruit a select group of fugitive slaves in the free states, then lead them in raids on plantations. Raiders would seize supplies, taking liberated slaves to strongholds in the mountains. Later, guides would lead most to safety in the North and Canada. However, the strongest and bravest would stay with Brown, forming scores of small strike units. In time, their raids would convince masters that their human property had little value, because they could not protect it. As prices fell, they would have no choice but to end slavery.[19]

Ten years is a long time. By 1857, the Fugitive Slave Act, Bleeding Kansas, and the *Dred Scott* decision had embittered too many people. Accordingly, Brown revised his plan and came to Boston. He now intended all-out war.

The plan had several parts, designed to fit together neatly, like pieces of a jigsaw puzzle. Its author expected masses of fugitives to join him when raiding began. Unused to war, they would need a professional soldier to train them. On a visit to New York City, Brown met Hugh Forbes, a former English officer. Desperate for money, Forbes was struggling to support his family in Europe as a fencing teacher. Brown hired him at a monthly salary of one hundred dollars, money donated by the Massachusetts Kansas Aid Committee. Brown did not tell the committee about Forbes, or that he paid him with money meant for use in Kansas.[20]

How to arm the slaves he expected to set free? To begin with, Brown signed a contract with Charles Blair, a blacksmith in Collinsville, Connecticut. Blair agreed to make one thousand pikes, at a dollar each. A pike was a type of spear that had been used in warfare since ancient times. It had an extra-long pole, or shaft, tipped with an iron head. The heads of Brown's pikes would be double-edged knife blades. Pikes, Brown told Blair, were ideal for Kansas farmers defending their homes against Border Ruffians. That was nonsense. Kansans had plenty of guns—too many—by 1857. Nobody in his right mind would go against a Sharps rifle or a Colt six-shooter with a pike. Brown never told his Boston friends that he had bought these weapons.

Yet pikes were easy to use by people untrained in handling firearms. Brown meant to give most of them to freed slaves, not Kansas farmers. He also wanted Forbes to train a select group with guns. Though friends of free Kansas had given him Sharps rifles, he needed many more for the army he had in mind. Where would he get them? Who kept thousands of military-grade rifles in one place? The federal government! It had all he needed at the arms depot in Harpers Ferry, Virginia. It is no accident that Brown chose this armory rather than any in another state. Virginia lay at the heart of the very place he hoped to begin his war.

All those pikes and rifles, Brown felt, made for the kind of uprising his abolitionist allies wished for but feared to carry out themselves. These were armchair revolutionaries, men of books and poems, more used to cozy Concord drawing rooms than battlefields. Brown would grab the rifles at Harpers Ferry and take them into the mountains. At the same time, he expected Virginia slaves to rally to him. Instead of sending the majority north, as in the original plan, he would drive south, gathering strength each day. Moving along the mountain ridges, he would cut through the Cotton Kingdom, invading each slave state in turn. These attacks, he said, would "strike terror into the heart of the Slave states," until "the whole country from the Potomac [River] to Savannah [Georgia] would be ablaze."[21]

No thoughts of failure troubled John Brown. The Lord, he believed, commanded him to destroy slavery. He also understood the American public's mood. Even if his plan failed, he expected the uprising to split the Union, igniting civil war. Brown told his son Salmon that the slave states, terrified and blaming Northern plotters for their troubles, would secede. The "North would then whip the South back into the Union without slavery." He told Franklin Sanborn much the same, saying he was "eager to begin it [civil war], [so] that it might be the sooner over."[22]

Meanwhile, the old man turned to another part of his plan. In January and February 1858, he spent three weeks in Frederick Douglass's home in Rochester, New York. Most days, he kept to his room (rented for three dollars a week, meals included), writing. Like his fellow abolitionists, he rejected the U.S. Constitution.

This pike, a replica of the ones John Brown commissioned, is nearly seven feet long with a ten-inch steel blade.

In its place, he wrote a constitution for the areas he expected to liberate. Covering nearly every aspect of daily life, the document even provided for black schools and churches. Many articles dealt with the new government's branches: executive, legislative, judicial. But there was a catch. Elected officials would choose the army's commander, who could veto any law. In effect, Brown's constitution called for a military dictatorship, with him as dictator. It went without saying that his forces would kill American soldiers opposing them.[23]

In February, Brown traveled to the mansion of Gerrit Smith, where he met Franklin Sanborn and Edwin Morton, a tutor to Smith's son. One evening, they gathered in an upstairs room to hear Brown outline his plan. He said he would raid Virginia and ignite a slave rebellion to provoke a national crisis. Yet he kept some secrets. Though Brown spoke freely about the coming raid to those he trusted, he never told the whole story. Nobody knew just where he would strike, not even his followers, who would learn their target only hours before going into action. At most, Brown would briefly mention Harpers Ferry as "a point" to seize, but not the exact point, then quickly change the subject.[24]

Though Smith and the others saw problems ahead, nothing they said shook the old man's confidence. Brown met each objection with a Bible quotation: "If God be for us, who can be against us?" The next day, while walking in the snowy woods near the mansion, Smith and Sanborn decided they must help him as a matter of honor. "You see how it is," said Smith. "Our dear friend has made up his mind to this course, and cannot be turned from it. We cannot give him up to die alone; we must support him."[25]

Support him they did. After returning to Boston, Sanborn invited the old man to meet with himself, Theodore Parker, Thomas Wentworth Higginson, George Luther Stearns, and Samuel Gridley Howe. Again, Brown vowed to set the South ablaze, but did not mention Harpers

Ferry. After five days of meetings (March 4–8), they approved the plan, promising to help with money and advice. To that end, they formed the "Secret Six," consisting of the five Bostonians and Gerrit Smith. Brown left town the next day under a false name, Shubel Morgan, Hebrew for "captive of God." He also wore a full white beard that the Lord, he said, ordered him in a vision to grow to deceive federal marshals.[26]

Early in May, he arrived in Chatham, Ontario, Canada, with twelve Kansas followers. Chatham was home to some one

John Brown in 1859, with the beard he grew to evade the federal marshals searching for him.

thousand fugitive and free blacks who had fled the States in fear of the Fugitive Slave Act. Brown had come to recruit fighters and gain approval of his constitution. At a secret "constitutional convention," held in a church, the whites met a delegation of thirty-four black men. After announcing his plan to invade Virginia, again not mentioning Harpers Ferry, Brown presented his constitution. Though only Osborne Anderson, a printer, eventually joined the raiders, the other blacks did vote for the document. Brown set July 4, 1858, the eighty-second anniversary of the Declaration of Independence, for the raid. As it turned out, he would miss that date by over a year.[27]

Kansas Interlude

While Brown was in Canada, the English soldier he had hired to train his raiders, Hugh Forbes, was making trouble in Washington. Believing Brown's plan too risky, he wanted to free as many slaves as possible, then lead them to Canada. He also demanded more money for his "starving" family in Europe. When Brown refused both demands, Forbes visited the nation's capital. Security in the Senate chamber had not improved since Charles Sumner's beating. Nobody challenged the ex-officer as he crossed the floor and went up to Massachusetts senator Henry Wilson. Forbes burst out that his employer

GEORGE L. STEARNS   GERRIT SMITH

FRANK B. SANBORN   T. W. HIGGINSON

THEODORE PARKER   SAMUEL G. HOWE

JOHN BROWN'S NORTHERN SUPPORTERS

was "a very bad man" who planned a slave uprising. Wilson wrote his friend, Dr. Howe, about the hysterical stranger. The senator may or may not have believed Forbes.[28]

The Secret Six, a group of Northern supporters of John Brown's aims. (dates unknown)

When Brown returned from Canada, the Secret Six met with him in Boston. Thomas Wentworth Higginson wanted to go ahead with the raid, but the others had second thoughts. Though they had blessed Brown's plan, they did not want to soil their reputations, and perhaps go to jail, by having their names linked to his. To discredit Forbes, they insisted that Brown disappear into Kansas for a year. In return, they promised $500 in gold, and another $3,000 when he returned to the East. Gerrit Smith wrote to Franklin Sanborn, "I do not wish to know Captain Brown's plans; I hope he will keep them to himself." While the landowner wished Brown success, such intentional ignorance would allow him to deny he knew what the old man meant to do.[29]

By June, Brown was back in Kansas. During the following months, he spent much of the time in bed with a high fever, most likely malaria, a common frontier disease. Kansas remained quiet, so he had little to do when the fever broke. That changed when he learned about a Missouri slave named Jim Daniels, whose owner intended to sell him, his pregnant wife, and their two children to different people. Outraged, Brown sprang into action. On the night of December 20–21, he led two raiding parties into Missouri. One party, under Aaron Stevens, a hot-tempered ex-soldier, attacked a farm, killing the owner, taking his valuables, and making off with his seven slaves. Meanwhile, Brown freed the Daniels family without firing a shot.

The raid, though meant as a humane act, threatened to undo the uneasy peace in Kansas. "We are settlers—you are not," a farmer bluntly told Brown. You make trouble, but we pay the price when the Missourians strike back. Kindly go away. Now![30]

Ahead of Brown and the Daniels family lay a 1,100-mile trek to Canada. It was winter. Subzero temperatures and snowdrifts exhausted everyone. A cavalry unit set out from Fort Leavenworth, Kansas, to intercept the fugitives, but free-staters from Topeka drove them off. Along the way, Mrs. Daniels delivered a son she called John Brown Daniels, the first of many black children to bear Brown's name. Once they crossed the frozen Missouri River into Iowa, it became smooth sailing. The Fugitive Slave Act was a dead letter there because of abolitionist opposition. In town after town, Iowans helped with money, food, and shelter.[31]

Feeling chipper and confident, Brown mocked the federal government. In Cleveland, Ohio, he walked the streets openly. Police officers knew he was a wanted man but looked the other way. Hearing that President James Buchanan had offered a $250 reward for his capture, Brown offered his own reward: $2.50 "for the safe delivery of the body of James Buchanan to any jail in the Free States." In Chicago,

Allan Pinkerton, head of a famous detective agency, arranged for the fugitives to go to Detroit by train. After eighty-two days, Brown saw the ferry take them across Lake Erie to Windsor, Ontario, on March 12, 1859. Now he turned to his business in "Africa."[32]

Brown returned to Cleveland and from there went to Ashtabula, where John Jr. had a farm. He told his son to prepare to send the Kansas recruits to a place in Maryland he would reveal later. From Ashtabula, he visited Gerrit Smith at his estate and other members of the Secret Six in Boston. At each stop, Brown asked for more money.

During the first week in June, he returned to North Elba for just a few days.

Brown came not only to see his family but also to enlist recruits for the upcoming raid. He was disappointed. Mary was not eager for more family members to go into harm's way. Nor were they all eager to go. John Jr. was busy on his Ohio farm. Jason and Salmon flat-out refused to go. Bleeding Kansas, they said, had made them "sick of fighting and trouble." Their brothers, Owen, thirty-five; Watson, twenty-five; and Oliver, twenty, decided to go in their place. Their brother-in-law Henry Thompson could not go, as his wife, Ruth, would not let him. Besides, he had seen enough killing in Kansas to last a lifetime. But Henry's brothers William, twenty-six, and Dauphin, twenty-one, felt they must go to uphold the family honor.[33]

The Kennedy farm, John Brown's home base during the time immediately before his raid on Harpers Ferry, just seven miles away. (c. 1859)

Final Preparations

Harpers Ferry lies on a narrow tip of flat ground where the Shenandoah River joins the Potomac River. Two bridges spanned the rivers, as they still do, the one over the Potomac serving the Baltimore & Ohio Railroad. The town is about fifty miles northwest of Washington, D.C., and sixty miles west of Baltimore, Maryland. Pinned to the riverbanks by high, steep cliffs, it owed its prosperity to the armory, where master gunsmiths made rifles, and an arsenal, or storehouse, holding some one hundred thousand rifles. The facility's only defense was a gate fastened by a chain, and a night watchman.

On July 3, 1859, Isaac Smith arrived in Harpers Ferry with two younger men, his sons. Plainly dressed, he had a Yankee accent and a short beard. "Smith" was John Brown, using another false name; before leaving North Elba, he had cut off his beard, leaving only an inch-long fringe. He said he came from New York and wished to rent a farm. Could anyone recommend a place at a fair price? Someone did: the Kennedy place in Maryland, about seven miles from Harpers Ferry. Nearby lay what would become two frightful Civil War killing grounds, Antietam Creek, ten miles to the north, and Gettysburg, Pennsylvania, fifty miles to the northeast.

Over the next two months, Brown's men arrived singly or by twos and threes, so as not to arouse the locals' suspicions. Of the twenty-one men who came, sixteen were white, three were free blacks, one was a freed slave, and one was a fugitive slave. The latter, Dangerfield Newby, thirty-nine, was the father of six children. His children and pregnant wife, Harriet, were still slaves on a farm thirty miles south of Harpers Ferry. Harriet's master wished to sell her farther south, into cotton country. Newby had offered to buy his family's freedom, but the master refused to sell at an affordable price. Desperate to reunite their family, Harriet wrote, "Oh dear Dangerfield, com this fall without fail monny or no Monny I want to see you so much that is the one bright hope I have before me." Her letter led him to join the raiders.[34]

John Brown wanted his wife to come to Virginia to cook for the raiders. Mary refused. From what little she knew of the plan, it seemed too risky. Besides, she had responsibilities at home. Though he called her refusal "a sorry disappointment," his fifteen-year-old daughter, Annie, came in her place, as did Oliver's pregnant sixteen-year-old wife, Martha.[35]

The young women spent most of their time watching for strangers. Should one appear, a signal sent the men rushing to the attic. The women stayed mostly indoors, talking, reading, and writing letters, going out only at night for exercise. Wherever they turned, they bumped into crates of rifles and pikes. John Jr. had sent the weapons by train from Tabor, Iowa, to the station at Chambersburg, Pennsylvania, forty miles to the northwest. From there, Brown had hauled the bulky crates, labeled *Tools,* to the farmhouse by wagon.

Waiting sharpened the men's belief in their mission. Now in a slave state, they saw firsthand the horrors of the peculiar institution. For example, Watson Brown learned that a slave had hanged himself in a nearby orchard after his master sold his wife to a cotton planter in the Deep South. "Cannot come home so long as such things are done here," he wrote his wife, Bell. He had left her and their newborn son, Freddy, to fight slavery, whatever the personal cost.[36]

The men wondered if their mission would succeed. Brown kept his secret until almost the last moment. He had led them to believe they would strike quickly and escape into the mountains with the slaves they freed. When he finally told them about the arsenal, they balked. Too dangerous, they said; we will be trapped, shot, or captured and later hanged. The old man offered to resign if they doubted him. However, he knew he had an emotional hold on them. These men looked up to him, needed him, and depended on him. "We have here only one life to live,

and once to die," he said, "and if we lose our lives it will perhaps do more for the cause than our lives could be worth in any other way." They quickly fell into line.[37]

They had more reasons to doubt their leader than they imagined. For all his confidence and study, Brown ignored the basics of military planning. He had not prepared local slaves for his arrival, assuming they would flock to him the moment he struck. Neither had he inspected the area around Harpers Ferry: it lay at the bottom of a "bowl" surrounded by hills, making the raiders easy targets from above. He had no escape plan. Even if they reached the mountains, the raiders had organized no defenses or stores of food or supplies. Worse, the mountains offered no refuge at all. Roads went through them; besides, the locals knew every likely hiding place and had bloodhounds to track fugitives. No matter. As Salmon noted, his father "wanted conditions to change for him." That made sense—to a man like John Brown. He fought in a sacred cause. God was on his side. So, he supposed, the Almighty would see that all turned out well.[38]

Though Brown never knew it, he was lucky, thanks to the bungling of John B. Floyd, secretary of war. From Massachusetts to Kansas, from New York to Canada, Brown had told scores of people that he planned to invade "Africa," but not

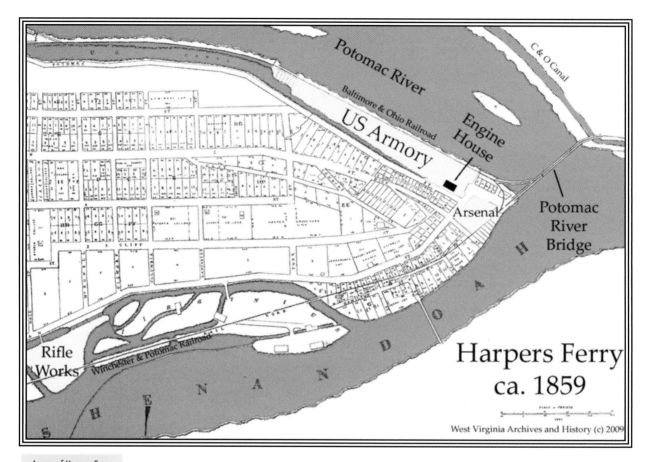

Harpers Ferry
ca. 1859

West Virginia Archives and History (c) 2009

A map of Harpers Ferry and its armory and arsenal, with respect to John Brown's hideout in the engine house. (c. 1859)

exactly where. David J. Gue, a Quaker from Springdale, Ohio, wanted to save him from certain disaster. Early in August, Gue wrote Floyd that *"old John Brown,"* lately of Kansas, was preparing a slave uprising. Most likely, he would begin by seizing a federal arsenal in Maryland. Since that state *had* no arsenal, Floyd ignored the warning.[39]

In mid-August, Brown invited Frederick Douglass to a meeting at an abandoned stone quarry near Chambersburg. Douglass brought Shields Green, twenty-three, a fugitive slave he had befriended.

Brown brought John Henry Kagi, a brilliant twenty-four-year-old serving as his second-in-command. Apparently, he did not trust any of his sons with this key post.

As the four men sat on the rocks, Brown revealed his plan, adding that he would take white hostages and start a massive slave uprising. Douglass could hardly believe his ears. Attack the federal government! At Harpers Ferry! In all the years they had been friends, Brown never mentioned *this*! Stunned, Douglass said Brown would be "going into a perfect steel trap." Later, he recalled telling

Brown that "Virginia would blow him and his hostages sky-high, rather than that he should hold Harpers Ferry an hour."[40]

They argued until sundown, and then returned for more of the same the next morning. Neither man would change his mind. When they had nothing more to say, they agreed to disagree. Before leaving, Douglass asked his companion what he intended to do. "I b'leve I'll go wid de ole man," Shields Green replied. Douglass returned to Chambersburg alone. Though later criticized for abandoning Brown, he had no regrets. Douglass still had vital work to do, and had no intention of dying in a futile adventure. Brown went to the Kennedy farm to make final preparations.[41]

Harpers Ferry

Sunday, October 16, 1859. Evening.

Having already sent Annie and Martha back to North Elba, the chief gathered his men. After reading his constitution (again) and leading them in prayer, Brown gave each his assignment. Three would haul weapons to a small schoolhouse midway between Harpers Ferry and the Kennedy farm, handing them to slaves who had learned of the raid and wished to fight. Other parties would take hostages, cut telegraph wires, and seize the bridges, while Brown's group took the main facility. Kill only in self-defense, he told

them, but "then make short work of it." At eight o'clock, Brown ordered: "Men, get on your arms; we will proceed to the Ferry."[42]

The plan went like clockwork. By midnight, the raiders had gained every objective without firing a shot. As his men broke the chain on the armory's gate, Brown told the watchman, "I must only burn the town and have blood" if anyone interfered. Other raiders soon arrived with three white hostages and their slaves. The whites were Colonel Lewis Washington, great-grandnephew of George Washington, and a neighbor, John Allstadt, and his son. "Your life is worth as much as mine," Brown told Washington. Hostages would share the same fate as his men if things went wrong.[43]

Colonel Washington's coachman, Jim, took a pistol and later, an eyewitness claimed, fought "with a good will." During the battle that followed, Jim fled, only to drown in the Shenandoah River. The other slaves, however, stared at the pikes, saying they knew "nuffin 'bout handlin' dem tings." Their feigned ignorance was really the first sign of trouble. Enslaved people knew all about Nat Turner; his story was part of their oral heritage. They also knew the fate awaiting captured rebels, and would not fight just because a white stranger asked them to.[44]

The Harpers Ferry Armory. (c. 1859)

Monday, October 17.

At 1:25 a.m., an eastbound Baltimore & Ohio passenger train started across the Potomac River Bridge. Brown's guards halted it, pointing their guns at the engineer's compartment. When Hayward Shepherd, baggage master at the Harpers Ferry station, heard the screeching brakes, he walked onto the bridge to investigate. Shepherd, a free black, was liked by all who knew him.

"Halt," a raider shouted. Seeing the armed men, Shepherd turned and ran toward the station. Seconds later, he fell, shot in the back, the bullet entering a little below his heart and exiting from his chest. Though he dragged himself to the station, the wound was mortal; he died in the afternoon. So it was that a free black man became the first victim of John Brown's crusade to free the slaves.[45]

At dawn, Brown allowed the train to go on its way. It is unclear why. He may have thought the crew could not give the alarm, as his men had put the telegraph out of service. If so, he was wrong; they had cut the wires only near Harpers Ferry. Upon reaching the next station, at Monocacy, eighteen miles down the line, the engineer sent a telegram to his supervisor in Baltimore, who relayed the information to Washington.

Meanwhile, the shots from the railroad bridge roused Harpers Ferry. A later version of Paul Revere, a Virginian this time, began spreading the news. Dr. John D. Starry, thirty-five, sprang into the saddle and rode off in the darkness. At each house and town he came to, he gave the alarm. The countryside stirred. Other men rode in all directions. Church bells rang. Farmers grabbed their rifles. Militia units assembled.

What Virginians had dreaded since Nat Turner's time had burst upon them. A slave uprising! For the rest of their lives, people remembered where they were when the word came. Jennie Chambers's experience was typical. After breakfast, the teenager began to walk to school, the Young Ladies' Seminary in the hills west of Harpers Ferry. When a rider told her to rush back home, she recounted, "my heart stopped beating and I dropped my books. . . . I didn't know what minute an abolitionist might jump out at me from behind a tree and eat me." Terror gripped Jennie's community: "Our people gathered all their families and put them in the cellars. The church was full of them . . .

the women and children crying and screaming."[46]

John Brown's plan had begun like clockwork but now lay in ruins, though he did not know it yet. By daybreak, everyone was hungry, so he ordered breakfast from the local tavern. However, when waiters brought the food, neither the raiders nor their captives touched it, fearing poison. Brown had not thought of taking food along, nor, apparently, had anyone else. They would not have a bite to eat for two days.

John Henry Kagi held the rifle works beside the Shenandoah River with two men, Lewis Leary and John Copeland, a free black from North Carolina. Kagi was growing more nervous by the minute. Already he could see groups of armed men across the way. He sent a note, urging Brown to leave before it was too late. "Captain Brown was all activity," Osborne Anderson recalled, "though at times he appeared somewhat puzzled." He did not budge, probably because he still expected a slave uprising.[47]

The "perfect steel trap" snapped shut. While Brown waited, militia companies arrived from Charles Town, Shepherdstown, and Winchester, easily retaking the bridges. Meanwhile, Harpers Ferry men shot at anything that moved on the armory grounds. Dangerfield Newby died first, shot by a sniper who had loaded his rifle with a six-inch iron spike instead of a bullet. The spike tumbled as it flew, cutting Newby's throat from ear to ear. Enraged townsmen sliced off the ears for souvenirs. Soon after the raid, Harriet Newby was sold to a New Orleans slave dealer.[48]

Firing increased throughout the morning. By ten o'clock, Brown knew he could not fight his way out. So he sent William Thompson under a white truce flag with a message. Brown offered to free the hostages in return for letting the raiders escape over the Potomac River bridge. To his amazement, townsmen ignored the flag, grabbing Thompson. Brown had no right to complain, as he had done the same to Henry Clay Pate in Kansas.

He tried again, at noon, sending his son Watson and Aaron Stevens with the same offer. Shots rang out as the two young men walked down the street with their truce flag. Stevens fell, wounded; townsmen dragged him away, a prisoner. Watson took a bullet in his stomach. Vomiting blood, he crawled back to the armory. By then, the raiders had retreated to the fire-engine house, later known as "John Brown's Fort," a solidly built brick building.

At 2:30 p.m., militiamen attacked the rifle works in force, sending Kagi and his men dashing toward the Shenandoah River. Escape was impossible. Shooters on the opposite bank riddled Kagi and Leary with bullets. Copeland reached a large, flat rock in a shallow part of the river, only to have townsmen drag him ashore kicking and screaming. An excited crowd was about to hang him when Dr. Starry, back from his ride, had him locked in a jail cell. Meanwhile, raider William Leeman, twenty, ran across the armory yard and dove into the Potomac. As he swam toward the Maryland shore, gunshots forced him to take cover on a tiny island. A Harpers Ferry man waded out to Leeman, who threw up his hands and cried, "Don't shoot." The man fired point-blank into Leeman's face.[49]

A firefight raged throughout the day. The engine house had heavy wooden double doors. Brown's men cut narrow slits in these, and through the brick walls on either side of the building. Whenever a townsman showed himself, they tried to pick him off. Brown watched closely. "Don't shoot; that man is unarmed," he shouted from time to time. Bullets pelted the building like hailstones. So many struck at once that some were bound to find a mark. One hit Oliver Brown as he stood beside his father. The young man lay on the redbrick floor, doubled up in agony.[50]

When a raider killed Fontaine Beckham, Harpers Ferry's beloved mayor, a frenzied mob went for William Thompson. "For God's sake, wait and let the law take its course," a woman cried as they dragged the prisoner away. It was no use.

They shot him in the head and threw his body into the Potomac.[51]

Night finally came, very dark and very cold. The shooting stopped. Four unwounded raiders and their chief kept their posts, exhausted and hungry, watching the hours drag by. Eleven white hostages huddled in fear at the rear of the engine house; these included the watchman, the paymaster, and others seized when they came to work. "Men, are you awake?" Brown asked now and then. His son Watson lay still, in shock, drenched with his own blood. Oliver begged his father to end his own misery with a bullet. Brown refused. "Oh, you will get over it," he said, adding, "If you must die, die like a man." Oliver stopped moaning. Brown called his name. No answer. "I guess he is dead," the old man said without emotion.[52]

Sometime during the night, hostage John Dangerfield, the armory paymaster, told Brown that the raiders were committing treason. Dauphin Thompson and Jeremiah Anderson, twenty-six, a free black, overheard the remark. "Are we committing treason against our country by being here?" they asked. Their chief did not hesitate. "Certainly," Brown snapped. Just as he had not revealed their destination until the last moment, he had failed to mention that attacking a federal facility was

Confederate general
Robert E. Lee on
his horse, Traveller.
(c. 1866)

treason. "If that is so," they replied, "we don't want to fight any more; we thought we came to liberate the slaves, and did not know that was committing treason." No matter, Brown said, except that they would die like dogs and not men if they refused to fight.[53]

First reports of a major event are usually inaccurate, filled with rumor, exaggeration, and errors. So it was with Harpers Ferry. As Brown admitted to treason, lights burned brightly in distant newspaper offices. Telegraph messages told of the raid, but little else. Nobody except the raiders knew their chief's identity. They had few facts, but reporters are paid to write stories that sell newspapers. Their early stories reflected the confusion. For example, the morning (October 18) edition of the *New York Herald* announced in bold headlines:

FEARFUL AND EXCITING INTELLIGENCE.
NEGRO INSURRECTION AT HARPERS FERRY.
EXTENSIVE NEGRO CONSPIRACY IN
VIRGINIA AND MARYLAND.
SEIZURE OF THE UNITED STATES
ARSENAL BY THE INSURRECTIONISTS.
ARMS TAKEN AND SENT TO THE INTERIOR.
THE BRIDGE FORTIFIED AND DEFENDED
BY CANNON.
TRAINS FIRED INTO AND STOPPED—
SEVERAL PERSONS KILLED.

Besides those about the seizure of the arsenal and the people killed, such head-lines were as true as the story of the man in the moon.

Tuesday, October 18.

At 11 p.m. on Monday, while printers set type for the early-morning editions, a train from Washington pulled into the Harpers Ferry station. It brought a ninety-man detail of U.S. marines, commanded by army colonel Robert E. Lee, a hero of the Mexican War. The colonel's instinct was to attack at once. Yet, as we have learned from recent hostage situations, rescuers have a special duty. Hostages' lives come first. Storming the darkened engine house at night, Lee knew, would kill some hostages, perhaps all. He must do everything possible to save them, but not allow the raiders to escape.

While waiting for daybreak, Lee asked Lieutenant Israel Green of the marines if he wanted the honor of "taking those men out." Green saluted smartly and thanked Lee. He immediately chose twelve marines to make the assault, and another twelve to stand by as a reserve. Tall men, they looked like dandies in their navy-blue coats, sky-blue trousers, pale blue caps, and white crossbelts. Yet they were tough professionals used to danger. Each carried a loaded rifle tipped with a bayonet. Fighting would be at close quarters, and Lee did not want to risk shooting hostages in error. Marines were trained to storm enemy positions with bayonets.

Green gave them orders to hold their fire but to stab any raider in their path.[54]

By seven o'clock on the morning of October 18, all was ready. Green's assault teams stood in two lines, one behind the other, while their comrades massed nearby. More than two thousand civilians and Virginia militiamen watched from a safe distance.

At Lee's signal, Lieutenant J. E. B. "Jeb" Stuart walked toward the engine house. The officer carried a note from Lee for the raiders' leader. It warned that if he refused to surrender, Lee could not answer for their safety. At a negative reply, Stuart had been instructed not to get into a debate. He must step aside and wave his cap, the signal for the marines to attack.[55]

As Stuart approached the doors, a civilian held an umbrella over his head, topped by a white handkerchief, a truce sign. Quickly, a door opened about four inches, and the lieutenant found himself looking down the barrel of a Sharps rifle. Behind it stood "Mr. Smith," whom Stuart recognized as Osawatomie Brown from Kansas. Three years earlier, Stuart had ridden with the unit that freed Brown's prisoners after the battle of Black Jack. Until that moment, only the raiders had known Smith's true identity.[56]

Stuart read Lee's message aloud. Brown would not budge. No surrender! He would release the hostages in return for a chance to escape! If Lee could not agree to that, Brown said, "I prefer to die just here." Then he slammed the door shut. Instantly, Stuart stepped aside, waving his cap.[57]

An illustration of the interior of the engine house, where John Brown and his crew hid with their hostages, armed with guns and pikes, just before the gate was broken down. (c. 1859)

Charge!

Three marines pounded the doors with sledgehammers. The doors swayed but did not open. Brown had fastened them with ropes, so the swaying absorbed the force of the blows. Just then, Lieutenant Green noticed a heavy ladder on the ground. On his command, the storming party used it as a battering ram to smash a hole in the right-hand door. A shot rang out and Private Luke Quinn, the first marine through the hole, fell dead. As Private Matthew Ruppert stepped over Quinn's body, a bullet tore through his face. Ruppert survived, horribly disfigured. His comrades kept coming.

In his official report, Colonel Lee, though a stickler for details, surprisingly said nothing about marines firing or raiders offering to surrender. However, a marine officer said some men fired as Private Quinn fell. As the marines squeezed through the narrow opening, John Brown supposedly cried, "Surrender!" Lieutenant Green recalled nothing of the kind. In the end, all we can say is that those present gave differing accounts of the fight. What is certain, however, is that Dauphin Thompson and Jeremiah Anderson, who had objected to committing treason, died by the bayonet.[58]

Was this murder? Again, we will never know for sure. We know from recent assaults on hostage takers that rescuers cannot afford to take unnecessary risks. They may not know, for example, how many enemies are inside, or the location of each. In the chaos of a break-in, turning one's back or pausing to make an arrest can prove fatal. Rescuers may eliminate any opponent they meet, for others could be lurking nearby, ready to shoot them from behind. Rather than capture an enemy, they kill quickly and move on.

Colonel Lewis Washington was the first person Lieutenant Green saw when he came through the broken door. Nearby, a man was down on one knee beside a fire engine, loading a Sharps rifle. "Hello, Green," cried Washington, an old friend. "This is Osawatomie," he yelled, pointing to the kneeling man.[59]

Suddenly Brown turned toward the lieutenant. Green raised his sword. It was not a heavy battle sword; in his haste to board the train with the marines, he had taken his light parade sword by mistake.

Green brought the blade down, slashing the back of Brown's neck. As Brown fell, the lieutenant lunged with the weapon, striking him in the belly and raising him completely off the ground. It was a killing blow, but Brown did not die. The thin blade had struck his belt buckle and bent double. Green hammered Brown's skull with the hilt until he passed out.[60]

It had taken just three minutes to smash the door, capture Brown, subdue his men, and free the hostages. Afterward, the marines lay the enemy casualties on the ground in front of the engine house. Nine were already dead. Townspeople gawked at the bloody bodies. One gallant fellow had a young woman on each arm. "Gentlemen," he said, "just give room here. Can't you stand back and let the ladies see the corpses?"[61]

Watson Brown lay among the dead, writhing in agony. "What brought you here?" a bystander asked. "Duty, sir," he said through clenched teeth. Another question: "Is it then your idea of duty to shoot men down . . . for defending their rights?" By that, the bystander meant the "right" to own slaves. Watson replied, "I am dying. I cannot discuss the questions. I did my duty as I saw it." He died early the next morning.[62]

Of the twenty-one men Brown led, ten lost their lives during the raid, along with four townsmen, including the mayor, and one marine. None of the hostages was injured, though Lieutenant Green called them "the sorriest lot of people I ever saw," having not eaten for over sixty hours. Six raiders were captured, tried, and eventually hanged. Five escaped. Slaves, too, were liberated by the marines, only to be returned to their masters.[63]

Despite his wounds, John Brown survived Harpers Ferry. He would fight another day, not with guns, but with words, ideas, and emotions.

VI

The Cause He Loved So Much

I think I cannot now better serve the cause I love so much than to die for it,
and in my death I may do more [than] in my life.
—John Brown, November 1859

The South on Trial

Had John Brown died in the engine house, you would not be reading about him here. Most likely, the fight at Harpers Ferry would have made headlines for a few more days, then quickly faded from public attention. In later years, history books might have given him brief mention, if any. Yet that was not to be. The old man survived to turn defeat into victory—or at least his version of victory.

Brown never wrote a detailed explanation of

why his raid failed. We do, however, have records such as trial reports, his court statements, and letters he wrote in jail. These suggest that he saw defeat as he would have seen victory: as God's will. Though sure the Lord wanted slavery destroyed, he began to see a divine purpose in his defeat. "I know," he said, "that the very errors by which my scheme was marred were decreed before the world was made."[1]

Brown shifted gears, believing his defeat God's way of attacking slavery through him, but from a different angle. His fate was certain; Virginia would hang him as surely as sunrise and sunset. So, rather than challenge the evidence, he decided to use the time he had left to shape his image for the American people and for history. The raider must show himself and his cause in the best light—holy, freedom-loving, humane. Meanwhile, he must turn the tables, putting the South on trial for "the sum of all villainies"—slavery. This would win Northerners' sympathy and enrage Southerners, speeding disunion and civil war, the only sure way to end slavery, he thought.[2]

Brown launched this campaign in the hours after his capture. Though he was in pain, his mind was sharp, his voice strong. Virginia's governor, Henry Wise, and a flock of state politicians and reporters had rushed to Harpers Ferry to question the prisoner. When Colonel Lee asked if he wanted the reporters removed, Brown said no. He welcomed the chance to tell his story as he wished the nation to hear it. For three hours straight, officials asked what any investigator would ask a terrorist today. Why did you come? From where? Who gave you money? How many men did you have? He refused to answer.[3]

When asked to explain what happened during the fight, Brown lied or slanted the facts, as he would during his trial. The marines "fired first" after "loud and long calls of 'surrender,'" he said. Brown received "bayonet stabs" in different parts of his body "after I had ceased fighting," he said. He never planned to ignite a slave uprising, but only "to gather them up from time to time and set them free," he said. In Kansas, "I killed no man except in fair fight," he said.[4]

Brown did answer some questions truthfully. These were not about the raid, but about the principles that guided his actions. To the question "How do you justify your acts?" he replied that he believed God sent him to Virginia to do sacred work. Brown added that he believed in the Bible, the Golden Rule, and the Declaration of Independence. Like any good person, he lived by their principles.[5]

That night, October 18, militiamen took Brown and the other prisoners to the county jail at Charles Town, eight miles southwest of Harpers Ferry. The Virginia authorities had decided to try the leader separately from his men. That way, they could rush him to the gallows without delay. In their haste, they set a trap—for themselves.

Americans would witness the trial through the eyes of the press. It was, we may say, our first nationwide media event. Brown understood the value of propaganda. As historian Paul Finkelman has observed, he aimed to "manufacture martyrdom"—that is, his own martyrdom. A martyr is one who suffers, even dies, for a belief and for the good of others. Many early Christians were martyred by their Roman persecutors.[6]

Reporters from the nation's major newspapers flocked to Charles Town. Brown meant to use them as mouthpieces

to put his case to the public. His behavior and personality impressed reporters. Wendell Phillips marveled at his skill in handling the press. "Having taken possession of Harpers Ferry," Phillips told an audience, "he began to edit the *New York Tribune* and the *New York Herald,*" America's largest newspapers. Brown did this not by writing articles but by calculating every move for maximum effect upon the reporters, and then upon their readers.[7]

On October 25, a grand jury charged him with three death-penalty offenses: conspiracy to incite a slave rebellion, treason against Virginia, and murder. Brown lay on a cot, eyes closed and head bandaged, a lone, battered figure against a mighty slave state. To win sympathy, he

The prison, guardhouse, and courthouse in Charles Town, Virginia (now West Virginia), where John Brown and his fellow raiders were held and tried. (c. 1859)

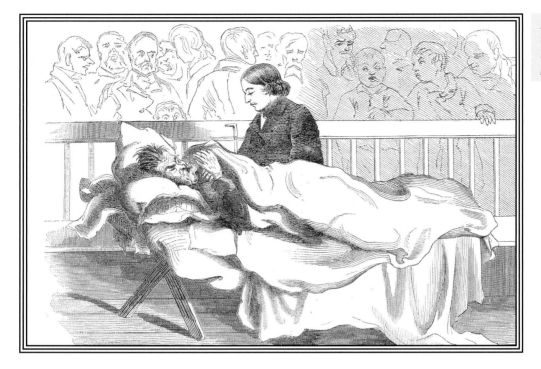

John Brown spent most of his trial on a cot, saying he was too ill to participate. (c. 1859)

told the court he was not up to the ordeal of a trial. He had pain, and his ears still rang from the noise of battle, he said.

Asked to plead innocent or guilty, Brown acted as if *he* were the wronged party. This was not a real court, he declared, as Virginia had no intention of giving him a fair trial. Away with the farce! Enough pretenses at justice! "If you seek my blood, you can have it at any moment, without this mockery of a trial. . . . I am ready for my fate." Such outbursts had the desired effect. When reported in the press, Northerners, even nonabolitionists, respected the "brave old man."[8]

Judge Richard Parker ordered that the trial begin immediately. Nearly six hundred people jammed the courtroom,

a small, grimy place like countless others in rural America. Spectators constantly opened peanuts, tossing the shells on the floor, where they crunched under their feet. Men smoked cigars and spat out streams of tobacco juice, then a common habit in America. A bailiff marched around the room, shouting at spectators to keep quiet. Now and then, they cursed the defendant, a "damned black-hearted villain! Heart as black as a stove-pipe!" State prosecutor Charles Harding, a drunkard, sat with his feet up on a table, napping whenever his eyelids grew heavy.[9]

Judge Parker assigned Brown two Virginia lawyers, but the defendant said he did not trust them. His Honor dismissed them. Free-state men soon took their places. Hiram Griswold, of Cleveland, Ohio, and Samuel Chilton, of Washington, D.C., were top-notch criminal defense lawyers. Boston abolitionists paid their fees. George H. Hoyt, twenty-one, a recent law school graduate, arrived from Boston. "A beardless youth," he was hired by John W. Le Barnes, a wealthy abolitionist who had given Brown money for his activities in Kansas.[10]

Acting prosecutor Andrew Hunter called his witnesses. Each described the raid from his point of view. They told of the seizure of the arsenal, the halting of the train, and the killing of Hayward Shepherd and Mayor Fontaine Beckham. Probably the most damaging testimony came from John Allstadt. The former hostage told of being awakened by armed men shouting, "Get up quick, or we will burn you up." Yet the testimony of Colonel Lewis Washington, the most prominent witness, cut both ways. On the one hand, he recalled Brown saying that "he was too old a soldier to yield the advantage he possessed in holding hostages." However, Washington also heard his captor "give frequent orders not to fire on unarmed citizens."[11]

Defense lawyers tried two tactics. First, they argued that Brown was not a citizen of Virginia and so could not be guilty of treason against it. Only the federal government, whose property Brown had seized, could try him. Judge Parker overruled the objection, noting most states had laws against treason. Brown lay on his cot, hardly moving, his eyes closed, as if the trial did not concern him.

The defense team's next argument got his attention—fast. It had collected letters from Brown's Ohio relatives that "proved" his insanity. For example, Jeremiah Brown wrote that his half brother John told him he would fight slavery "though it should destroy him and his family." Jeremiah also said that John "was satisfied he was a chosen instrument in the hands of God to war against slavery. From his manner and his conversation . . . I had no doubt he had become insane on the subject of slavery."[12]

Such letters stunned the defendant. Brown sprang from his cot, enraged. He resented the charge; it was a personal insult. Besides, he declared, "I am perfectly unconscious of insanity." His lawyers, humiliated by the client whose life they were trying to save, dropped the insanity plea.[13]

Brown surely had a deeper reason than pride for reacting as he did. Enemies would have used the jury's verdict of guilty due to insanity to discredit his life. Screaming headlines would have declared, "JOHN BROWN A LUNATIC!" and "JOHN BROWN COMMITTED TO AN INSANE ASYLUM!" Worse, his "insanity" would have implied that ending slavery was not a matter of justice, but a madman's fantasy.

We may still ask: Was John Brown insane? In his day, the study of mental illness was in its infancy. His belief that he acted on God's commands proves nothing. At a time when religion was still a dominant force in American life, many people "heard" God or "felt" Him acting through them; God "spoke" to William Lloyd Garrison and to Wendell Phillips. The record, though slim, shows Brown had few signs of what today's physicians would relate to mental illness. However, a question remains. Secret Six member Thomas Wentworth Higginson knew Brown quite well. Decades later, in 1906, Higginson wrote that he should have "perceived the madness that dwelled within him—the insanity that sat stealthily beside his great, selfless nobility." Higginson never mentioned what alerted him to Brown's "insanity."[14]

On October 31, the jury found Brown guilty of all charges. Two days later, Judge Parker asked if he had anything to say before sentencing. Yes, Brown had "a few words to say." After declaring his innocence, he gave what is among the greatest speeches in American history; Ralph Waldo Emerson later compared it to Abraham Lincoln's Gettysburg Address.

Brown spoke not only to the court but also to the reporters and, through them, to America. He did not see himself as the issue. He was simply a devout man doing the Lord's work. The real issue was slavery. How could anyone condemn him without first condemning slavery in a land of laws—yet a land with no legal way to end the horror without the masters' consent? Brown declared:

Had I . . . interfered in behalf of the rich, the powerful, the intelligent, the so-called great . . . it would have been all right; and every man in this Court would have deemed it an act worthy of reward rather than punishment. The Court acknowledges, too, as I suppose, the validity of the law of God. I see a book kissed, which I suppose to be the Bible . . . which teaches me that all things whatsoever I would that men should do to me, I should do even so to them. . . . I endeavored to act up to that instruction. I say I am yet too young to understand that God is any respecter of persons. I believe that to have interfered as I have done, as I have always freely admitted I have done in behalf of His despised poor, is no wrong, but right. Now, if it is deemed necessary that I should forfeit my life for the furtherance of the ends of justice, and mingle my blood farther

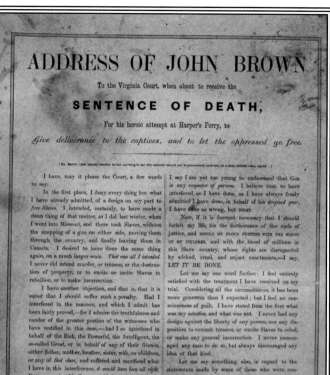

ADDRESS OF JOHN BROWN

To the Virginia Court, when about to receive the

SENTENCE OF DEATH,

For his heroic attempt at Harper's Ferry, to

Give deliverance to the captives, and to let the oppressed go free.

John Brown's address to the Virginia court before receiving the death sentence. (c. 1859)

Keeping the Deathwatch

If His Honor expected Brown to leave the world quietly, he was wrong. By giving him a month more to live, Judge Parker went against the politicians' wish to dispose of him quickly. For them, that decision was a serious error. But they could do nothing about it.

Brown slept little, but soundly, for, he said, he had a clear conscience. He spent most of each day reading the Bible and writing letters. Jailers also allowed him to receive visitors, mostly people he did not know—so many that the chief, Captain John Avis, had to take them into the tiny cell in groups. There they found the prisoner chained hand and foot, the chains fastened to an iron ring set into the stone floor. Guards had orders to shoot Brown in the case of a rescue attempt.[16]

Often the prisoner's words and manner gave visitors courage, rather than him taking courage from their good wishes. Upon leaving, they told waiting reporters about the incredible person they had seen. Reporters who interviewed Brown portrayed him as he wished they would. "In all his conversation Brown showed the utmost gentleness and tranquility, and a quiet courtesy," according to one. "He says God is with him, and fears nothing," said another.[17]

Brown wrote scores of letters to family, friends, and strangers who had written him. Those letters protested the injustice

with the blood of my children and with the blood of millions in this slave country whose rights are disregarded by wicked, cruel, and unjust enactments, I say let it be done![15]

He finished. Silence. You could hear a pin drop in the courtroom. Judge Parker then pronounced the sentence. John Brown would go to the gallows on December 2, in exactly one month.

of "my public murder." Yet if he must give his life for the oppressed, he would gladly do so. In a dig at the *Dred Scott* decision, he wrote, "I go joyfully in behalf of millions that 'have no rights' that this *great and glorious* Republic is 'bound to respect.'" Brown felt blessed "to die *for a cause,* not *merely* to pay a debt of nature as all must." He advised a correspondent, "Never in all your trials forget the poor that cry, and him that hath none to help him." The man's sincerity and dignity, tenderness and strength, even won over his jailers. Those who censored his letters wept as they read them.[18]

Though sent to private persons, those letters were really press releases. Brown knew the recipients would turn them over to the newspapers. Once they were printed, he expected the letters to reach tens of thousands of readers each day. The letters had such an effect that many wrote asking for his autograph, by return mail, to frame and hang in a place of honor in their homes.

One letter, however, struck a sour note. It came from Mahala Doyle, wife and mother of three of his Kansas victims. She was illiterate, so she had someone write it for her. Mahala was not in a forgiving mood: "I do feel gratified to hear that you were stopped in your fiendish career at Harper's Ferry, with the loss of your two sons. . . . O how it pained my heart to hear the dying groans of my

Husband & children." She added that her youngest son, John, whose life she had begged Brown to spare, was now grown. He would gladly put the noose around Brown's neck.[19]

The condemned man had not seen his wife for six months. Mary wanted to visit him, but he urged her not to come, as it would be too painful for both of them. Finally, Brown gave in. On December 1, Mary arrived at the Charles Town jail. Captain Avis's wife searched her before the captain opened the cell door. Though Avis had removed the prisoner's chains, he watched them the whole time.

Upon Mary's entering the cell, the couple "kissed and affectionately embraced," according to the *New York Times*. Mary said, "My dear husband, it is a hard fate" that he was to die and leave his family. "Well, well," he replied, "cheer up, cheer up, Mary. . . . I believe it is all for the best." After about an hour, they shook hands. "God bless you and the children," Brown said as they parted. Later that day, Brown told Captain Avis he wanted no proslavery minister to pray for his soul. He would prefer that "a dozen slave children and a good old slave mother" escort him to the gallows.[20]

Friday, December 2.

Jailers found Brown "perfectly calm and collected" when they came for him on December 2. He wore black: coat, trousers,

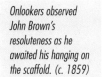

Onlookers observed John Brown's resoluteness as he awaited his hanging on the scaffold. (c. 1859)

vest, hat. On his feet he had loose-fitting red carpet slippers. As they walked to the front door, he handed a jailer a note. The man put it in his pocket. After the execution, he read Brown's message to America. For many years, Brown had thought only bloodshed could end slavery. Now he predicted the coming disaster with his last written words. The note said: "I John Brown am now quite *certain* that the crimes of this *guilty* land *will never* be purged *away* but with Blood. I had *as I now think, vainly* flattered myself that without *very much* bloodshed it might be done."[21]

Virginia took no chances. Militiamen kept all strangers out of Charles Town. They guarded Brown so closely that nobody could get near him, or to the open

wagon waiting at the foot of the jailhouse steps, without their permission. Guards helped Brown, his arms now tied behind him, into the wagon. Once aboard, they sat him on a long wooden box; Brown knew it contained his coffin. Off they drove, between lines of militiamen on each side of the road. "This *is* beautiful country. I never had the pleasure of seeing it before," Brown said, admiring the distant mountains.[22]

Carpenters had built the scaffold, a raised platform with a gallows, in a field at the edge of town. Fifteen hundred militiamen formed a square around it, ringed by squadrons of cavalry. Thomas J. Jackson, professor of mathematics at the Virginia Military Institute, stood with his cadets, facing the scaffold. Nearby, an actor named John Wilkes Booth stood with the Richmond Grays, volunteers from the Virginia state capital. Booth glared at the condemned man with the same "unlimited, undeniable contempt" in which he held an Illinois politician named Abraham Lincoln.[23]

Professor Jackson, a Mexican War veteran, admired Brown's "unflinching firmness." Without any sign of fear, he walked up the scaffold steps toward the gallows. The executioner tied his ankles, placed a white linen hood over his head, and adjusted the knot under his left ear. The hood prevented Brown from seeing anything, and onlookers from seeing the expression on his face as he died. Three slave states—South Carolina, Missouri, and Kentucky—had competed for the "honor" of furnishing the rope. Kentucky won.[24]

The executioner led Brown to the drop, a trapdoor with hinges on one side, held shut by a rope on the opposite side. At 11:35 a.m., he cut the rope with a hatchet. Brown fell through, then jerked to a stop as the knot broke his neck. "There was very little motion of his person," Professor Jackson wrote his wife, "after which the wind blew his lifeless body to and fro."[25]

Suddenly the voice of Jackson's friend Colonel J. T. L. Preston, also of the Virginia Military Institute, rang out. "So perish all such enemies of Virginia! All such enemies of the Union! All such foes of the human race!" This suggests that many Southerners had not, as yet, given up on the Union, and still saw themselves as patriotic Americans.[26]

FATE OF THE OTHER CAPTURED RAIDERS

John E. Cook, John Copeland, Edwin Coppoc, and Shields Green were tried together. Cook and Coppoc pleaded innocent, claiming (correctly) they knew nothing of Brown's plan to seize Harpers Ferry until the last moment. The other two did not defend themselves. Nevertheless, the jury convicted all of them of the same crimes as their leader. On November 16, 1859, Judge Parker sentenced them to death by hanging. They all died on the same day, December 16. Aaron Stevens was tried later, after recovering from his wounds, and was hanged on March 16, 1860. Albert Hazlett had escaped, but was caught near Carlisle, Pennsylvania, and returned to Virginia. After trial, he went to the gallows on the same day as Stevens.

The state of Virginia returned Brown's body to his wife, who had left for home after their last time together. On December 8, family, neighbors, and guests attended funeral services at the North Elba farm. As her husband had wished, Mary had him buried under his grandfather's gravestone—she simply added his name to the marker.

Wendell Phillips delivered the eulogy. "Marvelous old man! He has abolished slavery in Virginia," the fiery abolitionist said. "History will date Virginian Emancipation from Harpers Ferry. True, the slave is still there. So, when the tempest uproots the pine . . . it looks green for months—a year or two. Still, it is timber, not a tree. John Brown has loosened the roots of the slave system; it only breathes—it does not live."[27]

John Brown's grave and the "Big Rock" in North Elba, New York. (c. 1896)

Phillips was right. While Brown's raid had left slavery apparently as secure as ever, it helped bring on the crisis that would end it in America.

Aftershocks

Up in the North, Brown's closest allies had their own problems. After Brown's capture, Robert E. Lee sent patrols to search for his base camp. Within hours, they found the weapons stored in a disused schoolhouse: 102 Sharps rifles, 12 pistols, 10 kegs of gunpowder, and 483 pikes. At the Kennedy farm, a patrol made a more startling discovery. A cavalryman found a trunk in the cellar holding a carpetbag, a traveling bag made of carpet material. It contained a treasure trove of documents and maps with crosses marked on areas with many slaves. This strongly suggested

Illustrations in a November 1859 Harper's Weekly showing some of the raiders' weapons and the abandoned schoolhouse they used as an arsenal.

that Brown intended to arm these slaves with rifles taken from Harpers Ferry. Better yet, it held letters from the Secret Six. Lee sent these to the War Department. From there, copies found their way into the newspapers.[28]

So the old fellow had not acted alone! Important men were accessories before the fact, the legal term for those who aid a lawbreaker before a crime but who are not present when it is committed. The Secret Six had given Brown money, weapons, advice, and encouragement. These men knew he planned to ignite a slave rebellion, though not exactly where or when. Their aid and knowledge made them as guilty as him in the eyes of the law.

The Secret Six never thought Brown would leave such evidence behind. After the letters' discovery, they showed little courage. Upon reading his own words in the *New York Herald* and *New York Times*,

Gerrit Smith panicked. For all his talk of spreading fear of "fire and rape and slaughter" among slaveholders, he could not face the consequences. Prison was not for people like him! A millionaire used to praise and obedience, Smith could not bear the disgrace of prison or the idea of giving up his lifestyle.

"I am going to be indicted, sir, indicted!" the trembling Smith told a reporter. "If any man in the Union is taken, it will be me," he moaned. He did what others in his position had done, and would do again: ordered a cover-up. Smith sent his son-in-law, Charles Dudley Miller, to hunt for other dangerous papers. Miller burned anything he could find in Boston and Ohio linking Smith to Brown. Yet as his worries grew, Smith went "temporarily insane"—or so family doctors claimed. They sent him to the State Asylum for the Insane. There, doctors treated him with morphine, a highly addictive drug used to relieve pain, and cannabis, another name for marijuana, to reduce nervous stress. After seven weeks of treatment, he "recovered his reason" and returned to his mansion. By then, it was clear he would not be arrested. Until his dying day, Smith denied he and Brown had ever been close.[29]

Of the other members of the Secret Six, Theodore Parker applauded Brown's effort. He did so from the safety of Italy, where he had gone several months earlier, seeking relief from tuberculosis, a disease that claimed his life the following year.

Samuel Gridley Howe fled to Canada. The doctor returned after a few weeks, when lawyers assured him the federal government would not press charges, as it did not want to inflame North-South tensions. Upon his return, Howe said that he had known nothing of the Harpers Ferry scheme and that anyhow, Brown had acted "upon his own responsibility."[30]

George Luther Stearns fled and returned with his friend Howe. Years later, when it no longer mattered, he told the truth. Giving "good old John Brown" weapons was the finest thing he'd ever done, the millionaire said.[31]

After burning Brown's letters to him, Franklin Sanborn fled to Canada alone, then returned for the same reason that his comrades did. Like them, he never faced charges.

While not a member of the Secret Six, Frederick Douglass knew all about Brown's plan. After the raid, federal marshals went looking for him. Fearing for his life, the black leader fled to England, where he remained for nearly two years, until he felt it safe to return. Yet Douglass never forgave himself for being "most miserably deficient in courage" in fleeing after the raid.[32]

Only Thomas Wentworth Higginson stood firm. The others' actions disgusted him—so cowardly, so shameful were they, he thought. Rather than flee, he went about his daily life, daring the government to arrest him. It did not, for reasons officials chose not to share with the public. Higginson's only regret was his ignorance of Brown's plan to seize Harpers Ferry. Had he known, he claimed, he might have suggested another way to ignite a national explosion. "I think the bombing of a few fine southern buildings, or a few famous southern men, with notes crediting the blasts to some chosen northern abolitionist groups, would have done the job," he wrote years later. "Such action would have brought disunion quickly, and without risk to any from our side"—that is, would have safely provoked civil war over slavery. Higginson called this an exercise in "practical terror."[33]

Making an Abolitionist Martyr

Much as Higginson regretted the old man's death, he thought it a good thing. Nor was he alone in this belief. After the failure at Harpers Ferry, leading abolitionists saw John Brown dead more valuable than John Brown alive. His image as a martyr, they believed, would spread abolitionism faster than legions of speakers and printing presses could. His example would, they hoped, arouse free-state anger over slavery to the boiling point of disunion.

For this to happen, however, they

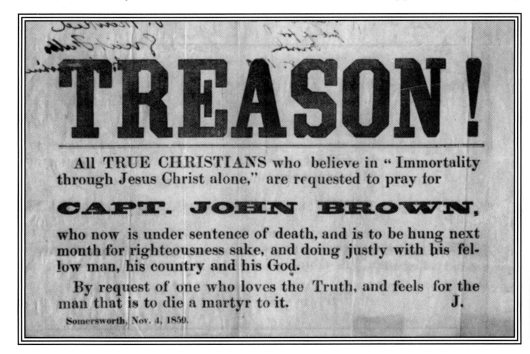

TREASON!

All TRUE CHRISTIANS who believe in "Immortality through Jesus Christ alone," are requested to pray for

CAPT. JOHN BROWN,

who now is under sentence of death, and is to be hung next month for righteousness sake, and doing justly with his fellow man, his country and his God.

By request of one who loves the Truth, and feels for the man that is to die a martyr to it.   J.

Somersworth, Nov. 4, 1859.

A flyer asking for prayers for John Brown after his death sentence was delivered. (1859)

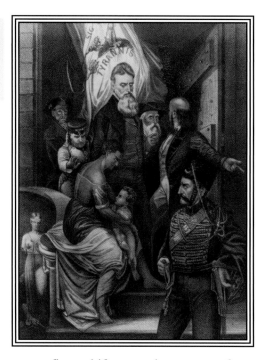

A melodramatic, and untrue, depiction of John Brown's last moments before his hanging. (c. 1863)

must first shift attention away from Brown's crimes by appealing to the sympathy people had for him. Brown had already prepared the ground with his letters, interviews, and court speech, as well as with his sad good-bye to Mary and his courage in facing death. Many Northerners had come to see him as he saw himself: devout, pure, simple, self-sacrificing. Abolitionists, then, could present him as a good man who *may* have done bad things, not for his own benefit, but in service to the higher law of conscience.

Henry David Thoreau set the tone in a famous speech on the evening of October 30, 1859, a day before the jury found Brown guilty. Thoreau praised him as "a superior man," "a man of ideas and principles," "an angel of light" sent from heaven

"to be the redeemer of those in captivity." Brown's critics, he said after the execution, were crude and rude, lacking human feelings. Why, they could not even recite poetry, let alone write it![34]

True, Brown had caused people's deaths. Yet, Thoreau said, he killed only when the slavery-protecting Constitution, slave codes, and slaveholder violence forced him to. "The question," he said, "is not about the weapon, but the spirit in which you use it." In plain English, Thoreau came to believe killing proper if the killer's character and motives were pure. Without realizing it, he and other abolitionists had crossed a dangerous moral boundary. The idea that we may do evil if we mean good has a long, dark history. It has justified torture and religious persecution such as the atrocities of the Spanish Inquisition. The atrocities of twentieth-century tyrannies, notably Joseph Stalin's Communist Russia and Adolf Hitler's Nazi Germany, were extreme expressions of this idea.[35]

Judge Parker's death sentence sparked a national debate. Cautious Southerners feared hanging Brown would backfire. "If old John Brown is executed," a Kentucky newspaper warned, "there will be thousands to dip their handkerchiefs in his blood; relics of the martyr will be paraded throughout the North." His death would surely inflame Northerners' opposition to slavery. Governor Wise would do best to spare his life and send him to the mad-house.[36]

Leading abolitionists worried that Virginia would *not* hang the old man. They wanted him to die for exactly the reason cautious Southerners feared. "I almost fear to hear of his deliverance," Thoreau wrote, "doubting if a prolonged life, if any life, can do as much good as his death." Franklin Sanborn, just returned from Canada, expected that Brown's death would "undoubtedly add millions to the righteous cause" of abolition. The Reverend Henry Ward Beecher, of the Sharps rifle "Bibles," agreed. "Let no one pray that Brown be spared," Beecher preached. "Let Virginia make him a martyr. . . . His soul was noble; his work miserable. But a cord and a gibbet [gallows] would redeem all that, and round up Brown's failure with a heroic success." When Brown read these words in his cell, he wrote "Good" next to them.[37]

Abolitionists gave Brown a marvelous send-off. They declared December 2, 1859, "Martyr's Day," the day a holy man died for his faith. Across the free states, especially in Massachusetts, men wore black mourning armbands, women heavy veils of the same color. Black streamers hung from windows and across streets. Peddlers did a brisk trade in colored prints of Brown and lapel buttons with his likeness. Church bells tolled. Minute guns—small cannons—fired, marking the minutes before the execution. Prayer meetings prayed for his soul.

Memorial meetings heard abolitionist leaders praise Old Brown as holy and damn Southerners as wicked. Wendell Phillips described him as God's law made flesh, licensed by the Almighty to destroy slavery. Ralph Waldo Emerson dubbed him the "new saint," whose death "will make the gallows as glorious as the cross." Others called him "St. John the Just," the "Christ of anti-slavery," and the "Prophet of God! Messiah of the Slave!" Harriet Tubman, the celebrated Underground Railroad conductor, noted, "When I think how he gave up his life for our people . . . it's clear to me it wasn't a mortal man, it was God in him."[38]

William Lloyd Garrison said what others felt in their hearts yet had trouble expressing. Two weeks after Brown's execution, he addressed an overflow gathering in Tremont Temple, a Boston meeting hall. Garrison had begun his career preaching nonviolence, but he no longer saw a peaceful end to slavery:

I am a non-resistant, and I not only desire, but have labored [tirelessly] to effect the peaceful abolition of slavery, by an appeal to the reason and conscience of the slaveholder. Yet, as a peace man . . . I am prepared to say, "Success to every slave insurrection at the South, and in every slave

*country." (Enthusiastic applause.) . . .
Whenever there is a contest between
the oppressed and the oppressor . . .
God knows that my heart must be with
the oppressed, and always against the
oppressor. . . . Rather than see men
wearing their chains in a cowardly and
servile spirit, I would, as an advocate
of peace, much rather see them
breaking the head of the tyrant with
their chains. . . . I see in every slave on
the Southern plantation* a living John
Brown. . . . *I see four millions of living
John Browns needing our thoughts,
our prayers, our noblest exertions
to strike off their [chains]. . . . There
is a law above . . . human codes, the
same throughout the world, the same
in all time: it is* the law of God written
by the finger of God upon the heart
of man; *and that law . . . [rejects]
with indignation the wild and guilty
phantasy that man can hold property in
man. (Loud applause.)*[39]

An illustration of the apocryphal story of John Brown kissing an African American infant before departing for the scaffold. (c. 1885)

Though Garrison wished success to every slave rebellion, his speech was mild compared to what others said. Their letters and articles, speeches and sermons, were verbal bullets shot at Southerners already terrified by Brown's raid. From Italy, Theodore Parker, never at a loss for angry words, wrote that he expected "the Fire of Vengeance" to sweep the South. "What shall put it out? *The white man's blood!*"[40]

Fellow abolitionists made similar statements—many others. For example, the Reverend George B. Cheever, of Boston, gave a sermon that Brown could easily have given himself. Sinners' lives meant nothing, their victims' lives everything! Like Brown, Cheever believed that all masters—men, women, children—should die if need be to rid America of slavery. "It is infinitely better that three hundred thousand slaveholders were abolished, struck out of existence, than that four million human beings, with their posterity forever, should be enslaved under them, compelled to a system which is the perpetual violation of God's law." Abolitionist Henry Clarke Wright, a noted opponent of war, called for a slave uprising. "It is the right and duty of the North," he said, "to instigate the slaves to insurrection."[41]

Meanwhile, Brown's fame grew. His death gave birth to a story, still repeated in some American history textbooks. Supposedly, before Brown boarded the wagon that would take him to the scaffold, a slave mother held her baby in front of him. With guards looking on, the man with the long Santa Claus beard kissed the infant. Though a good story, it is a myth. Brown did not have a long beard at the time of his execution. Nor could anyone have gotten past the militiamen surrounding him.

The myth's origins are unclear. Its idea may have come from Brown himself. In a letter, we recall, he wrote that he wished slave children and an old slave mother to escort him to the scaffold. That letter appeared in the newspapers. Three days after his execution, the *New York Tribune* printed the first version of the kissing story. It is probably no accident that the *Tribune*'s founder and editor was Horace Greeley, an abolitionist whose editorials helped shape public opinion. Still, it is a mystery who wrote the original story,

or why. It grew more elaborate as other newspapers printed their own versions.

The kissing legend perfectly fit the image Brown's admirers sought to create. It spread like wildfire, inspiring countless drawings and poems. The most famous poem, by abolitionist poet John Greenleaf Whittier, described the nonevent this way:

John Brown of Osawatomie,
They led him out to die;
And, lo!—a poor slave mother
With her little child pressed nigh.
Then the bold, blue eye grew tender,
And the old, harsh face grew mild,
As he stooped between the jeering
  ranks,
And kissed the negro's child![42]

This kissing story, while untrue, is important: it shows how repetition, and people's will to believe, can gain a myth acceptance as historical fact. When I taught junior high school in the late 1960s, our American history textbook had a picture of the scene, without explaining that it never happened. Apocryphal stories like this one can reveal something about a society's views, even if the actual story is untrue.

Brown's death also created a demand for relics, objects once linked to a holy person. Many religious people prized relics because they were a tangible memorial and could be venerated. After the execution, Northerners sought anything linked to Brown: splinters from the gallows, bits of the hanging rope, pieces of clothing, locks of his hair, pikes. People bought these without realizing they were throwing good money away. Brown's personal effects went to his family. The other objects were fakes. After the execution, Virginia authorities had the rope burned and the gallows taken down, its pieces mixed in with regular lumber. That did not prevent Harpers Ferry blacksmiths from making fake "John Brown pikes" and selling them to eager relic hunters. However, a scrawny man with white stringy hair down to his shoulders and a wild glint in his eyes managed to get hold of the real things. Edmund Ruffin, a Virginian, took several pikes for a special purpose, as we will see later.[43]

John Brown's body would have been the best relic. A fellow abolitionist told Wendell Phillips the body should be "put into a metal coffin enclosed except the face in ice," to prevent rotting. After an impressive funeral in Boston, abolitionists could show it in Northern cities as propaganda and a fund-raiser for the cause. Phillips thought it too soon for that; Widow Brown wanted her husband buried on the farm. At the right time, Phillips intended to persuade Mary to donate the body to Boston for reburial near Bunker Hill, where Brown's grave would become a sacred spot for abolitionist pilgrims to renew their faith. Nothing came of the scheme. Mary wanted her husband's remains to stay at home. Thomas Wentworth Higginson lost his temper, and discouraged others from giving money to aid her family.[44]

The Harpers Ferry raid and its leader's execution left Americans fearful about the future. Where was the country heading? An African American minister, J. Sella Martin, gave the best answer. On December 2, as Brown's body swayed in the breeze, Martin addressed his Boston congregation. Like a Bible prophet, he warned, "John Brown . . . shall slay more in his death than he ever slew in all his life." For, the minister knew, the old man had set in motion the worst tragedy, and the noblest triumph, in American history. The Civil War began less than eighteen months later.[45]

VII

High Noon for the Union

Whereas ten years [ago], there were thousands who could not endure my lightest word of rebuke of the South, they can now swallow John Brown whole, and his rifle into the bargain. In firing his gun, he has merely told us what time of day it is. *It is high noon, thank God!*
—William Lloyd Garrison, January 1860

Fear

The Harpers Ferry raid was to the Civil War what Japan's 1941 attack on Pearl Harbor was to the United States' involvement in the Second World War. It was the first clash of arms, starting a chain of events that would change America forever. Harpers Ferry, as a Southerner put it, "proved that the North and South are standing in battle array," poised for civil war.[1]

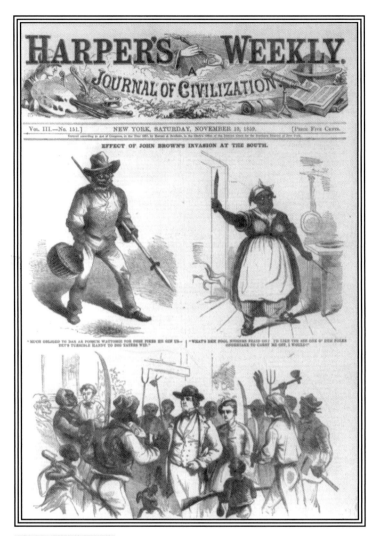

The cover of Harper's Weekly *illustrating the supposed effect of John Brown's invasion: slaves up in arms, empowered by his actions. (1859)*

Fear poisoned reason. Although his plan had failed, Old Brown had struck a tender nerve. All levels of white Southern society felt the effects of his raid. It stunned slaveholders, and also the vast majority of those who owned no slaves. The very idea of armed blacks roaming the countryside was terrifying, a waking nightmare.

Harpers Ferry revived awful memories. It was as if Nat Turner's revolt had happened yesterday, stirring the same feelings as in 1831. Beautiful Constance Cary, a belle of Virginia high society, captured the mood. Her family lived far from the arsenal, but "there was the fear . . . dark, boding, oppressive, and altogether hateful." Fear seeped into whites like an evil spirit. The worst time was after sundown. "I can remember taking it to bed with me at night, and awakening suddenly [in] nervous terror. The mutterings of the distant thunderstorm, even the rustle of the night wind in the oaks that shaded my window, filled me with nameless dread. . . . In short, peace had flown from the borders of Virginia."[2]

In this world of fear, certain events took on sinister meaning. For several weeks after the raid, Virginia had a rash of mysterious fires. Flames from barns, stables, and silos lit up the night sky. "The heavens," a Richmond newspaper said, "are illuminated by the lurid glow of burning property." There is no proof that slaves started these fires. Yet anxious whites saw them as plots by slaves and abolitionists. Fear sparked rumors, which spread like epidemics. For example, newspapers reported (wrongly) the discovery of barrels of strychnine meant to poison wells throughout the South. A chalked graffiti image of John Brown's face with the words "The martyr—God bless him" triggered a local panic in Virginia.[3]

Vigilance committees set out to identify and punish "disloyal" slaves. Committees doubled their night patrols, searched slave quarters for weapons, and hanged suspects without trial. Free blacks fared little better than their brethren. Freedom of assembly, guaranteed by the Bill of Rights, vanished as officials denied permits for gatherings. Free black sailors on ships docking at Southern ports had to stay in jail until their ships sailed. In one case, a Georgia court illegally ordered a black English sailor sold into slavery for a made-up offense. Mississippi and neighboring states passed laws forcing free blacks to make a dreadful choice: enslave yourself to any master who will have you, or leave the state. Those who refused to leave within the time allowed went to the auction block.[4]

Northern things, ideas, and people raised suspicions. Since Northern newspapers "corrupted" minds, having one spelled trouble. In a Georgia town, for example, a man found with a clean shirt wrapped in a New York newspaper had to flee for his life. Anyone who spoke with a Northern accent might get a tar-and-feather party. A barrel of tar was brought to a boil and *the application made to his nude person,* said a *New York Times* report. When the sticky goop covered the victim from head to toe, a feather pillow emptied over him made him look like some weird chicken. Abolitionists, of course, were marked men. Newspapers told of irate Southerners throwing them off moving trains, clubbing them, and dunking them in rivers until they nearly drowned.[5]

The carpetbag found at the Kennedy farm fueled fear and fury. The papers it held showed that John Brown and the Secret Six had aimed to launch a massive slave uprising. How widespread was their conspiracy? Did Northerners scorn the conspirators as "ABOLITIONISTS RUN MAD"? For many Southerners, the answers to such questions would test Northern goodwill and intentions and, finally, national unity. For reassurance, Southerners demanded that Northerners condemn abolitionists in the strongest terms.[6]

But instead of outrage, Southerners read sermons, speeches, and articles praising Old Brown as a "martyr and saint." This played right into the hands of the "fire-eaters," extreme supporters of disunion or, as Southerners called it, secession. Mostly wealthy slaveholders, politicians, and newspaper editors, the fire-eaters wanted to create an independent Southern nation based on slavery. Some even dreamed of ruling a slave empire in Cuba and Central America. It would be easy, they thought, to seize these fertile lands with a few determined volunteers, creating "a great cotton slave Republic" that would last for centuries. The raid on Harpers Ferry came as a gift, the perfect way for them to win mass support.[7]

Fire-eaters worked to sharpen Southerners' fears and anger. They depicted all Northerners as abolitionists—all reckless, all bloodthirsty, all anti-Southern fanatics. This was untrue. Many Northerners did hate slavery and honor John Brown. But because there were no opinion polls in the 1850s, it is impossible to form an accurate picture of public opinion. However, Northern newspaper reports do suggest that the majority thought the raider did deserve to hang.

Fire-eaters sought to create panic by printing the most violent abolitionist statements. For good measure, they reprinted gory thirty-year-old reports of Nat Turner's killings. According to Senator Jefferson Davis, of Mississippi, abolitionists sent John Brown "to incite slaves to murder helpless women and children." To prod them along, Edmund Ruffin, a fanatical secessionist, sent every Southern governor a John Brown pike. Each bore a label reading, *Sample of the favors designed for us by our Northern brethren.* This was Ruffin's way of saying that the South must secede or face mass murder. If civil war followed, then let it![8]

It is easy to jump to the conclusion that John Brown caused the Civil War. That would be wrong; no individual is ever totally responsible for a great historical event. The Civil War arose from deep disagreements between North and South, as old as the Union, that had nothing to do with him. However, his actions helped drive the nation to the brink of conflict. The presidential election of 1860 would push it over the brink. In the coming political battles, Southern fears and anger would focus on the young Republican

Ardent secessionist Edmund Ruffin sent one of John Brown's pikes to the governor of each Southern state, and fired one of the first—if not the first—shots of the Civil War. (c. 1861)

Party and its candidate, Abraham Lincoln. If Harpers Ferry shook their trust in their fellow citizens, Lincoln's election destroyed it totally.

Lincoln

From the earliest days of the Republic, America had had two chief political parties. Borrowing their name from an English party, the Whigs favored a strong federal government to help build up the economy. The Democrats favored states' rights, or a minimum of interference from Washington. Leaders of both parties favored slavery, or at least wished to keep it out of national politics. "Let sleeping dogs lie" was their attitude.

The Kansas-Nebraska Act of 1854 ignited a firestorm, as we saw. Even before the law went into effect, both Whigs and Democrats opposed to the spread of slavery began to form the Republican Party. Their motto said it all: "WE ARE REPUBLICANS BUT NOT ABOLITIONISTS." Republicans opposed slavery not out of regard for blacks, but to protect the interests of whites by preventing slaves from competing with them. Proudly calling themselves "the white man's party," they wanted slavery left alone where it existed but kept out of the West. No one favored this aim more than Abraham Lincoln.[9]

In the usual schoolbook history,

"Honest Abe" Lincoln came out of the wilderness to wage a crusade against slavery. This explanation is too simplified. Lincoln was a complicated man who, despite certain guiding beliefs, acted for different reasons at different times.

Born into a poor farm family in 1809, Lincoln was nine years younger than John Brown. Raised in Kentucky, Indiana, and Illinois, he decided to become a lawyer. A legal career had several attractions for an ambitious youngster living on the frontier. Lawyers always had work: preparing wills, land deeds, and bills of sale, or settling property disputes in court. Better yet, there were no formal education requirements. The nation had few law schools at this time, so few lawyers went to college. You simply "read law" on your own, as Lincoln did, or in the office of a licensed attorney who guided you. In return for the latter, you copied piles of legal documents "in fine hand"—neatly. When you felt ready, you took an oral license exam, given by district judges.

In his law practice, Lincoln met hundreds of people who came to admire and trust him. That, in turn, became a stepping-stone to politics. Over the years, he served in the Illinois state legislature and in the U.S. House of Representatives. In 1858, Stephen A. Douglas defeated him in a bid for a Senate seat from Illinois.

Lincoln never had the slightest doubt

about slavery. It was evil. Period. In 1864, as president, he explained: "I am naturally anti-slavery. If slavery is not wrong, nothing is wrong. I can not remember when I did not think so, and feel."[10]

Lincoln was a child during the early years of the Second Middle Passage, when masters moved their slaves to the rich cotton lands of the Deep South. Lincoln saw slaves herded along the dirt road that passed in front of his Kentucky home. One day, a trader asked Tom, his father, if he could bed down the slaves for the night in his barn. The child never forgot how "all of the slaves, men, women, and children," lay chained together as they slept, and how "some mothers held babies in their arms."[11]

Years later, in 1841, Lincoln went by steamboat down the Mississippi River to New Orleans. On deck, the young lawyer saw a dozen slaves "chained six by six together . . . like so many fish upon a trot line." These men, he wrote, "were being separated forever from the scenes of their childhood, their friends, their fathers and mothers, brothers and sisters, and many of them, from their wives and children, and going into perpetual slavery [and] the lash of the master."[12]

The Declaration of Independence reinforced Lincoln's hatred of slavery. From the moment he read it, it became his guiding star. "I have never had a feeling politically that did not spring from the sentiments embodied in the Declaration of Independence," he told an audience in 1861. Lincoln believed "all Men" are created equal, but not in all ways. People differ in appearance, intelligence, strength, abilities, and character. However, these differences amount to little, compared to the "inalienable" natural rights they have as human beings to "life, liberty, and the pursuit of happiness."[13]

Yet Lincoln despised both slavery *and* abolitionism. His attitude toward abolitionism sprang from his devotion to the Constitution, for him humankind's finest achievement in government. Lincoln was above all a man of the law. He believed with all his heart that law was the glue that held society together. Obedience to the law allowed people to live together, despite social class, rank, or wealth.

Slavery, like it or not, was legal. Under the Constitution, Congress could not interfere with the peculiar institution in the states. But that was exactly what abolitionists raged against, appealing to the higher law of conscience. Resisting sin, even violently, meant more to them than any written law. It followed for Lincoln, as for Daniel Webster, that if each person judged right and wrong for himself or herself, democracy would be impossible. Society would collapse into anarchy—disorder, confusion, and violence.[14]

This attitude was contrary to everything Lincoln believed. For that reason, he loathed "the self-righteousness of the Abolitionists," their belief in their own goodness and their arrogance in judging others. Lincoln called them "fanatics," "fiends," and "deluded men" who would make things worse for the enslaved, endangering the entire nation. The spectacle of William Lloyd Garrison burning the Constitution offended Lincoln deeply. The Garrisons of the world, he warned, would gladly smash the Union, "even burn the last copy of the Bible, rather than slavery should continue a single hour."[15]

It is no surprise that Lincoln should condemn John Brown. The old man got what he deserved, under the law. In February 1860, two months after the execution, Lincoln analyzed Brown's state of mind. He described him as an "enthusiast," a fanatic who "broods over the oppression of a people till he fancies himself commissioned by Heaven to liberate them," ending in his own death.[16]

Lincoln and Brown also differed in their attitudes toward race. Brown thought black people as good as anyone else, and treated them as equals. Lincoln, however, proved that one could believe two opposing ideas at once. Though he despised slavery, like most nineteenth-century white Americans he held racist ideas. Lincoln thought black people "inferior," and said so in public—often. He opposed "amalgamation," an evil-sounding term for interracial marriage. He called "mix-

An 1860 campaign button for a beardless Abraham Lincoln and his running mate, Hannibal Hamlin. (c. 1860)

ing blood" an unnatural act. "There is," he claimed, "a natural disgust in the minds of nearly all white people to the idea of . . . amalgamation of the white and black races."[17]

That "natural disgust" infected him. Lincoln supported his state's black laws. When free blacks in Illinois circulated a petition demanding the right to testify against whites in court, he refused to sign. Even as president, insults like "nigger," "darky," "Sambo," and "Cuffy" were part of his everyday speech. Lincoln had a keen sense of humor, and he relished vulgar black-dialect jokes. He also liked minstrel shows, where white actors posed as blacks by darkening their skin with burnt cork and painting their lips bright red. During these shows, actors portrayed black people as shiftless buffoons who sang in plantation dialect. One song, "Zip Coon," made fun of "larned" black "skolars," free blacks who "put on airs," trying to rise above their station by daring to read. (*Coon* is short for *raccoon*, and is an offensive slang term for a black person.)

O ole Zip Coon he is a larned skolar,
O ole Zip Coon he is a larned
    skolar . . .

Sings possum up a gum tree and coony
    in a hollar.[18]

Though Lincoln branded the Fugitive Slave Act "ungodly," that did not stop him from arguing both sides of the issue. As a lawyer, he felt that clients, whether he believed them right or wrong, deserved his best efforts. Lincoln had just two fugitive slave cases. In the first, he won freedom for a woman brought to Illinois by her master. In the second, he represented Kentucky slave trader Robert Matson, who had sued to recover a slave named Jane Bryant and her four young children. Bryant's lawyer demanded their freedom because they, too, had been brought to free-state Illinois. This time, Lincoln lost and Jane and her children went free.[19]

When it came to the spread of slavery, Lincoln, like his fellow Republicans, had no qualms about it in the South. He despised slavery, yet if whites wanted it, the Constitution allowed them to have it. But the West was different. Lincoln explained, in his folksy way, why white people must have "a clean bed with no snakes in it"— that is, a place without any blacks, slave or free. White workers would then not have to compete with blacks who worked for very little pay, or for no pay at all. Another time, he said he did not want the territories changed "into asylums for slavery and niggers." Nor did Lincoln think well of Mexicans, calling them "most decidedly a race of mongrels," people of mixed Native American and Spanish heritage.[20]

The territories, Lincoln insisted, belonged to the American people. They had paid for them in blood and treasure. Thus, it was up to the entire nation, not merely a minority of Southern slaveholders, to decide how best to use them. Moreover, locking slavery into the South spelled its end, its "ultimate extinction," as he put it. Time was against the peculiar institution. Since growing cotton exhausted the soil, slavery must fade away if confined to where it already existed. The laws of nature, not government actions, guaranteed its "natural death."[21]

The election of 1860 promised to be an exciting event. Old Brown knew it. Shortly before the Harpers Ferry raid, he predicted: "If the Republican Party elects its President next year, there will be war. . . . We are on the eve of one of the greatest wars in history."[22]

The Election of 1860

Abraham Lincoln, living, owed much to John Brown, dead. In May 1860, the Republican Party held its convention in Chicago. Few expected Lincoln to win its presidential nomination. Party leaders thought him too inexperienced to hold the nation's highest office. Luckily for him, the leading contender, New York senator William Henry Seward, had abolitionist friends who admired Brown. This allowed Democrats to paint the entire party as "Black Republicans," hateful abolitionists. To blunt their charges, the Democrats denounced the Harpers Ferry raid as "the gravest of crimes." Lincoln, however, seemed a safe choice. He was no abolitionist, or fan of Brown's. After a series of behind-the-scenes deals, the convention gave him the nomination. Thus, as historian David S. Reynolds has said, "John Brown was, in effect, a hammer that shattered Lincoln's opponents into fragments."[23]

Meanwhile, the slavery issue split the Democrats. Northern Democrats nominated Lincoln's old rival, Stephen A. Douglas. Southern Democrats, thinking Douglas too moderate, chose John C. Breckinridge, of Kentucky, as their candidate. The Whigs changed their name to the Constitution Party and nominated a Tennessee politician named John Bell. In this way, a divided opposition cleared Lincoln's path to the White House.

A campaign banner for Lincoln and Hamlin advocating "free territory for a free people." (c. 1860)

Yet it was a bumpy path. The campaign of 1860 was perhaps the ugliest in American history. Democrats, South and North, brazenly appealed to racial bigotry. Douglas supporters called Lincoln a black man pretending to be white, and his father a gorilla brought from Africa. A Democrat poster showed the "BLACK REPUBLICAN ARGUMENT": a large pike "addressed by Old John Brown to the People of the South."[24]

The Republican faithful made black

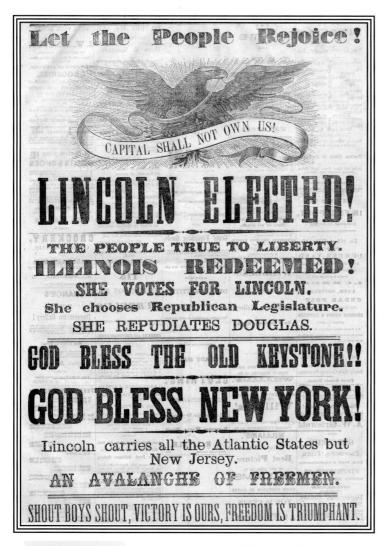

Let the People Rejoice!

CAPITAL SHALL NOT OWN US!

LINCOLN ELECTED!

THE PEOPLE TRUE TO LIBERTY.

ILLINOIS REDEEMED!

SHE VOTES FOR LINCOLN.

She chooses Republican Legislature.

SHE REPUDIATES DOUGLAS.

GOD BLESS THE OLD KEYSTONE!!

GOD BLESS NEW YORK!

Lincoln carries all the Atlantic States but New Jersey.

AN AVALANCHE OF FREEMEN.

SHOUT BOYS SHOUT, VICTORY IS OURS, FREEDOM IS TRIUMPHANT.

The Freeport Wide Awake, a campaign newspaper from Illinois, ran this banner celebrating Abraham Lincoln's presidential victory and the election of a Republican legislature. (1860)

people, not opposition candidates, their target. They staged huge torchlight parades under banners with slogans like "NO NEGRO EQUALITY IN THE NORTH," "AMERICA IS A WHITE MAN'S COUNTRY," and "NO MORE SLAVE STATES."[25]

These slogans reflected Lincoln's long-held views. The candidate had al-ready set the stage during an 1858 debate with Douglas:

> *I will say . . . that I am not, nor ever have been, in favor of bringing about in any way the social and political equality of the white and black races— that I am not nor ever have been in favor of making voters or jurors of negroes, nor of qualifying them to hold office, nor to intermarry with white people; and I will say in addition to this that there is a physical difference between the white and black races which I believe will forever forbid the two races living together on terms of social and political equality. And inasmuch as they cannot so live, while they do remain together there must be the position of superior and inferior, and I as much as any other man am in favor of having the superior position assigned to the white race.*[26]

The Republican candidate won no friends among abolitionists. Many de-tested him as a fraud and a traitor to the Declaration of Independence. Wendell Phillips could barely control his fury, in-sulting Lincoln personally. "Who is this huckster in politics?" he asked, mean-ing this dishonest seller of cheap goods. Phillips went on to brand the candidate "ABRAHAM LINCOLN, THE SLAVE-

HOUND OF ILLINOIS." Lincoln repaid the insults, exclaiming, "I don't see why God lets him live." We suspect Lincoln would rather have had a demon of a toothache than have been on the receiving end of Phillips's invective.[27]

On Election Day, November 6, 1860, Lincoln carried the free states with 1,864,735 votes. The other candidates combined received 2,821,157 votes. This meant that the future sixteenth president received around 39 percent of the vote, hardly a ringing endorsement. He received zero votes in ten Southern states where the Republican Party did not appear on the ballot. Party speakers had stayed away, fearing a coat of boiling tar and feathers if they dared venture into the South.[28]

Secession

The thought of a Lincoln presidency terrified white Southerners. His election "proved" the North was a land of wild-eyed abolitionists bent upon destroying their way of life. The United States seemed an oxymoron. No longer united by shared ideals and values, it had become two feuding regions incapable of settling their differences.

Southerners "were sure" Lincoln would appoint abolitionist justices to the Supreme Court. Once in the majority, they would declare the Fugitive Slave Act

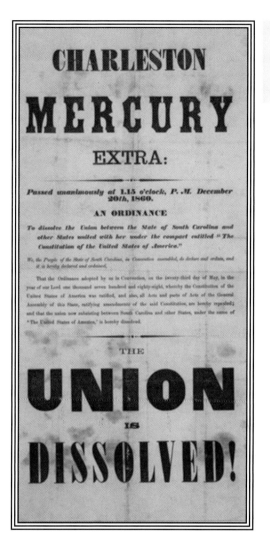

The December 20, 1860, headline in the Charleston Mercury announcing the secession of the South.

and *Dred Scott* decision unconstitutional. With slavery unable to expand, economic disaster must follow. It would take longer than the likes of Wendell Phillips wished, but the result was inevitable. Three billion dollars' worth of human property, the largest single investment at the time, would vanish. Said the *Mercury,* of Charleston, South Carolina, "Slave property is the

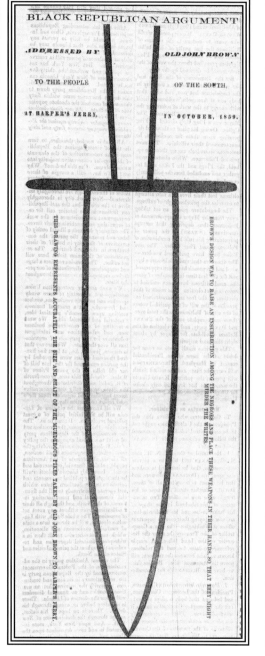

This image in the campaign newspaper the Pennsylvania Statesman allegedly reproduces the size and shape of the knife used by John Brown, and is meant to associate the violent abolitionism of John Brown with the Republican Party. (c. 1860)

will sell out. . . . Confusion, distrust and pressure must remain."[29]

Economic collapse, dreadful as it would be, seemed trivial when measured against the destruction of Southern society. Whites dreaded losing control of black people, whether enslaved or free. Racist fears, inflamed by the fire-eaters, ran wild, creating horrible images in whites' minds. Like Thomas Jefferson, most feared that freeing blacks would lead to a war of races.

In this war, Southerners imagined the spirit of John Brown lurking in black people's hearts. Hatred of the old man automatically turned into hatred of Abraham Lincoln. Never mind that he despised abolitionists; fire-eaters described him as an abolitionist as bloodthirsty "as John Brown himself." Expressions like "they will John Brown us" and "they will Brown us all" became common. Another phrase, "I'll be John Brown," meant "I'll be damned." Jefferson Davis raised the panic level further, promising that Lincoln's Black Republicans would abandon the South to a horrible fate. "Then John Brown, and a thousand John Browns, can invade us, and the Government will not protect us." Finally, other fire-eaters warned of the worst imaginable outrage: "Abolition preachers will be at hand to [marry] your daughters to black husbands."[30]

"Secession fever" swept the South. It

foundation of all property in the South. When security in this is shaken, all other property [is affected]. Banks, stocks, bonds, must be influenced. Timid men gripped Charleston, where delegates from across South Carolina met to discuss the situation. Citing Northern support for John Brown, on December 20, 1860, they voted to secede from the Union. Later that day, the *Charleston Mercury*'s special edition announced, "THE UNION IS DISSOLVED!" Between then and February 1, 1861, another six states—Georgia, Florida, Alabama, Mississippi, Louisiana, and Texas—seceded. On February 4, their delegates met in Montgomery, Alabama, to form the Confederate States of America; they chose Jefferson Davis as president. The other slave states—Virginia, Kentucky, Missouri, Tennessee, North Carolina, Arkansas, Maryland, and Delaware—remained in the Union, at least for now.

The president-elect tried to keep the fever from spreading. In the weeks before his inauguration, Lincoln said nothing publicly about the Confederacy. One thing, he knew, would restore the Union: a promise to let slavery expand into the territories. This he could not give. Privately,

The first inauguration of President Abraham Lincoln (standing under the wood canopy, his white shirt visible) at the U.S. Capitol, Washington, D.C., on March 4, 1861.

he told Republicans in Congress, "I am inflexible. I am for no compromise which assists or permits the extension of the institution on soil owned by the nation." It was a matter of democracy for him. Having won the election on a pledge not to extend slavery, he felt that compromising would brand him a liar. Who, then, would believe *any* politician's promises? Besides, his action would embolden slaveholders to ask for more concessions without end.[31]

Washington, D.C., March 4, 1861. Inauguration Day. High noon. A crowd of thirty thousand stood before a platform built on the east front of the yet-unfinished Capitol. Tension ran high, for threats had been made against Lincoln's life, and the army was not taking chances. Files of soldiers lined the streets leading to the Capitol, and snipers on rooftops stood ready to fire at the slightest wrong move. Just across the Potomac River, in Alexandria, Virginia, a slave auction was in progress. Free blacks who had failed to pay local taxes were being sold into temporary bondage to work off their debts.[32]

In his inaugural address, Lincoln spoke directly to the slave states. He declared: "I have no purpose, directly or indirectly, to interfere with the institution of slavery where it exists. I believe I have no lawful right to do so, and I have no inclination to do so." This was basic; slavery was permitted where it already existed,

but Lincoln would never allow slavery to expand. Yet things seemed so bleak that he thought he must address the South in words that came straight from his heart:

I am loath to close. We are not enemies, but friends. We must not be enemies. Though passion may have strained, it must not break our bonds of affection. The mystic chords of memory, stretching from every battle-field, and patriot grave, to every living heart and hearthstone, all over this broad land, will yet swell the chorus of the Union, when again touched, as surely they will be, by the better angels of our nature.[33]

When he finished, Chief Justice Roger Taney administered the oath of office. In doing so, Taney was, in a sense, closing a circle: the author of the *Dred Scott* decision had sworn in Abraham Lincoln, who would eventually strike the deathblow to American slavery.

If Lincoln thought his speech would calm Southerners' fears, he was wrong. Most did not believe anything he said. They saw all those "mystic chords of memory" and "better angels" as sweet words for a bitter reality. Those favoring secession read the phrase "slavery where it exists" as a death sentence for their peculiar institution. The *Richmond Enquirer* exploded with indignation. Virginia and her sister slave states must join the Confederacy! There was no other way to avoid the disaster "Black Republicans" planned for them. The day after Lincoln took office, it declared, "Civil war must now come. . . . To war! To arms!"[34]

Throughout the South, panicking whites closed ranks behind the fire-eaters. Slaveholders and those without slaves, rich and poor, even those who had once called for hanging enemies of the Union, joined forces. Now they greeted secession and a Southern confederacy as their only hope of safety, of avoiding being "John Browned" to death.

On March 6, as the First Family prepared to move into the White House, the Confederacy prepared for war. In Montgomery, its congress called for an army of one hundred thousand volunteers; the draft would come later. States began seizing federal property: forts, arsenals, and dockyards.

Leaders on both sides clung to their illusions, believing what they wished to believe. Southerners told themselves they were a soldierly race, trained from childhood to ride horses and shoot guns. Northerners were a race of cowards—sniveling shopkeepers, soft-handed bankers, and oppressed factory workers. One Southerner was worth ten Yankees! Northerners, however, had their own beliefs. The peculiar institution supposedly made Southerners pampered dandies unable to exert themselves. Time would teach each side that its view of the other was nonsensical.

Many abolitionists welcomed the gathering storm. Like John Brown, they hated slavery more than they loved the Union. True to their motto, "No union with slaveholders," they cheered disunion as joyfully as fire-eaters cheered secession. "Will the South be so obliging as to secede from the Union?" William Lloyd Garrison asked. In short, slave states, please destroy the nation and go your own way! Efforts to patch up the quarrel were "simply idiotic," the editor of the *Liberator* declared.[35]

Wendell Phillips spoke loudest, as usual. The veteran abolitionist thanked God for the crisis. "All hail Disunion!" he cried after South Carolina seceded. "I would not give slavery a spoonful of earth to stay in the Union—not one; not a blade of grass," he declared. Let the South march out of the Union with drums beating and trumpets blaring! Give it forts and arsenals! Give it jewels of gold and silver! Give it anything, but just let it go—quickly! For good measure, Phillips taunted the South by hailing John Brown: "Sleep in peace, Martyr of Harpers Ferry! Your life was not given in vain."[36]

Secession soothed abolitionists' consciences, Phillips added, relieving them of shame for the South's evil ways, and for the North's sin of allowing them to continue for so long. Yet he also admitted that secession meant enslaved people would have to fend for themselves, for "we can no longer extend to the black race at the South our best sympathy and our best aid." Worse, he expected the Confederacy to reopen the Atlantic slave trade and seize Central American lands for cotton plantations. Thus, secession meant more slaves, and a slave empire south of the border. So be it, Phillips said, if secession brought the end of American slavery. Just how this would happen, he did not explain clearly. We may note that cutting off Southern exports during the Civil War actually increased slavery elsewhere in the world. Encouraging cotton farming in

Egypt put thousands more black Africans under Arab masters.[37]

Civil War

Events in South Carolina ignited the Civil War. When the state seceded, it seized all federal property except Fort Sumter, a large stone structure on an island in Charleston Harbor. Though it was now in Confederate territory, Lincoln said the fort still belonged to the American people. He could not abandon it, as Jefferson Davis demanded and Wendell Phillips urged. Nor did Lincoln wish to start a war over it. If war came, let the other side shoot first! That would show who the

The interior of Fort Sumter, where the first shots of the Civil War were fired on April 12, 1861.

aggressors were, branding themselves as rebels. Lincoln would then have Northern public opinion on his side.[38]

The Confederates obliged. On April 12, 1861, their gun batteries stood ready to bombard Fort Sumter. The honor of firing one of the first shots (as he claimed, the very first shot) went to Edmund Ruffin. That fire-eater stood behind a cannon, grasping a John Brown pike with his left hand. At 4:30 a.m. sharp, with his right hand Ruffin jerked the rope that released the weapon's firing mechanism. After thirty-four hours of nonstop shelling, the fort lay in ruins. Miraculously, only one man died, a Union private accidentally killed after Major Robert Anderson, the fort's commander, raised the surrender flag. On April 14, the Confederates allowed the Yankees to leave with flags flying, a courtesy to enemies who have fought well. So ended the all but bloodless start of the bloodiest war in American history.

The next day, Lincoln ordered the navy to blockade Confederate ports and called for seventy-five thousand army volunteers. This move drew another four states into the Confederacy, for a total of eleven states. Within days, Virginia, North Carolina, Arkansas, and Tennessee seceded. The remaining slave states—Kentucky, Missouri, Maryland, and Delaware—stayed loyal to the Union

throughout the war. Known as the border states, these lay in an east-west line along the Confederacy's northern border. Part of Virginia, including the area around Harpers Ferry, seceded from the state, rejoining the Union as a separate state, West Virginia. During the Civil War, Harpers Ferry changed hands a dozen times. By war's end, it lay in ruins, a mass of rubble reeking with the smell of death.

Fort Sumter ignited an explosion of Northern patriotism. Volunteers flocked to recruiting offices, often escorted by family members. In Boston, for example, a Harvard professor wrote, "The whole population, men, women, and children, seem to be in the streets with Union favors and flags." In New York, a Massachusetts volunteer, asked how many from his state were coming, exclaimed: "How *many*? We're *all* a-coming!" This was no exaggeration. In towns across the North, every male of military age, eighteen to forty, enlisted. The army also accepted twelve-year-olds as drummers, fifers, and flag bearers.[39]

Those who knew and loved John Brown did their part for the Union war effort. The surviving members of the Secret Six helped in various ways. Gerrit Smith, George Luther Stearns, and Franklin Sanborn raised money for good causes, especially to help soldiers' families. Samuel Gridley Howe acted as an adviser to the could not get an officer's commission. He refused to enlist as a common soldier, remaining a private citizen. Owen and Jason had no interest in serving, and were too old for the draft. In 1863, their sister Annie went south as a teacher of freed slaves. During her travels in Virginia, she heard about a black baby born on the plantation of Governor Henry Wise. The infant's name was John Brown Wise. Mary Ann Brown praised President Lincoln for carrying her husband's work forward. When the Emancipation Proclamation went into effect, the widow said, "God bless Abraham Lincoln. And give God the glory for the day of Jubilee has come."[40]

Many Northerners took John Brown as the ideal example of a fighter, not a martyr. New Yorker George Templeton Strong, a wealthy attorney and leader of high society, missed the old man. "Osawatomie John Brown," Strong wrote in his diary, "would be worth his weight in gold just now. What a pity he got himself prematurely hanged!" But his spirit lived.[41]

A song captured Northerners' hearts. On April 17, 1861, three days after Fort Sumter's surrender, the Twelfth Massachusetts Regiment massed at Fort Warren, near Boston. As the volunteers drilled, they sang a fast-paced hymn called "Say, Brothers, Will You Meet Us?" A member of the unit, a jolly Scotsman named John Brown (no relation), often reported for drill late. Comrades began to tease him.

Union army's medical department and did charity work in Boston. Thomas Wentworth Higginson took part in the fighting. In 1861, he raised a company of Massachusetts troops, leading it as captain. The next year he became colonel of the First South Carolina Volunteers, the Union army's first black outfit. Higginson served until 1864, and recorded his adventures in a book based on a diary he wrote while campaigning in the South, *Army Life in a Black Regiment* (1870). The book is a classic of Civil War literature.

Old Brown's family welcomed the outbreak of the war. John Brown Jr. received a captain's commission in a Kansas regiment. His brother Salmon, though,

"This can't be John Brown; why, John Brown is dead," they sang to the hymn's tune. "Yes, poor old John Brown is dead." Soldiers gradually changed the hymn's lyrics but kept the tune, creating an entirely new song—"John Brown's Body":

> John Brown's body lies a-mold'ring in
>   the grave,
> John Brown's body lies a-mold'ring in
>   the grave,
> John Brown's body lies a-mold'ring in
>   the grave,
> His soul goes marching on.
> Glory, glory, hallelujah!
> Glory, glory, hallelujah!
> Glory, glory, hallelujah!
> His soul is marching on!
> He captured Harpers Ferry with his
>   nineteen men so true,
> He frightened old Virginia till she
>   trembled through and through,
> They hung him for a traitor, themselves
>   the traitor crew,
> His soul is marching on.
> Glory, glory, hallelujah!
> Glory, glory, hallelujah!
> Glory, glory, hallelujah!
> His soul is marching on!

"All over the country," the *Illinois Weekly Mirror* (August 6, 1862) reported, "the John Brown song may be heard at all times of the night or day in the streets of Chicago and all other cities; it is the pet song among the soldiers in all our armies."

The song also inspired countless variations, famously "The Battle Hymn of the Republic" by poet Julia Ward Howe, wife of Secret Six member Samuel Gridley Howe. Throughout the North, schoolchildren were taught the song. Nearly a century after the war, in New York City, my fourth-grade teacher taught our class to sing it.[42]

Why They Fought

Wendell Phillips used to say, "All civil wars are a struggle of opposite ideas, and armies are but tools." He was right. The Civil War was a clash of ideas about the meaning of America.[43]

Lincoln surely saw it as such. On Independence Day 1861, he set out the Union's case in a special message to Congress. The president defined the war as "essentially a People's contest," concerning not only Americans, but "the whole family of man." Lincoln believed in what we call today "American exceptionalism." This belief holds that the United States has a God-given mission to further self-government under the rule of law. Yet history was not encouraging. Republics like the ancient Greek city-states and Rome had ended in violence, leading to the rule of emperors and kings, nobles and dictators. Later, in the 1840s, attempts to form republics in Europe ended with military rule and further oppression. Lincoln asked: "Is there, in all republics, this inherent, and fatal weakness? Must a government . . . be too *strong* for the liberties of its own people, or too *weak* to maintain its existence?" We still debate these matters.[44]

Lincoln was deeply committed to republicanism. This had nothing to do with the Republican Party, a political organization, but with the principles of the Constitution. This document opens with these stirring words: "We the People of the United States, in Order to form a more perfect Union . . . and secure the Blessings of Liberty to ourselves and our Posterity, do ordain and establish this Constitution for the United States of America." To achieve these aims, the Founders set up a republic governed by the people's elected representatives. Thus, the Union was based on free elections and majority rule.

But for majority rule to succeed, the minority, the losers of a free election, must accept the rule of the winners until (if ever) the nation changes its mind in a future election. The issue after Fort Sumter was whether Americans could allow violence to settle their disputes. They could not, Lincoln insisted. As he said in 1863, "Among free men, there can be no successful appeal from the ballot to the bullet."[45]

The president's words reflected opinion in the free states. Most people were as committed as he to America's founding principles, as imperfectly realized as they were. We see this in the letters and diaries of Union soldiers. These were written not for future publication, but to explain to relatives and friends their reasons for enlisting. The writers were not career warriors, but citizen soldiers. Ordinary men, many barely able to read and write, they did not cheer secession, as abolitionists did; they branded abolitionists foolish, fanatical, and unpatriotic. Nor did they care about slavery—at least not right away.

For "Billy Yank," the average Union "G.I. Joe," the Civil War was the War for the Union. This was because the Union stood for liberty under law: majority rule, free speech, freedom of the press, freedom of religion, economic opportunity. Secession meant, for Billy Yank, the end of republican government and majority rule. More, it meant the end of America, which Lincoln called "the last, best hope of earth."[46]

Europe's emperors and kings, nobles and dictators, welcomed the war. By smashing the Union, it would crush humanity's last, best hope, proving ordinary people unfit to govern themselves. A minister of Tsar Alexander II, Emperor of All the Russias, put the case simply. He declared, "The republican form of government, so much talked about by the Europeans and praised by the Americans, is breaking down. What can be expected from a country where men of humble origin are elevated to the highest positions?" By "men of humble origin," he meant the likes of Abraham Lincoln.[47]

In their imagination, Union soldiers marched beside the ghosts of George Washington's ragged troops. In 1861, the Revolution was not merely an event read about in textbooks. It was real, vivid, timely—as recent as if it had just occurred. "Remember," an Ohio soldier wrote his wife, "that thousands went forth and poured out their life's blood in the Revolution to establish this government; and twould be a disgrace to the whole American people if she had not noble sons enough who had the spirit of seventy six in their hearts." A Missouri volunteer wrote his parents, "We fight for the blessings bought by the blood and treasure of our Fathers. I will fight till I die if necessary for the liberties which you have so long enjoyed." Unlike in 1776, the enemy was not a foreign army. Now Americans fought "this monstrous rebellion," "this wicked rebellion," "this infernal rebellion" called secession.[48]

Above all, the War for the Union was a war for future generations. "Without Union & peace," a Billy Yank wrote, "our freedom is worthless, [as] our children would have no warrant for liberty. . . . [For] of what value will be house, family, and friends?" We fight for our sacred inheritance of liberty, another wrote, and "for the sake of the country's millions who are to come after us." Finally, as if echoing the commander in chief, a corporal told his wife: "If I do get hurt I want you to remember that it will be not only for my country and my Children but for Liberty all over the World that I risked my life, for if Liberty should be crushed here, what hope would there be for the cause of Human Progress anywhere else?" Four months later, he fell in battle.[49]

"Johnny Reb," the Confederate common soldier, saw things differently. His was a war for security, liberty, *and* slavery. Few expected to conquer the Union. The Confederacy had neither the resources nor the people to do that. Already an economic giant, the Union had 85 percent of the nation's factories and 98 percent of its shipping. It produced thirteen times more iron and had thirty-two times as many weapons as the Confederacy. As if that were not enough, in 1860 the North had a population of 22,339,989, compared to the Confederacy's 8,971,329, of whom 3,521,109 were slaves and 132,760 free blacks. In one state, blacks far outnumbered whites: South Carolina had 292,388 whites, compared to 412,320 blacks, enslaved and free.[50]

A cover for the sheet music for "The Bonnie Blue Flag." (c. 1861)

as he understood it. A favorite marching song, "The Bonnie Blue Flag" (a banner with a white star on a blue field), put it this way:

> *We are a band of brothers, and native*
> *to the soil,*
> *Fighting for our liberty, with treasure,*
> *blood and toil,*
> *And when our rights were threatened,*
> *the cry rose near and far:*
> *Hurrah for the Bonnie Blue Flag that*
> *bears a single star!*
> *Hurrah! Hurrah!*
> *For Southern rights, hurrah!*
> *Hurrah for the Bonnie Blue Flag that*
> *bears a single star.*
> *As long as the Union was faithful to*
> *her trust,*
> *Like friends and like brethren, kind*
> *were we and just,*
> *But now, when Northern treachery*
> *attempts our rights to mar,*
> *We hoist the Bonnie Blue Flag that*
> *bears a single star.*
> *Hurrah! Hurrah!*
> *For Southern rights, hurrah!*
> *Hurrah for the Bonnie Blue Flag that*
> *bears a single star.*
> *Then here's to our Confederacy, strong*
> *we are and brave,*
> *Like patriots of old we'll fight, our*
> *heritage to save;*

To restore the Union, Lincoln's troops, nicknamed "Lincolnpoops" by Johnny Rebs, had to crush the Confederacy. They had to invade its territory and defeat its armies, in the process wrecking the country. It is no surprise, then, that Southerners, whatever their social class, joined the Confederate armies.

Northerners found that invading the South was like knocking down hornet nests. Johnny Rebs were not pushovers. A New York soldier wrote that they fought to defend "their liberties, homes, firesides, wives and children." They "fight like Devils in tophet [hell]," an Illinois sergeant said, "fighting to keep an enemy out of [their] own neighborhood & protect [their] property."[51]

Johnny Reb also fought for liberty

And rather than submit to shame, to die
  we would prefer,
So cheer for the Bonnie Blue Flag that
  bears a single star.

Johnny Reb's idea of liberty was states' rights—the right of each state to follow its interests without interference from the federal government. Unlike Lincoln, he thought the states, not the American people as a whole, had formed the Union. Nor would the South have joined in the first place, had it felt it could never leave. Like George Washington's men, Johnny Reb fought for his rights against an "oppressive" government. These rights included independence and, as the Declaration of Independence said, "life, liberty, and the pursuit of happiness."

Liberty included the natural right to own property. In 1861, property included human beings. Even many who owned no slaves spoke of the "divine right of slaveholding." What is more, the wealthy planters shaped Southern attitudes. By working and saving their profits, poor whites hoped to buy a few slaves, produce more cotton and food crops, and, if lucky, join the planters' ranks. To them, depriving an owner of slaves was stealing. Besides, the South needed its peculiar institution. An officer in a Mississippi regiment wrote his wife, "This country without slave labor would be completely worthless. . . . If the negroes are freed the

Alexander H. Stephens, the vice president of the Confederacy. (c. 1865–1880)

country . . . is not worth fighting for." Another Johnny Reb denounced the North for wanting to deny Southerners the "right to keep our slaves in peace and quietness."[52]

Abraham Lincoln had no patience with such claims. "The *perfect* liberty they sigh for," he snapped, "is the liberty of making slaves of other people." Logically, if Confederates had the right to do that, then others, stronger than they, had the same right to enslave them.[53]

Confederate leaders left no doubt that the conflict was mainly about slavery. Had slavery not been *the* issue, there would have been nothing to fight a civil war about. The breakaway nation was dedicated to slavery. It never tried to hide that fact. The Confederate constitution guaranteed that black people would be enslaved forever, making it illegal for any state to abolish the peculiar institution, even by popular vote. Unlike the U.S. Constitution, the document repeatedly referred to "negro slavery."[54]

Two weeks after Lincoln's inauguration, Confederate vice president Alexander H. Stephens, of Georgia, officially dedicated his country to racism. The Declaration of Independence had only one meaning, Stephens announced: "all Men" were not created equal in *any* way. The idea of natural equality was "an error." The Confederacy aimed to correct the so-called error: "Our new government is founded . . . upon the great truth that the negro is not equal to the white man; that slavery, subordination to the superior race, is his natural and normal condition. This, our new government, is the first in the history of the world based upon this great physical, philosophical, and moral truth." When "those at the North . . . assume that the negro is . . . entitled to equal privileges and rights with the white man," they are "attempting to make things equal which the Creator [has] made unequal." In short, they are interfering with the laws of God and nature.[55]

Thus, two principles stood opposed at the start of the Civil War. The first was republican liberty, the right of the majority to choose its government and live under the rule of law in a united nation. The second was the right of states to leave the Union when they felt threatened by the majority, especially when it came to holding other people in bondage. It was unclear, in 1861, which principles would prevail. Nor could anyone guess if, how, or when slavery would end in America.

VIII

Wiped Out in Blood

I hear Old John Brown knocking on the lid of his coffin & shouting, "Let me out,"
"let me out!" The doom of slavery is at hand. It is to be wiped out in blood. Amen!
—Abolitionist Henry Stanton, April 1861

A War to End Slavery?

Abolitionists hailed the outbreak of the Civil War with the same zest with which they preached disunion and greeted secession. Wendell Phillips, who had never seen a battle, let alone fought in one, wondered if its horrors were worse than slavery. "Where is the battlefield . . . ," he asked, "that is not white—compared with the blackness of that darkness which has brooded over [America] for two hundred years? . . . Add all the horrors of cities sacked and lands laid waste. Weigh it now against some young, trembling girl sent to the auction block . . . and tell me if [a battle] can claim one tear . . . compared with this daily system of hell." Thus, the war must serve a higher moral goal than simply saving the Union. It must be an abolition war, whatever the cost in lives and treasure. "We go for the abolition of slavery first, whether the Union survives it or not," he declared.[1]

Frederick Douglass, however, realized that the war had not begun as an antislavery crusade. To turn it into one, he set out to prove that ending slavery was a practical weapon, and probably the only way of saving the Union. "The very stom-

ach of this rebellion is the Negro in the condition of a slave," he wrote in the July 1861 issue of *Douglass' Monthly*. "Arrest that hoe in the hands of the Negro, and you smite rebellion in the very seat of its life. . . . The Negro is the key to the situation—the pivot upon which the whole rebellion turns."[2]

John Brown's friend was right. Slaves were a source of both strength *and* weakness to the enemy. Though they did not fight, they enabled whites to do so. The enslaved did countless war-related jobs. Besides raising the Confederacy's food crops, they wove its cloth, made its boots, sewed its uniforms, and repaired its railroads. Slaves also helped arm its troops. Black miners dug the coal and iron ore that black gunsmiths made into weap-

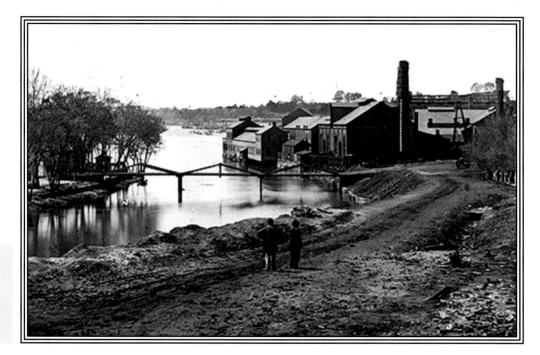

Slaves at Tredegar Iron Works, pictured here, produced many of the weapons for the Confederate army. (date unknown)

ons. Black workers at Virginia's Tredegar Iron Works, the South's largest, produced much of the enemy's artillery and repaired damaged guns.

In the field, Johnny Reb depended on slaves to set up his tents, cook his food, wash his clothes, cut his hair, drive his wagons, tend his horses, dig his trenches, fill his sandbags, and build his fortifications. During battle, slaves helped load cannons and brought water to the troops on the firing line. About half the nurses in Confederate military hospitals were black men and women. Slaves were so important to the war effort that the Confederate congress passed laws allowing them to be drafted into labor battalions.[3]

Slaves were also the chink in the Confederacy's armor. By 1861, many had learned about John Brown, and how he had died for them. They also knew about Abraham Lincoln, and that their masters feared he would "John Brown" them. One historian estimates that at least 10 percent of the people at any Southern political rally were black bystanders. They heard everything, and spread the word. Slaves knew that Lincoln had won the presidential election. On Inauguration Day, on some plantations, they stopped work out of respect for him. On that day, too, some sang an old hymn, and got whipped for it:

We'll fight for liberty
Till de Lord shall call us home;

We'll soon be free
Till de Lord shall call us home.

As a runaway told Thomas Wentworth Higginson, "Dey tink *'de Lord'* mean for say de Yankees."[4]

The Confederate government had counted on having six hundred thousand men under arms by July 1861. However, fear of being "John Browned" gripped the Southland. So, when the war began, governors kept state-owned weapons from the army. Fearing "disturbances among the blacks," they held these in reserve or gave them to local militia units. As a result, generals sent two hundred thousand volunteers home because they had no weapons for them. Had the Confederacy used its full military power at this critical early stage, it might have gained a quick victory, ending the war on its own terms. But a lengthy struggle allowed the Union to mobilize its superior resources.[5]

Shortages gradually eased, thanks to European arms smuggled through the naval blockade and weapons captured from the Yankees. Yet that, too, created problems. The ability to arm more men placed a heavy burden on Southern women. With more men away in the army, women had to run plantations and farms. That meant supervising slaves, who grew more restless as the war dragged on.

Slaves quietly ignored mistresses' orders, or became "uppity"—answered in a tone few had dared use before the war. Women lived in fear of an uprising. "I lay down at night," an Alabamian wrote a friend, "& do not know what hour . . . my house may [be] broken open & myself & my children murdered." Wives' letters to soldier husbands were filled with tales of woe, ending with a plea: "Come home!" Johnny Rebs deserted to help them and to guard against slave uprisings. Desertion and draft evasion were serious problems throughout the war.[6]

Meanwhile, the struggle had a deep emotional effect on thousands of Union soldiers. Few Billy Yanks had ever traveled more than a hundred miles from their birthplace. Mostly farmers' sons, they had little knowledge of the wider world. The war changed all that. During the early campaigns in Virginia, and later in the Deep South, they came face to face with the peculiar institution. It angered them, much as seeing the Nazi death camps angered their great-grandsons in the Second World War.

As Billy Yank advanced, he saw living proof of sexual abuse by slaveholders. Lieutenant George Landrum spoke for his comrades. Landrum never forgot a slave child "as white as I ever was; light curly hair, blue eyes. . . . There are many such here. I have seen them in every town we have come through, slaves as white as any white man can be." Yet their owner-fathers had every right to sell them, if hard up for cash.[7]

Soldiers came to plantations and found thumbscrews, chains, handcuffs, leg shackles, and iron collars. They saw "offenders" missing ears, or disfigured by red flesh-knobs raised by the branding iron. They saw whipping posts, and what a leather whip could do to bare skin. "Some of them," a soldier writing about slaves reported from Louisiana, "were scarred from head to foot where they had been whipped. One man's back was nearly all one scar, as if the skin had been chopped up and left to heal in ridges. Another had scars on the back of his neck, and from that all the way to his heels every little ways. . . . That beat all the antislavery sermons ever preached."[8]

Experience made many Billy Yanks see slaves not as the brutes of racist myth, but as fellow human beings. "Abolitionized" by what he saw, an Ohio officer vowed, "By G-d I'll *fight* till hell *freezes* over and then I'll cut the ice and fight on." A Massachusetts captain held a special grudge against South Carolina, which had started the war. He wrote his mother, "I want to sing 'John Brown' in the streets of Charleston, and ram red-hot abolitionism down their unwilling throats at the point of the bayonet."[9]

We do not know how widespread such attitudes were, but we *do* know that terrible sights did not erase bigotry. However, while many Billy Yanks still resented blacks, they hated slavery with a fury that grew as the war continued. It was not always a matter of sympathy for the suffering or of defending human rights. A civilian in uniform, Billy Yank was a most practical fellow. Unlike for the professional soldier, the army was not his career, but an interruption. Yes, he would do his duty to the Union, but he wanted to return to civilian life as quickly as possible, and in one piece. Like Frederick Douglass, he soon understood that slavery aided the enemy's war effort. While it existed, Johnny Reb could go on fighting. A private in the First Minnesota Regiment put it best: "The war will never end until we end slavery."[10]

Two Union commanders shared this view. John C. Frémont was a politician turned general. In 1856, he had run as the Republican Party's first presidential candidate, losing to Democrat James Buchanan. In July 1861, in Missouri, Frémont freed slaves whose masters aided the Confederacy. Ten months later, in May 1862, General David Hunter declared all slaves freed in Georgia, Florida, and South Carolina, where he held a few small areas along the coast. Abolitionists praised these actions. The commander in chief did not.

President Lincoln was not ready to

Soldier and explorer John C. Frémont lost the presidential election of 1856 to James Buchanan. (c. 1856)

free slaves—yet. "Emancipation," he said, "would be equivalent to a John Brown raid, on a gigantic scale." For that reason, he canceled the generals' orders. Furthermore, he ordered generals to return fugitive slaves to Confederate masters. In Washington, D.C., he enforced the Fugitive Slave Act to the letter. Military police had to arrest runaways and turn them over to the city police, who jailed them. Rebel masters placed ads describing runaways in city newspapers, offering rewards for their return. The police obliged, pocketing the cash. Brazen slave catchers even kidnapped free blacks off Pennsylvania Avenue, the city's main thoroughfare. According to one report, a slave broke away, but he was grabbed again as he hobbled up the steps of the Capitol in leg irons.[11]

Allowing such things to happen was part of the burden of office. As president, Lincoln had to do what he thought best for the entire country. If the situation changed, so must he. "I claim not to have controlled events," he wrote, "but confess plainly that events have controlled me." He feared that if generals continued freeing slaves, the border slave states would join the Confederacy. Losing these raised the odds of losing the war. Having Maryland in rebel hands would make it impossible to hold Washington. Rebel control of Kentucky would open an invasion route to Illinois, Indiana, and Ohio.[12]

Abolitionists cared little about the problems Lincoln faced. As always, for them, ending slavery was an absolute moral goal and came first. If the president did not see things their way, they thought it because he was weak-willed and ignorant. William Lloyd Garrison tore into the "weak, besotted" president. Frederick Douglass openly voiced "disgust" with Lincoln's "spineless" policy. Wendell Phillips lashed out with a fury unusual even for him. Lincoln, he sneered, was a "senile, lick-spittle" coward—"a first-rate *second-rate* man" with "no mind whatever."[13]

Phillips was wrong. Lincoln had a mind. A very keen one. It just worked along different lines from the abolitionists'. Despite his racist beliefs, he had always known that slavery was wrong and ending it was right. Yet, as president, he was not free to do as he pleased. America was a land of laws, not men. The Founders had seen to that. Thus, the president must separate his private beliefs from his legal duty as head of the government.

For Lincoln, as for any leader in a democracy, it was not enough to know what was "right" and do it. By ignoring the existing law to do "right," he feared doing far greater wrong. In a discussion with Secretary of the Treasury Salmon P. Chase, on whether to free the slaves because he felt it was morally right, Lincoln asked, "Would I not thus give up all footing upon constitution and law? Would I not thus be in the boundless field of absolutism?" That is, of tyranny. Slavery was legal. Lincoln felt he could not end it without breaking his oath to "preserve, protect, and defend the Constitution of the United States." Yet abolitionists also had a valid argument. By not acting, Lincoln was prolonging the war and keeping millions of innocents in bondage.[14]

What to do? How to end slavery without breaking the law and becoming a tyrant?

Emancipation

The war itself answered these questions for Lincoln. It was not going well for the Union. Though outmanned and outgunned, the Confederacy had begun with an advantage in military talent. Colonel Robert E. Lee disapproved of secession, calling it "nothing but revolution." When Virginia joined the Confederacy, Lincoln chose him to lead the Union armies and gave him the rank of general. Yet Lee decided to go with Virginia, "my mother State." In time, he became leader of the Army of Northern Virginia, the South's main fighting force, taking his place beside history's foremost generals.[15]

General Lee built a first-rate fighting team. Professor Thomas J. Jackson became his top combat commander. Nicknamed "Stonewall," Jackson stood like a stone wall, refusing to give ground. Deeply religious, like John Brown, Stonewall

General Robert E. Lee, originally asked by Lincoln to lead Union soldiers, chose to fight for his homeland, the South, instead. (c. 1864)

General Thomas J. "Stonewall" Jackson was Robert E. Lee's top combat commander. (c. 1860–1870)

Lieutenant J. E. B. "Jeb" Stuart aided Robert E. Lee in the confrontation of John Brown's raiders at Harpers Ferry, and later served as Lee's cavalry commander. (c. 1860–1864)

Jackson called his troops the "army of the living God." He rode into battle with his eyes raised to heaven, his lips moving as he "spoke" with the Almighty. He was a brilliant officer, as was Jeb Stuart, who became Lee's cavalry commander. Of the three Confederate greats, only Lee survived the war.[16]

Repeatedly, Union armies drove toward Richmond, the Confederate capital, only to flee in defeat and disgrace. Of the nine major battles fought between July 1861 and June 1862, the Confederates won eight: First Bull Run, the Seven Days' Battles (six battles fought in a week), and Second Bull Run. The battle

of Seven Pines ended in a draw. Each battle left thousands of dead and wounded on both sides. Despite their material advantages, Northerners began to doubt their cause. Many wondered whether saving the Union justified this butchery, or if it might be best to let the South go its own way.

On July 13, less than two weeks after the Seven Days' Battles, Lincoln took a carriage ride with Secretary of the Navy Gideon Welles and Secretary of State William Henry Seward. Appropriately, they were going to a funeral. The president had reached a crossroads. He had tried everything to restore the Union, from promising to protect slavery where it existed to fighting. Nothing worked. He had decided, Welles noted in his diary, "that it was a military necessity absolutely essential for the salvation of the Union, that we must free the slaves or be ourselves subdued." The only thing left was to free the rebels' slaves in a way that did not violate the Constitution.[17]

The Constitution is not a suicide pact, providing for the country's own death. National survival ranked higher than any right to own fellow humans. As commander in chief, Lincoln had the authority to invade rebel states, kill their soldiers, and seize any property useful to their war effort. Slaves were property. Johnny Reb used them in countless ways. Under the war powers given to the president by the

Constitution, he could abolish slavery in the rebel states as a *military necessity*. It might drive the border states out of the Union, but now he must take that risk.

On July 22, 1862, Lincoln read a draft of the preliminary Emancipation Proclamation to his cabinet. So that it would not seem like a desperate gamble by a defeated government, Secretary Seward urged him to delay issuing it until the military situation improved. That would also look better to foreign countries, particularly England and France, whose economies were still suffering from the cutoff of Southern cotton. Their governments leaned toward recognizing the Confederacy as a nation, which would open the way to massive military aid. The president welcomed the delay, hoping to use it to prepare public opinion for his emancipation bombshell.

Lincoln moved carefully. He had no choice. In a democracy, a leader cannot go faster or further than voters will allow. However, he or she may sometimes think it necessary to go in a direction contrary to voters' wishes. To do so, the leader must first change minds, a difficult and delicate task that can backfire and result in loss of support.

An effective leader, sensitive to people's concerns, calms their fears to win their support. Yet to lead is to choose. No leader can convince everyone. Sometimes it may be necessary to offend some to gain

or hold others' support. We do not know if this is what Lincoln thought, because he never said so. Yet his actions suggest that he felt he must offend the free black minority to reassure the white majority about his next move. Most whites supported the war to defend republicanism, not to free slaves. Given the extent of Northern bigotry, the president had to stress saving the Union, while using emancipation as a means to that end.

On August 14, Lincoln invited five black ministers to the White House. The meeting was not a free exchange of ideas; he did not ask for his guests' opinions. Instead, he lectured them as if reciting a script he had memorized. Nor was the meeting secret: a stenographer sat in a corner, taking down every word. Lincoln made sure his remarks appeared in the press the next day. Obviously, he had staged the event to make a point.[18]

The president began by noting, "You and I are of different races." Both races suffered by living beside one another. Right or wrong, that was the reality. "See our present condition—" he said, "the country engaged in war!—our white men cutting one another's throats. . . . But for your race among us there could not be war. . . . I repeat, without the institution of Slavery and the colored race as a basis, the war could not have an existence. It is better for us both, therefore, to be separated." He urged the ministers to persuade free blacks to settle in places like Central America, or return to Africa. Though outwardly polite, inwardly the ministers seethed with anger. Meanwhile, Lincoln's handwritten draft of the Emancipation Proclamation lay in his desk drawer.[19]

The meeting made headlines in newspapers across the nation. For example, the *New York Tribune,* on August 15, said:

> *SPEECH OF THE PRESIDENT*
> *He Holds that the White and Black*
> *Races Cannot Dwell Together*
> *He Urges Intelligent Colored Men to*
> *Exert Themselves for Colonization*
> *He Suggests Central America as the*
> *Colony*

After reading about the meeting, Frederick Douglass railed against Lincoln's "pride of race and blood, his contempt for Negroes and his canting hypocrisy." Blaming blacks for the Civil War was "illogical and unfair," like blaming a stolen horse for the horse thief's crime. Nobody asked to come to America in chains. But now it was black people's country as much as any others', more so perhaps since they had been in America long before the ancestors of most whites reached its shores. The black leader boiled down the president's meaning to a sentence: "He says to colored people: I don't like you, you must clear out of the country."[20]

Lincoln *had* shown his pride of race,

and his wish to rid America of blacks if it would save the Union. Yet the White House meeting also enabled him to reach beyond a black audience. The president's offensive tone sent a message to millions of whites. Do not worry about *me*! I hate slavery, as you know I do! However, my personal belief has nothing to do with the way I fight this war. Know that I will always act in the Union's best interests, not those of black people. Like you, I would gladly get rid of them!

Lincoln reinforced this message in a reply to Horace Greeley, founder and editor of the *New York Tribune*. Greeley had written an open letter, "The Prayer of Twenty Millions," criticizing Lincoln's foot-dragging on emancipation. Three days later, on August 22, 1862, the president sent his own open letter, printed in the *Tribune* and most other Union newspapers. Using Greeley's letter to further prepare the nation, he wrote:

> *I would save the Union. I would*
> *save it the shortest way under the*
> *Constitution. . . . My paramount object*
> *in this struggle* is *to save the Union,*
> *and is* not *either to save or to destroy*
> *slavery. If I could save the Union*
> *without freeing* any *slave I would do*
> *it, and if I could save it by freeing* all
> *the slaves I would do it; and if I could*
> *save it by freeing some and leaving*
> *others alone I would also do that. What*

I do about slavery, and the colored race, I do because I believe it helps to save the Union; and what I forbear, I forbear because I do not *believe it would help to save the Union. . . . I have here stated my purpose according to my view of* official *duty; and I intend no modification of my oft-expressed* personal *wish that all men every where could be free.*[21]

Thus, Lincoln drew a clear line between his personal beliefs and his duty as president under the law. All should understand that he would do anything, even free the slaves, to save the Union.

A few days after the Greeley letter, Robert E. Lee invaded Maryland, hoping to swing the people of that border slave state to the rebel side. On September 17, his Army of Northern Virginia met Union forces at Antietam Creek, just north of Harpers Ferry. It was the bloodiest single day in American history: combined losses totaled 4,710 dead, 18,400 wounded, and 3,041 missing. *Missing* usually meant a soldier had been blown into pieces too small to identify. Union forces fought Lee to a standstill, forcing him to retreat into Virginia. "God had decided the question in favor of the slaves," Lincoln said when he received the news.[22]

On September 23, he issued the preliminary Emancipation Proclamation. It declared that unless the rebel states re-

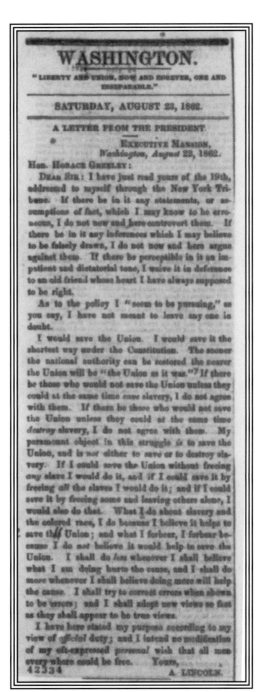

Abraham Lincoln's printed response to newspaper editor Horace Greeley's criticism. (August 23, 1862)

turned to the Union by January 1, 1863, their slaves "shall then, thenceforward, and forever, be free." The Confederacy's

The Battle at Antietam, the bloodiest battle of the Civil War. (c. 1865)

fate lay in its own hands. If it took Lincoln's offer, it could keep its peculiar institution, though not carry it into the territories. But, if Southerners had not trusted Lincoln's pledge in his inaugural address, they trusted him even less after so much bitter fighting.[23]

Southern cartoonists had a field day criticizing the preliminary Emancipation Proclamation. A well-known cartoon shows the president at his desk, writing the document. His left foot rests on the Bible, symbolizing his "crimes," while a winged devil holds the inkwell for him. A portrait of "Saint Osawatomie" grasping a John Brown pike hangs on the wall above him, a reminder of the old man's crimes in Kansas. Beside it, another painting,

titled *St. Domingo,* depicts slaves torturing whites.

Antislavery people wondered if Lincoln would sign the final proclamation. He was so cautious, they feared any military setback would change his mind. They need not have worried. As New Year's Eve drew near, he revealed his true intentions to Senator Charles Sumner, a trusted foreign policy adviser. Lincoln assured him that he "could not stop the proclamation if he would, and would not if he could." He also told Massachusetts congressman George Boutwell that a promise, once made, was a matter of honor with him: "My word is out to these people, and I can't take it back."[24]

New Year's Eve came. Still, only his

Abraham Lincoln with
General George B.
McClellan and a group
of officers at Antietam,
just two weeks after
the grisly battle there.
(c. October 2, 1862)

closest advisers knew what Lincoln would do. Throughout the North, antislavery people held nightlong services asking God to guide the president in doing the right thing. New Year's Day dawned, and still no word came from the White House. The tension mounted.

In the afternoon, Lincoln slipped away from a reception and went to his office. There he found the cabinet waiting to witness the signing. Dipping his pen into the inkwell, the president bent over the Emancipation Proclamation and, with shaking hand, wrote *Abraham Lincoln* at the bottom of the page. After a moment, he declared, "I never in my life felt more certain that I was doing the right thing than I do in signing this paper." Signing

emancipated Lincoln, too. It put him at peace with himself, for he had done the right thing in the right way. The president had been true to his belief that slavery was wrong *and* to his faith in the rule of law.

A caricature by
Adalbert John Volck
of Abraham Lincoln
writing the Emancipation
Proclamation, with one
foot trampling a Bible
and a framed painting
of John Brown holding
a pike behind him.
(c. 1864)

Ent'd according to Act of Congress, A. D. 1863, by W. T. Carlton, in the Clerk's Office of the District Court of the District of Mass.

No longer must he live with the inner conflict of defending republican liberty without fighting slavery.[25]

Telegraph messages spread the news. In Washington, free blacks surrounded the White House, calling for the president to come out so they could "hug him to death." Thousands kneeled on Pennsylvania Avenue, singing:

Oh, go down, Moses,
Way down in Egypt's land;
Tell King Pharaoh
To let my people go.

Church bells rang. People shouted, "Glory! Hallelujah! We are free! We are free!"[26]

Four hundred miles to the north, in Boston, a huge crowd waited in Tremont Temple. When the news came, a black minister led the people in song:

Sound the loud timbrel
O'er Egypt's dark sea,
Jehovah hath triumphed,
His people are free.[27]

That night, William Lloyd Garrison hosted a celebration at the mansion of Secret Six member George Luther Stearns. Though Lincoln had signed the Emancipation Proclamation, Garrison gave the credit to John Brown, who had set the nation's feet on the freedom road. After many speeches, Wendell Phillips unveiled a marble bust of the Harpers Ferry raider. A few days before his execution, Mrs. Stearns had sent a sculptor to visit the old man in jail to sketch his image. Guests

said the figure looked like Moses, who had led the children of Israel out of Egyptian bondage. In New York, an overflow crowd at Shiloh Church, a black church, burst into "John Brown's Body" and a hymn, "Blow Ye the Trumpet, Blow," whose refrain began, "The year of jubilee is come." This was Old Brown's favorite hymn, used to lull his young children to sleep.[28]

Celebrants knew the Emancipation Proclamation was imperfect. Again, Lincoln could only go as far as he thought public opinion would allow. Thus, "forever free" applied only to slaves in areas within the control of Union forces. This left in bondage millions of blacks in the border states and the areas of the South unoccupied by the Union. Slavery was still legal there, since only an amendment to the Constitution could abolish it nationwide.

Nevertheless, Union loyalists realized Lincoln's action was a down payment on the future. It turned the Civil War into more than the War for the Union. As a former slave explained, *"We'se free now, bress de Lord! Dey can't sell my wife and child any more, bress de Lord! No more dat! No more dat! No more dat, now! Preserdun*

A painting of a reenactment of the signing of the Emancipation Proclamation showing, from left to right, Edwin M. Stanton, secretary of war; Salmon P. Chase, secretary of the treasury; President Lincoln; Gideon Welles, secretary of the navy; Caleb B. Smith, secretary of the interior; William H. Seward, secretary of state; Montgomery Blair, postmaster general; and Edward Bates, attorney general. Simon Cameron and Andrew Jackson are featured as paintings. (c. 1864)

A Harper's Weekly illustration of newly freed slaves leaving plantations en masse after the signing of the Emancipation Proclamation. (c. 1863)

Lincum have shot [shut] de gate!" He had shut the door on compromise. Now there could be no turning back. It was to be an abolition war after all.[29]

Blacks in Blue

Though many Billy Yanks protested that they had not enlisted to fight an abolition war, many more greeted the Emancipation Proclamation with "shouts & Hurrahs." They knew it had dealt the enemy a stunning blow. From now on, there would be no returning of fugitives to their masters. Better yet, wherever Union armies went in the Confederacy, they would destroy slavery as a practical war measure *and* in the name of freedom.[30]

Masters were unable to keep news of the proclamation from their slaves. As ever, they got the news within days or weeks of its appearance. Word spread through the slave quarters like fire in dry grass. The result, a Billy Yank wrote, "played hell" with the rebel war effort. The problems that had appeared at the start of the war grew worse, costing the Confederacy thousands of workers. No longer did enslaved people flee by ones and twos, as in the days of the Underground Railroad. Now they left in batches, often crowded into wagons "liberated" from their masters. "They go in droves every night," a Missouri slaveholder whined. In Tennessee, "whole families are stampeding and leaving their masters."[31]

Recent research, however, reveals another, grimmer side to the story. This shows that for all too many liberated slaves, the thrill of freedom quickly faded, the unexpected and unintended consequences of the Emancipation Proclamation.

The main objective of Lincoln, Congress, and the U.S. military was to save the Union. Like most Americans at the time, national leaders did not consider the federal government responsible for the health and well-being of civilians. These were duties of families, churches, charities, and local authorities. As a result, they gave little thought to, much less made detailed plans for, feeding, clothing, and sheltering people fleeing bondage. And when a public health crisis arose, their efforts were too little and too late.

The Civil War era was still in the Dark Ages as far as hygiene and medicine were concerned. Although there had been advances in science, most physicians saw little connection between dirt and disease. As a result, army camps, usually filthy and overcrowded, became breeding grounds for "fevers." This explains a shocking fact: Despite the horrendous battles, more soldiers died of diseases such as typhoid fever, pneumonia, dysentery, and smallpox than from bullets.

Encouraged to flee by the Emancipation Proclamation, hordes of former slaves followed the Union armies or wound up in encampments called "contraband camps." "They arrived worn out," noted Maria Mann, a teacher, "with swellings, open sores, and eaten up with vermin." Poorly fed, ragged, exposed to the elements, they succumbed en masse to malnutrition and disease.[32]

We have many examples of their plight. In one case, a Virginia slave who fled to Washington lay dying on a straw mattress. Moments before the end, he murmured, "Is this freedom?" In a typical account, a Union officer reported from Tennessee that former slaves were "dying by scores—that sometimes 30 per day die & are carried out by wagon loads without coffins, and thrown promiscuously, like brutes, into a trench." Around one million former slaves—that is, one in four—became "sick from freedom." Through no fault of their own, they suffered serious illness or died during and immediately after the Civil War.[33]

Others died on the battlefield. Whatever biases Billy Yanks had toward black people, they also knew bullets are colorblind. A black man wearing a blue uniform could stop a rebel bullet as easily as a white man. So make him a soldier! The Emancipation Proclamation called for just that. In it, Lincoln promised to recruit former slaves into the armed forces of the United States. By doing so, he took the first step toward making America into a multiracial society. Surely, after former slaves had fought for the Union, they could not return to slavery or be forced to leave the land of their birth.

Black men had served with distinction in the American Revolution and the War of 1812. Accordingly, from the first days of the Civil War, free blacks rushed to enlist in the Union army. Yet recruiters, unlike the common soldier, would not have them, saying, "This is a white man's war!"[34]

Frederick Douglass urged blacks to keep trying. The abolitionist believed we value nothing so much as when we earn it. To earn the rights of citizenship, blacks could not allow whites alone to fight for their freedom. Moreover, military service would strengthen former slaves' pride in their manhood. "Once let the Black man get upon his person the brass letters U.S.," Douglass said, "let him get an eagle upon his button, and a musket on his shoulder, bullets in his pocket, and there is no power on earth . . . which can deny that he has earned the right to citizenship in the United States." Citizenship brought the right to vote, "the keystone of the arch of human liberty," for it gave one a say in how the nation was governed.[35]

President Lincoln, ever cautious, held back. Centuries of living under the lash had crushed the slave's spirit, he thought. Slaves lacked courage and drive, he thought. Arming blacks, he feared, would just be a roundabout way of putting guns into rebel hands. Yet there is no arguing with facts. By 1863, Union soldiers were dying at an alarming rate. Lincoln needed fighting men, and he could not be fussy about their color. In the North, he

A call for newly freed men to enlist in the Union army. (c. 1863)

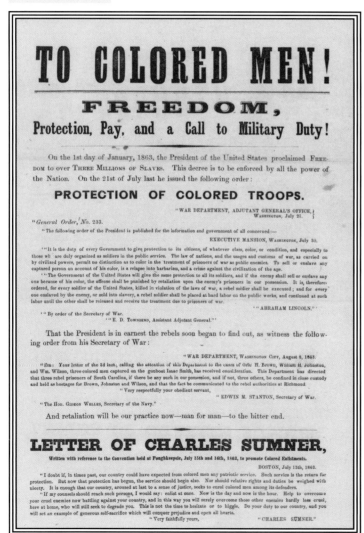

asked free blacks to enlist in segregated units under white officers. In the South, the Emancipation Proclamation became a tool for recruiting fugitive slaves.[36]

When recruiting lagged, Lincoln turned to Frederick Douglass. By 1864, John Brown's friend had become the black community's leading spokesman, a national figure in his own right. On August 19, 1864, he visited the White House at the president's invitation. Lincoln knew of Douglass's past criticisms of him, but these did not matter now. Douglass immediately felt Lincoln was "an honest man," one he could trust, and who trusted him.

The president asked Douglass to organize a band of black scouts "somewhat after the original plan of John Brown." These would slip into rebel territory and encourage slaves to flee to the Union lines.[37]

By the end of the war, roughly 186,000 black men (10 percent of the Union army) had served in the ranks. Among these were Douglass's sons Charles and Lewis. Another 20,000 blacks served aboard warships. Black women became army cooks, laundresses, nurses, and guides. Harriet Tubman, of Underground Railroad fame, served as a guide for the Union army. Such guides were worth

This former slave, shown at left in ragged clothing, became a drummer boy in a sharp Union uniform in the Seventy-Ninth U.S. Colored Infantry in Louisiana. (c. 1863–1865)

This former slave, shown at left in ragged clothing, became a drummer boy in a sharp Union uniform in the Seventy-Ninth U.S. Colored Infantry in Louisiana. (c. 1863–1865)

their weight in gold, since they knew the country better than white Billy Yanks did. A few enslaved women served as spies. In Northern Virginia, one did housework for a group of General Lee's commanders, including Stonewall Jackson. They spoke freely in front of her, a mistake, since she signaled the direction of rebel troop movements by placing garments on a clothesline in special patterns.[38]

We often read how the simple act of putting on a uniform and performing military drills changed former slaves' views of themselves. Elijah Marrs, Twelfth U.S. Colored Heavy Artillery, felt the change instantly. When his sergeant called the roll, he said, "and when he called 'Marrs, Elijah' . . . I felt freedom in my bones. . . . Then all fear vanished."[39]

Soldiers like Private Marrs needed no excuse for singing "John Brown's Body." They sang it lustily, throughout the war. Nor is it surprising that one of the first blacks killed in action had changed his name to John Brown.[40]

The rebels' nightmare had become reality. What Old Brown wished for, Abraham Lincoln did. Turning black men into soldiers struck at the core belief of the Confederacy, that blacks were inferior to whites. Now thousands of armed blacks opposed the rebels in regular military units. Outraged, in May 1863, Jefferson Davis threatened to punish white officers

The Fourth U.S. Colored Infantry at Fort Lincoln. (c. 1863–1866)

who were captured leading black troops. Like Old Brown, these officers faced the gallows for inciting rebellion. Black prisoners would get a sound whipping before being returned to slavery or, in some states, executed.

Abraham Lincoln would have none of this. A humane person, he often pardoned youthful deserters. Yet, when aroused, he showed the harder side of his nature. In July 1863, the president issued his "Order of Retaliation." To make sure everyone got the message, he had thousands of copies printed as a poster. Lincoln declared that for every white officer executed for leading black troops, a Confederate prisoner of equal rank would hang. For every

black soldier enslaved, a rebel soldier would do forced labor.[41]

The Confederates never officially carried out their threat. Though Johnny Rebs hated whites who led blacks, very few murdered them. However, some did, especially when enraged by a hard-fought battle with men they regarded as "so many devils." At such times, they refused to give quarter—a military term for allowing an enemy to surrender.[42]

The worst atrocity took place at Fort Pillow, Tennessee, in April 1864. Johnny Rebs stormed the fort shouting, "No quarter! No quarter!" Overcome by hatred, they murdered over three hundred blacks and their white officers, shooting them, bayoneting them, even burning some alive. Their commander, General Nathan Bedford Forrest, a former slave trader, either ordered the massacre or did nothing to prevent it.[43]

Since it was unclear where the blame lay, Lincoln refused to order reprisals. Instead, he had his generals set aside a number of enemy prisoners and give the rebel army their names. This action carried a silent warning: dare to kill more prisoners, and see what happens. But Lincoln hoped the enemy would not test him. If he hanged hostages, the rebels would feel justified in doing the same, setting off a chain of prisoner killings.[44]

Union field officers checked prisoner abuse with their own methods. When rebels made black captives dig trenches during a Union bombardment, officers made rebel captives work under Confederate artillery fire. That ended the practice. Black soldiers, however, never forgot or forgave Fort Pillow. A Billy Yank wrote that rebels feared black troops more than they feared whites. "When they charge they will not take any prisoners, if they can help it. Their cry is, 'Remember Fort Pillow!' "[45]

Making War John Brown's Way

Abolitionists urged Lincoln to fight as they thought John Brown would have. Frederick Douglass used his friend's exact words to describe the proposed strategy. Only by *"carrying the war into Africa"* could the Union win a decisive victory. Lincoln's armies must lay waste to the South, creating such hardship that civilians would demand peace.[46]

At first, Lincoln hesitated to use such drastic means. Yet circumstances made him change his mind, as they had about

General Ulysses S. "Unconditional Surrender" Grant (above) and General William Tecumseh "Uncle Billy" Sherman (facing page) were tapped by Abraham Lincoln in 1864 to lead the Union military to victory.

emancipation and recruiting black soldiers. A new strategy, however, would require effective leaders to replace the incompetents he had fired after each setback. By 1864, Lincoln had found the team of Ulysses S. Grant and William Tecumseh Sherman.

Robert E. Lee said he understood Lincoln's generals, and thus could beat them or at least fight them to a draw. Yet he feared that, one day, the president would find one he did not understand. General Grant was that man. Nicknamed "Unconditional Surrender," he was an aggressive fighter able to make a plan and stick to it, despite setbacks. According to Lincoln, two words said all one needed to know

about Grant: "He fights!" Oddly enough, Grant's family had a connection to John Brown's family. As a youngster, Grant's father, Jesse, had lived in the Brown home, learning the leather business from the future raider's father.[47]

Soldiers called William Tecumseh Sherman "Uncle Billy," because he always looked after their welfare. A believer in "hard war," Sherman acted as if John Brown's spirit lived within him. War is always brutal, "all hell," he declared. The Civil War, however, was a new kind of war—a total war between entire peoples. "We are not only fighting armies," Sherman said, "but a hostile people, and must make old and young, rich and poor, feel the hard hand of war, as well as their organized armies."[48]

Lincoln named Grant general in chief of the armies of the United States, with Sherman as his deputy. Together, the generals devised a master plan. Though operating hundreds of miles apart, their armies would work toward a single objective. Grant would hurl his Army of the Potomac against Lee's Army of Northern Virginia. Forcing Lee to abandon Richmond would be a stunning defeat for the rebels. Yet Grant's real aim was to keep Lee busy while Sherman cut the Confederacy in half. Uncle Billy would drive southward from Tennessee, pillaging the country as he went. Next, Sherman

The Fifty-Fifth Massachusetts Infantry Regiment singing "John Brown's Body" as they march through the streets of Charleston. (February 21, 1865)

promised to "make Georgia howl!" He would march through the state to the sea, then swing northward, plunging into the Carolinas. If all went well, Union armies would crush the enemy in the jaws of a gigantic vise.

While Confederates fought with their usual skill, Sherman's larger force swept them out of its path. Its march became a triumphal "John Brown parade." Even in the Deep South, by 1864 few enslaved people did *not* know about Brown and Harpers Ferry. "We Negroes in the South never call him John Brown," a woman told passing troops, "we call him *our* Savior. *He died for us.*"[49]

Sherman's army took "John Brown's Body" as its marching song, adding fresh verses as it advanced. Some verses went like this:

> *He's gone to be a soldier in the army of*
> *the Lord,*
> *He's gone to be a soldier in the army of*
> *the Lord,*
> *He's gone to be a soldier in the army of*
> *the Lord,*
> *His soul goes marching on.*
> *John Brown died that the slaves might*
> *be free,*
> *John Brown died that the slaves might*
> *be free,*
> *John Brown died that the slaves might*
> *be free,*
> *His soul goes marching on.*

The song was a kind of password; enslaved people cheered Sherman's men whenever they heard it. When, for example, a regiment took a rest stop at Shady Dale, Georgia, its band struck up the tune. Instantly, an eyewitness reported, scores of young black women "formed a circle around the band, and in a solemn and dignified manner danced to the tune." Later, as other regiments passed, their bands played the same tune, with the same results.[50]

Southerners could not get that "danged" song out of their heads. Each day, parties of soldiers called "bummers" left Sherman's marching columns to strip the countryside of supplies, cut telegraph lines, burn bridges, and tear up railroad tracks. Black soldiers made it a point to shoot any bloodhounds, those trackers of fugitive slaves, that they found. They did their mischief to the sound of "John Brown's Body." In November 1864, as the army left Atlanta, Georgia's largest city, in flames, Uncle Billy said he had never heard "Glory, glory, hallelujah" sung with more spirit.[51]

Sherman's troops marched with confidence, knowing they had friends in slave country. Blacks helped them in countless ways. Some became "talking maps," telling them about every back road, shortcut, and ambush spot. Escaped prisoners, or troops separated from their units, knew they could stop at any slave cabin to find safety, a meal, and a guide. "God bless the poor slaves," a former prisoner said. "If such kindness will not make one an Abolitionist then his heart must be made of stone."[52]

Each day, hundreds, often thousands, of slaves reached Sherman's army. Asked why they came, one replied: "I's want to be a free man, cum when I please, and nobody say nuffin to me or order me roun'." Sometimes soldiers dealt out rough justice, as when a fugitive pointed out a brutal master. Soldiers tied the master to a tree and gave him a taste of his own whip.[53]

On December 13, Sherman reached the coast, seizing Savannah, Georgia, a major seaport. Wheeling to the north, his

A card showing an African American beating a white man, whip in hand, with a stick. (c. 1863)

army spent the next six weeks burning its way across South Carolina. Soldiers despised the Palmetto State. "Here is where treason began," one cried, "and, by God, here is where it shall end!" On February 18, 1865, Charleston fell. A black soldier led the advance troops on a mule, carrying a banner with a single word: *Liberty.* Black infantrymen marched behind him singing "John Brown's Body." Retreating rebels had set fire to the cotton warehouses along the waterfront. The flames leaped out of control, consuming hundreds of buildings. "Serves 'em right," soldiers growled.[54]

When things settled down in Charleston, Sherman held a victory parade. The all-black Fifty-Fifth Massachusetts Infantry Regiment sang "John Brown's Body" in the city they called the "hell-hole of secession." Former slaves joined the parade with a banner reading, "The spirit of John Brown still lives." Horse-drawn floats bore various displays. One depicted a mock slave auction. "How much am I offered for this good cook?" the auctioneer asked when the float stopped. "She is an excellent cook, gentlemen." Laughing Billy Yanks called out their bids. Blacks burst into hysterical tears. "Give me back my children!" women cried. "Give me back my children!" Slavery was still too close, its memory too raw, to joke about.[55]

Sherman presented Charleston to Lincoln as a "gift" for his election to a second

This cartoon by Frank Bellew in Harper's Weekly *celebrates Lincoln's victory by depicting the tall president as having grown even taller—in political stature—after his reelection. The original caption read "Long Abraham Lincoln a Little Longer." (c. 1864)*

term as president. On March 4, 1864, Lincoln gave his second inaugural address. In it, he echoed John Brown's last jail message, in which he said America could only wipe away the sin of slavery with blood. Lincoln, like Brown, had come to see himself on a sacred mission. "In his own mind," says historian Don E. Fehrenbacher, "he was God's holy instrument carrying out a Divine mandate of liberty and justice for all." Like Brown, Lincoln now believed he was doing God's work.[56]

The Lord, Lincoln said, sent the nation "this terrible war" as punishment for slavery. America had it coming: "Fondly do we hope—fervently do we pray—that this mighty scourge of war may speedily pass away. Yet, if God wills that it continue, until all the wealth piled up by the bond-man's two hundred and fifty years of unrequited toil shall be sunk, and until every drop of blood drawn with the lash shall be paid for by another drawn with the sword, as was said three thousand years ago, so still it must be said 'the judgments of the Lord are true and righteous altogether.' "[57]

Both sides had passed through the fire

Abraham Lincoln delivering his second inaugural address on March 4, 1865.

of suffering, Lincoln continued. Soon, God willing, the rebellion would be a bad memory. Americans must welcome peace in the spirit of brotherhood, not vengeance: "With malice toward none; with charity for all; with firmness in the right, as God gives us to see the right, let us strive on to finish the work we are in; to bind up the nation's wounds; to care for him who shall have borne the battle, and for his widow and his orphan—to do all which may achieve and cherish a just and lasting peace, among ourselves, and with all nations."[58]

A start had already been made in binding up the nation's wounds. Lincoln worried that a future president or majority in Congress might cancel the Emancipation Proclamation as an out-of-date war measure. He wanted to make it permanent, applying it nationwide. As Sherman drove toward Charleston, in January 1865

General Philip H. Sheridan (standing at center) in front of his tent with Civil War generals, from left to right, Henry E. Davies, David McM. Gregg, Wesley Merritt, Alfred Torbert, and James H. Wilson. (c. 1864)

Congress passed the Thirteenth Amendment to the Constitution, abolishing slavery on American soil. New Yorker George Templeton Strong gave the credit to John Brown. "Who thought four years ago that John Brown would march so fast?" he wrote in his diary.[59]

After the war, Congress added two other amendments. The fourteenth gave citizenship to all persons born in the United States. The fifteenth declared that no citizen could be prevented from voting due to race. These amendments settled forever the meaning of "all Men." With the amendments, the descendants of African slaves, who Justice Taney said had no rights whites need respect, became African Americans—legally equal to any citizen.

Meanwhile, the Confederacy was on its last legs. As Sherman marched through Georgia, Grant turned to his cavalry commander, General Philip H. Sheridan. The son of Irish immigrants, "Little Phil," as soldiers called him, stood five feet five inches tall. Unlike Grant and Sherman, the bowlegged general charged with his men, pistol in hand, risking his life as they did.

Grant sent Little Phil into the Shenandoah Valley, the "Breadbasket of the Confederacy," an area that grew most of the Army of Northern Virginia's food. Grant's orders were brief and brutal. Turn the valley into a wasteland, so that crows flying over it would have to bring their own food along. Sheridan obeyed. "The people must be left nothing," he told his men, "but their eyes to weep with over the war." From August 1864 to March 1865, his cavalry destroyed everything of value. Crops in the fields and silos filled with grain went up in flames. Farmhouses, barns, stables, flour mills, wagons, and plows: all were torched. When Sheridan finished, he joined Grant for the final drive on Richmond.[60]

The end came quickly. By late March, Sherman's army had begun to smash through North Carolina. Knowing that Sherman would attack him from behind while Grant struck from the front, General Lee decided to take an all-or-nothing gamble. He must abandon Richmond, put his exhausted men aboard trains, and join the few remaining rebel forces in North Carolina. If all went well, he would defeat Sherman, then return with a combined force to deal, somehow, with Grant. It was the Confederacy's only chance, and, he knew, a very slim one.

On April 2, Lee abandoned Richmond. As his troops pulled out, they set fire to tons of ammunition they could not take along. Explosions rocked the city. Hot cinders rained down, setting fires that raged out of control. The following day, Grant's lead units arrived.

A regiment of black cavalrymen came first. As the troopers wheeled into Main Street, one shouted: "Richmond at last!" The city's black people turned out to cheer them. "The cavalry," a white onlooker wrote, "return the greeting with a will, rising in their stirrups, waving their flashing sabers, their white eyes and teeth gleaming from dark visages, and rending the air with wild huzzas." Moments later, a black infantry regiment swung by, singing "John Brown's Body" at the top of their voices.[61]

The next day, April 4, Abraham Lincoln visited Richmond. Fires still burned, but after four years the nightmare was just about over. Former slaves crowded around his carriage. When one kneeled in gratitude, the president told him to kneel only to God, adding, "I am but God's humble instrument."[62]

Black people were not alone in greeting the president. As his carriage rolled past, a white man shouted, "Abraham Lincoln, God bless you! You are the poor

The ruins after the war in Richmond, Virginia. (c. 1865)

man's friend!" Farther on, a beautiful white girl of about seventeen handed him a bouquet of roses with a card reading: "From Eva to the Liberator of the Slaves." Clearly, not all Southern whites favored slavery.[63]

Robert E. Lee lost his gamble. On April 9, Grant cornered his ragtag army at Appomattox Court House, forcing him to surrender, effectively ending the Civil War. Though the Confederacy's western army had not surrendered, it was so crippled that its end came within a few

days. The North celebrated. But Abraham Lincoln would not live to deal with the problems of Reconstruction, the process of rebuilding the nation after the guns fell silent.

On April 14, a color guard raised the Stars and Stripes over Fort Sumter, where the war had begun. That evening, Lincoln, his wife, Mary, and two guests attended a performance of an English comedy, *Our American Cousin*, in Ford's Theatre. During the third act, a figure dressed in black slipped into the presidential box, stood

A poster offering a reward for capture of Lincoln's assassination conspirators John Wilkes Booth and his two accomplices, John H. Surratt and David E. Herold. (1865)

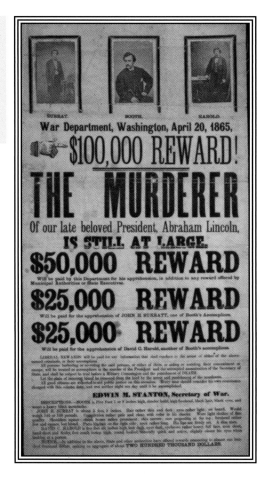

A poster offering a reward for capture of Lincoln's assassination conspirators John Wilkes Booth and his two accomplices, John H. Surratt and David E. Herold. (1865)

and willingness to kill for his beliefs. In Booth's warped mind, Lincoln was to blame for all that had gone wrong since 1859. Slavery abolished! The traditional Southern way of life gone! The South's men killed, its lands ravaged! Lincoln, Booth told his sister, "is walking in the footprints of old John Brown." Yet Brown had also become a "great hero" to the assassin, "a man inspired, the grandest character of the century!" And, like Brown, Booth had a divine call to kill, for "God simply made me the instrument of His

behind Lincoln, and fired a bullet into his brain. As the assassin fled, he shouted the Latin motto of Virginia, *"Sic semper tyrannis!"*—Thus always to tyrants! His victim died early the next morning, without regaining consciousness.

We have already met the assassin. He was none other than John Wilkes Booth. During Lincoln's second inauguration, the actor stood in the crowd, as he had among the Richmond Grays at John Brown's execution. Since then, Booth had grown to admire Brown's sincerity

The last photograph of Abraham Lincoln, taken just over two months before his assassination. (c. February 5, 1865)

punishment." Within days of Lincoln's assassination, federal troops had trapped Booth in a Virginia barn and killed him.[64]

In the decades after Lincoln's death, African Americans linked Brown's name to the slain president's. "Lincoln and John Brown are two martyrs whose memories will live united in our bosom," wrote the editor of a black newspaper shortly after the assassination. With time, however, some came to see this as an idealized view of the "Great Emancipator."[65]

Foremost among these was Frederick Douglass. This lifelong champion of human rights knew and appreciated both Lincoln and Brown. Still, Douglass had no illusions about the sixteenth president. On April 14, 1876, the eleventh anniversary of the assassination, he gave the keynote speech at the unveiling of the Freedmen's Monument in Lincoln Park, Washington, D.C. Lincoln, he said, was a white man devoted to white people's interests. Black people, Douglass continued, "are at best only his step-children; children by adoption, children by forces of circumstances and necessity."[66]

Yet Douglass justly gave credit where it was due. Though often critical of Lincoln, he recognized that a leader in a republic cannot do whatever he wishes, however good the cause. Given political realities, and the realities of racial bigotry, he saw Lincoln as a genius. Lincoln's mission had always been to save the Union,

A cartoon depicting John Brown exhibiting Confederate president Jefferson Davis, wearing a dress and holding a sour apple, in a birdcage. Union soldiers had been singing about "hanging Jeff Davis from a sour apple tree" since the onset of the Civil War. (c. 1865)

and thus government by the people, for future generations. Had he put the abolition of slavery above that, he would have split the Union further, saving the Confederacy *and* slavery: "Viewed from the genuine abolition ground, Mr. Lincoln seemed tardy, cold, dull, and indifferent, but measuring him by the sentiment of the country, a sentiment he was bound as a statesman to consult, he was swift, zealous, radical, and determined."[67]

Though Douglass respected and admired Lincoln, he loved John Brown. On May 30, 1881, he spoke at Storer College in Harpers Ferry, a school founded to educate young African Americans. The college would sell copies of the speech and use the money to set up a professorship in

John Brown's honor. Douglass praised his friend as "a grand, brave and good man," and "our noblest American hero." Long before most abolitionists, Brown realized moral arguments and political deals alone could not end slavery. Only force could do that. Yet Brown, unlike his friend, actually bore arms. "I could live for the slave," said Douglass, "but he could die for him."[68]

"Did John Brown fail?" Douglass asked in closing. His answer still rings true: "If John Brown did not end the war that ended slavery, he did at least begin the war that ended slavery," and made America a better country. "Until this blow [at Harpers Ferry] was struck, the prospect for freedom was dim, shadowy and uncertain. . . . [But] when John Brown stretched forth his arm the sky was cleared. The time for compromises was gone . . . and the clash of arms was at hand."[69]

However, the great abolitionist chose not to address two troubling questions. We must at least raise them. First, may individuals do whatever they think necessary to right dreadful wrongs? Second, most would agree that Douglass's hero had the right to sacrifice himself for the liberty of enslaved people. But did he also have the right to sacrifice others for that cause, whether they wished it or not? These questions are still with us. They will endure while oppression endures, and while people with "righteous rage" feel bound to right wrongs by violence.

 **IX**

Legacy

Nothing in all the world is more dangerous than sincere ignorance and conscientious stupidity.
—Dr. Martin Luther King Jr., *Strength to Love,* 1963

John Brown's legacy has become more relevant in the last half century. He inspired extremists in the civil rights movement of the 1960s and 1970s. Though the Civil War ended slavery, the promise of equality remained unfulfilled. The descendants of former slaves faced segregation, discrimination in employment, denial of voting rights, and police brutality. Like William Lloyd Garrison in the 1830s, moderate civil rights leaders like Martin Luther King Jr. argued that violence breeds more violence. If we demand an eye for an eye and a tooth for a tooth, we all will end up blind and toothless. The best way to gain equality, King insisted, is by appealing to the oppressor's conscience through debate, peaceful demonstrations, and disobeying unjust laws but willingly accepting punishment for doing so.

Like many abolitionists in the 1850s, black militants believed it useless to argue with bigots. Only force and threats of force could reach minds closed to reason and humanity, they insisted. Not surprisingly, militants took inspiration from the memory of John Brown. They hailed him as the only white man worthy of respect. In 1965, Malcolm X, an eloquent spokesman for the Black Muslims, de-

clared: "If you are for me and my problems—when I say me I mean *us,* our people—then you have to be willing to do as old John Brown did."[1]

Militants founded the Black Panther Party in 1966. Huey P. Newton, a party leader, called for a convention, like John Brown's of 1858, to write a new constitution. "If we are to remain a part of the United States," Newton said, "then we must have a new Constitution that will strictly guarantee our Human Rights to Life, Liberty and the Pursuit of Happiness."[2]

Other militants demanded "Black Power," urging African Americans to take control of their communities, and thus their own lives. The Harpers Ferry raiders' actions squared perfectly with their beliefs. H. Rap Brown noted in his book *Die Nigger Die!* that "John Brown was the only white man I could respect and he is dead. The Black Movement has no use for white liberals. We need revolutionaries." Fellow militant Eldridge Cleaver wrote in *Soul on Ice,* "From the beginning of the contacts of blacks and whites, there has been very little reason for a black man to respect a white, with such exceptions as John Brown and others lesser known."[3]

John Brown's example has inspired recent American terrorists, too. Paul Hill was a Protestant minister who hated what he called the "sin" of abortion. In July 1994, Hill shot a doctor outside a Florida abortion clinic. Sentenced to death for murder, he had no regrets. His conscience, Hill told the court, was higher than any written law, because he took a life to save lives. "There's no question in my mind," he said, that shooting the doctor "was what the Lord wanted me to do . . . to prevent him from killing unborn children." John Brown had been his role model: "[The abolitionist's] example has and continues to serve as a source of encouragement to me. . . . Both of us looked to the scriptures for direction . . . and our general understandings of the . . . means to deliver the oppressed have resulted in my being encouraged to pursue a path which is in many ways similar to his."[4]

Not all Brown-inspired terrorists claimed to get their orders from God. Timothy McVeigh, a former soldier, thought that the U.S. government had murdered scores of innocents, including children, by burning the compound of an armed religious group near Waco, Texas. To avenge those innocents, in April 1995 McVeigh detonated an explosives-filled truck outside a federal building in Oklahoma City. The blast killed 168 people, including children in a nursery school. As a journalist noted, "McVeigh saw himself as John Brown." Another wrote, "One of his big heroes was John Brown, who committed some very violent acts in the 1800s . . . to eliminate slavery in our country."[5]

Many who may never have heard John Brown's name hold similar ideas. Like him, they believe God calls them to make war upon what they consider evil. September 11, 2001, reminded Americans of "holy terrorism." On that day, hijackers crashed jet airliners into the Pentagon, the nation's military nerve center, and the twin towers of the World Trade Center in New York City, and were probably on their way to send another plane into the U.S. Capitol before its passengers resisted, forcing it to crash in a field in Somerset County, Pennsylvania. The hijackers and three thousand innocents died. The terrorists, all Muslims, belonged to al-Qaeda, a group led by Osama bin Laden, a wealthy Saudi Arabian turned terrorist. The attacks seem to have stunned and disgusted the vast majority of Muslims. They knew that the Prophet Muhammad had preached jihad, Arabic for "struggle." The word *jihad* can refer to one's personal struggle to live a devout, moral life. It can also mean holy war to defend the faith or expand it by conquest. As he did with slavery, the Prophet made rules for waging holy war: no indiscriminate killing, and no directly attacking women, children, or the elderly.

Osama bin Laden broke with traditional Muslim teaching. Like John Brown, he believed God ordered his actions. Instead of killing slaveholders, bin Laden attacked the United States, which he considered godless, decadent, and out to seize Muslim lands for their oil. He said, "The killing of Americans and their allies—civilian and military—is an individual duty of every Muslim." An al-Qaeda spokesman added, "We have the right to kill four million Americans—two million of them children. . . . Furthermore, it is our right to fight them with chemical and biological weapons." This call for mass murder is reminiscent of John Brown, who said it would be better that a generation of Americans died than to allow slavery to continue.[6]

John Brown remains a force in American life, no matter how we may regard him. He was a man of many faces. Gentle and harsh, martyr and fanatic, freedom fighter and terrorist, devout Christian and murderer. He raised thorny questions about the use of violence at a time when democracy seemed ineffective and the road to justice blocked by self-interest, brutality, and racism.

What, then, can we learn from God's Angry Man? Of course, we must remember him as a righteous person, but also as a warning against terrorism for a "good" cause. We live in a democracy, a land of laws, where, as Abraham Lincoln said, the bullet must never replace the ballot. If ever it does, chaos and dictatorship will follow as surely as sunrise and sunset.

Lerone Bennett Jr., the eminent African American historian, summed up Old Brown's importance best. In 1964, Bennett wrote: "It is to John Brown that we must go, finally, if we want to understand the limitations and possibilities of our situation. He was of no color, John Brown, of no race or age. He was pure passion. . . . He was an elemental force like wind, rain, and fire."[7]

Notes

PROLOGUE: A HOUSE DIVIDING

1. Roy P. Basler, ed., *The Collected Works of Abraham Lincoln,* 9 vols. (New Brunswick, NJ: Rutgers University Press, 1953–55), 2:461–62.

2. John Bernard, *Retrospectives of America, 1797–1811* (New York: Benjamin Blom, 1969), 90–91.

3. Ken Chowder, "The Father of American Terrorism," *American Heritage* 51, no. 1 (February/March 2000).

4. Basler, *The Collected Works of Abraham Lincoln,* 1:112.

5. Henry David Thoreau, *A Plea for Captain John Brown, Read to the Citizens of Concord, Mass., Sunday Evening, October 30, 1859* (Boston, 1859), 19.

6. David Goldfield, *America Aflame: How the Civil War Created a Nation* (New York: Bloomsbury Press, 2011), 238–39.

7. Eugene V. Debs, "John Brown: History's Greatest Hero," *Appeal to Reason,* November 23, 1907; Dale Fetherling, *Mother Jones, the Miners' Angel* (Carbondale: Southern Illinois University Press, 1974), 7–8; David S. Reynolds, *John Brown, Abolitionist: The Man Who Killed Slavery, Sparked the Civil War, and Seeded Civil Rights* (New York: Alfred A. Knopf, 2005), 500; Zoe Trodd and John Stauffer, eds., *Meteor of War: The John Brown Story* (Maplecrest, NY: Brandywine Press, 2004), 214.

I. A VOLCANO BENEATH THE SNOW

1. The sixteen states were Delaware, Pennsylvania, New Jersey, Georgia, Connecticut, Massachusetts, Maryland, South Carolina, New Hampshire, Virginia, New York, North Carolina, Rhode Island, Vermont, Kentucky, and Tennessee.

2. David Brion Davis, *Inhuman Bondage: The Rise and Fall of Slavery in the New World* (New York: Oxford University Press, 2006), 149.

3. James M. McPherson, *Ordeal by Fire: The Civil War and Reconstruction* (New York: Alfred A. Knopf, 1982), 5.

4. William Seale, *The President's House: A History,* 2 vols. (Washington, DC: White House Historical Association, 1986), 81, 472.

5. F. B. Sanborn, ed., *The Life and Letters of John Brown: Liberator of Kansas, and Martyr of Virginia,* 3rd ed. (Concord, MA: F. B. Sanborn, 1910), 12.

6. Richard O. Boyer, *The Legend of John Brown: A Biography and a History* (New York: Alfred A. Knopf, 1973), 167.

7. Avery Craven, *The Coming of the Civil War* (Chicago: University of Chicago Press, 1969), 127.

8. Benjamin P. Thomas, *Abraham Lincoln: A Biography* (New York: Alfred A. Knopf, 1952), 9; Richard Drinnon, *Facing West: The Metaphysics of Indian-Hating and Empire-Building* (New York: Schocken Books, 1990), 100.

9. B. Clive Ponting, *A Green History of the World: The Environment and the Collapse of Great Civilizations* (New York; St. Martin's Press, 1991), 168.

10. Boyer, *The Legend of John Brown,* 175.

11. Sanborn, *The Life and Letters of John Brown,* 12–13.

12. Ibid., 13.

13. Ibid., 14; Boyer, *The Legend of John Brown,* 188.

14. Sanborn, *The Life and Letters of John Brown,* 13.

15. Evan Carton, *Patriotic Treason: John Brown and the Soul of America* (New York: Free Press, 2006), 24.

16. Sanborn, *The Life and Letters of John Brown,* 14–15.

17. Ibid., 15.

18. Reynolds, *John Brown, Abolitionist,* 19; Sanborn, *The Life and Letters of John Brown,* 15.

19. Stephen B. Oates, *To Purge This Land with Blood: A Biography of John Brown* (New York: Harper & Row, 1970), 13.

20. Boyer, *The Legend of John Brown,* 240.

21. Sanborn, *The Life and Letters of John Brown,* 17, 33.

22. Carton, *Patriotic Treason,* 65; Boyer, *The Legend of John Brown,* 249.

23. Paul Finkelman, ed., *His Soul Goes Marching On: Responses to John Brown and the Harpers Ferry Raid* (Charlottesville: University of Virginia Press, 1995), 17; Boyer, *The Legend of John Brown,* 251–52; Craven, *The Coming of the Civil War,* 83.

24. Sanborn, *The Life and Letters of John Brown,* 628; Oswald Garrison Villard, *John Brown, 1800–1859: A Biography Fifty Years After* (Gloucester, MA: Peter Smith, 1965; first published 1910), 392.

25. Boyer, *The Legend of John Brown,* 64–65; Sanborn, *The Life and Letters of John Brown,* 627.

26. Sanborn, *The Life and Letters of John Brown,* 628; Louis Ruchames, ed., *A John Brown Reader* (New York: Abelard-Schuman, 1959), 379.

27. Edward J. Renehan Jr., *The Secret Six: The True Tale of the Men Who Conspired with John Brown* (New York: Crown, 1995), 84.

28. Oates, *To Purge This Land with Blood,* 20.

29. Villard, *John Brown,* 22.

30. Oates, *To Purge This Land with Blood,* 19–20, 202–3.

31. Trodd and Stauffer, *Meteor of War,* 69.

32. Sanborn, *The Life and Letters of John Brown,* 93.

33. Boyer, *The Legend of John Brown,* 237–38.

34. Sanborn, *The Life and Letters of John Brown,* 92.

35. Ibid., 92.

36. Ibid., 37.

37. Finkelman, *His Soul Goes Marching On,* 17; Sanborn, *The Life and Letters of John Brown,* 94; Trodd and Stauffer, *Meteor of War,* 69.

38. Boyer, *The Legend of John Brown*, 211.

39. "The History of Medicine: The Revolutionary War," International Wellness Directory, www.mnwelldir.org/docs/history/history02.htm.

40. Boyer, *The Legend of John Brown*, 343.

41. Villard, *John Brown*, 35.

42. Sanborn, *The Life and Letters of John Brown*, 44.

43. McPherson, *Ordeal by Fire*, 13.

44. Sanborn, *The Life and Letters of John Brown*, 88.

45. Boyer, *The Legend of John Brown*, 337–41.

46. Oates, *To Purge This Land with Blood*, 35–49; Villard, *John Brown*, 26–41.

47. Villard, *John Brown*, 34.

II. THE FOULEST BLOT: RISE OF THE AFRICAN SLAVE TRADE

1. *The Politics of Aristotle*, trans. Benjamin Jowett (New York: Colonial Press, 1900), 4.

2. Murray Gordon, *Slavery in the Arab World* (New York: New Amsterdam Books, 1989), 18; A. H. M. Jones, "Slavery in the Ancient World," *Economic History Review* 9, no. 2 (1956): 187.

3. Gordon, *Slavery in the Arab World*, 100.

4. James Pope-Hennessy, *Sins of the Fathers: The Atlantic Slave Traders, 1441–1807* (Edison, NJ: Castle Books, 1967), 88; Basil Davidson, *The African Slave Trade* (Boston: Little, Brown, 1980), 38. Two good general accounts of African slavery before the international slave trade are "Slavery in Africa," http://autocww.colorado.edu/~blackmon/E64ContentFiles/AfricanHistory/SlaveryInAfrica.html; and Dr. Akosua Perbi, "Slavery and the Slave Trade in Pre-Colonial Africa" (paper presented at the University of Illinois, April 5, 2001), www.latinamericanstudies.org/slavery/perbi.pdf.

5. Olaudah Equiano, *The Interesting Narrative of the Life of Olaudah Equiano, Written by Himself* (New York: St. Martin's Press, 1994; first published 1789 in London), 40–41.

6. Gordon, *Slavery in the Arab World,* 133.

7. Suzy Hansen, "Islam's Black Slaves," *Salon,* April 5, 2001, www.salon.com/2001/04/05/segal; Gordon, *Slavery in the Arab World*, 56; Ronald Segal, *Islam's Black Slaves: The Other Black Diaspora* (New York: Farrar, Straus and Giroux, 2001), 38.

8. Segal, *Islam's Black Slaves*, 41; Hansen, "Islam's Black Slaves."

9. Andrew G. Bostom, ed., *The Legacy of Jihad: Islamic Holy War and the Fate of Non-Muslims* (Amherst, NY: Prometheus Books, 2005), 93.

10. Segal, *Islam's Black Slaves,* 22; Gordon, *Slavery in the Arab World,* 159–60.

11. Segal, *Islam's Black Slaves*, 133–34, 136.

12. Gordon, *Slavery in the Arab World,* 65.

13. Fawn M. Brodie, *The Devil Drives: A Life of Sir Richard Burton* (New York: W. W. Norton, 1967), 149.

14. Church Missionary Society, *The Slave Trade of East Africa* (London: Church Missionary Society, 1869), 11–12.

15. Segal, *Islam's Black Slaves,* 69.

16. Ibid., 159.

17. "Slavery in Islam," www.bbc.co.uk/religion/religions/islam/history/slavery_1.shtml; Gordon, *Slavery in the Arab World*, 37–41; Segal, *Islam's Black Slaves,* 35–37.

18. Gordon, *Slavery in the Arab World,* 37.

19. Peter Russell, *Prince Henry "the Navigator": A Life* (New Haven: Yale University Press, 2000), 35–37.

20. E. F. Benson, *Sir Francis Drake* (London: John Lane, 1927), 19; Peter Macinnis, *Bittersweet: The Story of Sugar* (London: Allen & Unwin, 2002), 79, 83, 45.

21. Pope-Hennessy, *Sins of the Fathers,* 123.

22. Hugh Thomas, *The Slave Trade: The Story of the Atlantic Slave Trade, 1440–1870* (New York: Simon & Schuster, 1997), 804.

23. Marcus Rediker, *The Slave Ship: A Human History* (New York: Viking, 1973), 253, 6.

24. Ibid., 72, 205, 267; Pope-Hennessy, *Sins of the Fathers,* 246–47.

25. Tunde Obadina, "Slave Trade: A Root of Contemporary African Crisis," Africa Economic Analysis, www.africaeconomicanalysis.org/articles/38/1/Slave-trade-a-root-of-contemporary-African-Crisis /Page1.html; Macinnis, *Bittersweet,* 99; Pope-Hennessy, *Sins of the Fathers,* 229.

26. Rediker, *The Slave Ship,* 141–42.

27. Pope-Hennessy, *Sins of the Fathers,* 50.

28. Anthony Benezet, *Some Historical Account of Guinea . . . : An Inquiry into the Rise and Progress of the Slave Trade, Its Nature and Lamentable Effects* (Philadelphia, 1772), Chapter 1.

29. Rediker, *The Slave Ship,* 244–45, 7.

30. Henry Louis Gates Jr., "Ending the Slavery Blame-Game," *New York Times,* April 22, 2010.

31. Frederick Douglass, "African Civilization Society," February 1859, http://teachingamericanhistory .org/library/index.asp?document=1031.

32. Major William Gray, *Travels in Western Africa: In the Years 1818, 19, 20, and 21, from the River Gambia . . . to the River Niger* (London: John Murray, 1825; reprint, London: British Library, 2011), 290–91, 292–93, 296.

33. Equiano, *The Interesting Narrative of the Life of Olaudah Equiano,* 53.

34. Ibid., 54; David Northrup, ed., *The Atlantic Slave Trade* (Lexington, MA: D. C. Heath, 1994), 14; Winthrop D. Jordan, *White over Black: American Attitudes Toward the Negro, 1550–1812* (Chapel Hill: University of North Carolina Press, 1968), 7.

35. Jordan, *White over Black,* 9–10, 11; Brodie, *The Devil Drives,* 209; Pope-Hennessy, *Sins of the Fathers,* 32; Equiano, *The Interesting Narrative of the Life of Olaudah Equiano,* 54; William D. Piersen, "White Cannibals, Black Martyrs: Fear, Depression, and Religious Faith as Causes of Suicide among New Slaves," *Journal of Negro History* 62, no. 2 (April 1977): 147–48.

36. John Thornton, "Cannibals, Witches, and Slave Traders in the Atlantic World," *William and Mary Quarterly* 60, no. 2 (April 2003): 273–94; Rediker, *The Slave Ship,* 287.

37. Rediker, *The Slave Ship,* 275; Alexander Falconbridge, *An Account of the Slave Trade on the Coast of Africa* (London: J. Phillips, 1788), 32.

38. Equiano, *The Interesting Narrative of the Life of Olaudah Equiano,* 56.

39. Falconbridge, *An Account of the Slave Trade on the Coast of Africa,* 23; Thomas Howard, ed., *Black Voyage: Eyewitness Accounts of the Atlantic Slave Trade* (Boston: Little, Brown, 1971), 83.

40. Falconbridge, *An Account of the Slave Trade on the Coast of Africa,* 25.

41. Eric Williams, *Capitalism and Slavery* (Chapel Hill: University of North Carolina Press, 1944).

42. Obadina, "Slave Trade: A Root of Contemporary African Crisis."

III. AN OBJECT VAST IN ITS COMPASS

1. Engel Sluiter, "New Light on the '20. and Odd Negroes' Arriving in Virginia, August 1619," *William and Mary Quarterly* 54, no. 2 (April 1997): 395–98; Benjamin Woolley, *Savage Kingdom: The True Story of Jamestown, 1607, and the Settlement of America* (New York: HarperCollins, 2007), 353–54.

2. Ben Kiernan, *Blood and Soil: A World History of Genocide and Extermination from Sparta to Darfur* (New Haven: Yale University Press, 2007), 241, 242.

3. Douglas Harper, "Slavery in Massachusetts," in *Slavery in the North,* www.slavenorth.com /massachusetts.htm.

4. Douglas Harper, "Northern Profits from Slavery," in *Slavery in the North,* www.slavenorth.com /profits.htm; Harper, "Slavery in Massachusetts"; Janet Halley, "My Isaac Royall Legacy" (speech, Harvard Law School, Cambridge, MA, September 17, 2006), www.law.harvard.edu/students/orgs /blj/vol24/Halley/pdf; Abram English Brown, *Faneuil Hall and Faneuil Hall Market; or, Peter Faneuil and His Gift* (Boston: Lee Shepard, 1900), 22–50; Paras D. Bhayani, "Beneath the Ivy, a Legacy of Chains," *Harvard Crimson,* October 27, 2006.

5. William Goodell, *The American Slave Code in Theory and Practice . . .* (New York: American and Foreign Anti-Slavery Society, 1853), Part 1, Chapter 13, Chapter 6, http://dinsdoc.com /goodell-1-1-13.htm; Willie Lee Rose, ed., *A Documentary History of Slavery in North America* (New York: Oxford University Press, 1976), 106–7; Reynolds, *John Brown, Abolitionist,* 57.

6. Frederick Douglass, *Autobiographies* (New York: Library of America, 1994; first published 1845, 1855, 1893), 290.

7. Member of the Washington Bar, *The Slavery Code of the District of Columbia . . .* (Washington, DC: L. Towers, 1862), http://www.loc.gov./exhibits/treasures/trm009.html.

8. Margaret Leech, *Reveille in Washington, 1860–1865* (New York: Harper and Brothers, 1941; reprint, New York: Book of the Month Club, 1989), 260, 264; Adam Goodheart, "A Capital under Slavery's Shadow," *New York Times,* February 24, 2011.

9. Federal Writers' Project, *Slave Narratives: A Folk History of Slavery in the United States from Interviews with Former Slaves* (Washington, DC: Library of Congress, 1941), 17:54.

10. Irving H. Bartlett, *Wendell Phillips: Brahmin Radical* (Boston: Beacon Press, 1961), 44.

11. Frederick Douglass, "Lecture on Slavery, No. 1," December 1, 1850, in *Frederick Douglass: Selected Speeches and Writings,* ed. Philip S. Foner, abr. Yuval Taylor (Chicago: Lawrence Hill Books, 1999), 167.

12. John W. Blassingame, ed., *Slave Testimony: Two Centuries of Letters, Speeches, Interviews, and Autobiographies* (Baton Rouge: Louisiana State University Press, 1977), 133; Henry Bibb, *Narrative of the Life and Adventures of Henry Bibb, An American Slave, Written by Himself* (New York: Published by the Author, 1849), 177.

13. Goodell, *The American Slave Code in Theory and Practice*; Rose, *A Documentary History of Slavery in North America,* 106–7; McPherson, *Ordeal by Fire*, 35–36.

14. C. Vann Woodward, ed., *Mary Chesnut's Civil War* (New Haven: Yale University Press, 1981), 29.

15. David Brion Davis, *The Problem of Slavery in Western Culture* (Ithaca, NY: Cornell University Press, 1966), 291.

16. Matthew Spalding, "How to Understand Slavery and the American Founding," Heritage Foundation, August 26, 2002, www.heritage.org/research/reports/2002/08/how-to-understand-slavery-and-americas.

17. The five committee members were Thomas Jefferson (Virginia), John Adams (Massachusetts), Benjamin Franklin (Pennsylvania), Robert Livingston (New York), and Roger Sherman (Connecticut).

18. Garry Wills, "Lincoln's Black History," *New York Review of Books,* June 11, 2009, www.nybooks .com/articles/archives/2009/jun/11/lincolns-black-history, review of Henry Louis Gates Jr., ed., *Lincoln on Race and Slavery* (Princeton, NJ: Princeton University Press, 2009), xxiii.

19. Thomas Jefferson, "Query 14," *Notes on the State of Virginia,* in *Thomas Jefferson: Writings* (New York: The Library of America, 1984), 264–67; Paul Finkelman, "Jefferson and Slavery: 'Treason Against the Hopes of the World,'" in *Jeffersonian Legacies,* ed. Peter Onuf (Charlottesville: University Press of Virginia, 1993), 181–221; John Chester Miller, *The Wolf by the Ears: Thomas Jefferson and Slavery* (New York: Free Press, 1977), 1–11, 38–45.

20. Joseph J. Ellis, *Founding Brothers: The Revolutionary Generation* (New York: Alfred A. Knopf, 2001), 91.

21. Lawrence Goldstone, *Dark Bargain: Slavery, Profits, and the Struggle for the Constitution* (New York: Walker, 2005), 3.

22. Max Farrand, ed., *The Records of the Federal Convention of 1787,* rev. ed. (New Haven: Yale University Press, 1937), vol. 3, art. 1, sec. 9, clause 1, August 25, press-pubs.uchicago.edu/founders documents.html.

23. Don E. Fehrenbacher, *The Slaveholding Republic: An Account of the United States Government's Relations to Slavery* (New York: Oxford University Press, 2001)*,* 24; David Barton, "The Founding Fathers and Slavery," WallBuilders, www.wallbuilders.com/LIBprinterfriendly.asp?id=122; Goldstone, *Dark Bargain,* 112–129; Garry Wills, *"Negro President": Jefferson and the Slave Power* (Boston: Houghton Mifflin, 2003), 1–3.

24. Lynne Withey, *Dearest Friend: A Life of Abigail Adams* (New York: Simon & Schuster, 2001), 60.

25. Bernard Rosenthal, "Puritan Conscience and New England Slavery," *New England Quarterly* 46, no. 1 (March 1973): 80.

26. Eric Foner, *The Fiery Trial: Abraham Lincoln and American Slavery* (New York: W. W. Norton, 2010), 16.

27. Oscar Sherwin, *Prophet of Liberty: The Life and Times of Wendell Phillips* (New York: Bookman Associates, 1958), 50–52; Leon F. Litwack, "The Abolitionist Dilemma: The Antislavery Movement and the Northern Negro," *New England Quarterly* 34, no. 1 (March 1961): 50; Leon F. Litwack, *North of Slavery: The Negro in the Free States, 1790–1860* (Chicago: University of Chicago Press, 1961), 65, 69, 72–73, 75–76, 93–94, 97; James Brewer Stewart, *Holy Warriors: The Abolitionists and American Slavery* (New York: Hill & Wang, 1976), 141–42.

28. Stewart, *Holy Warriors,* 24–25; Eugene H. Berwanger, "Negrophobia in Northern Proslavery and Antislavery Thought," *Phylon* 33, no. 3 (1972): 266–75.

29. Ellis, *Founding Brothers,* 95–96; Jordan, *White over Black,* 319–20.

30. Ulrich Bonnell Phillips, *American Negro Slavery: A Survey of the Supply, Employment, and Control of Negro Labor as Determined by the Plantation Regime* (Baton Rouge: Louisiana State University Press, 1966; first published 1918), 181–82.

31. Craven, *The Coming of the Civil War,* 110.

32. D. B. Davis, *Inhuman Bondage,* 46.

33. James Mellon, ed., *Bullwhip Days: The Slaves Remember* (New York: Weidenfeld & Nicolson, 1988), 302.

34. John Hope Franklin, *From Slavery to Freedom: A History of Negro Americans* (New York: Alfred A. Knopf, 1960), 255; David M. Potter, *The Impending Crisis, 1848–1861* (New York: Harper & Row, 1976), 135.

35. Jacqueline L. Tobin and Raymond G. Dobard, *Hidden in Plain View: A Secret Story of Quilts and the Underground Railroad* (New York: Anchor Books, 2000), 53–83; "Follow the Drinking Gourd," Owen Sound's Black History, www.osblackhistory.com/drinkinggourd.php.

36. Reynolds, *John Brown, Abolitionist,* 52; Herbert Aptheker, ed., *From Colonial Times through the Civil War,* vol. 1 of *A Documentary History of the Negro People in the United States* (New York: Citadel Press, 1951), 162–208.

37. Adam Hochschild, *Bury the Chains: Prophets and Rebels in the Fight to Free an Empire's Slaves* (Boston: Houghton Mifflin, 2005), 257; Martin Ros, *Night of Fire: The Black Napoleon and the Battle for Haiti* (New York: Sarpedon, 1994), 5–6.

38. Hochschild, *Bury the Chains,* 267.

39. Eleven new states were created from the Louisiana Purchase: Minnesota, Iowa, Missouri, Arkansas, Louisiana, North Dakota, South Dakota, Nebraska, Kansas, Oklahoma, and Montana. Lands from the Louisiana Purchase also formed parts of four other states: Wyoming, Colorado, New Mexico, and Texas.

40. Eugene D. Genovese, *From Rebellion to Revolution: Afro-American Slave Revolts in the Making of the Modern World* (Baton Rouge: Louisiana State University Press, 1979), 128.

41. David Walker, *Walker's Appeal, in Four Articles; Together with a Preamble, to the Coloured Citizens of the World . . .* (Boston: David Walker, 1830), 37, 38, 81, http://docsouth.unc.edu/nc /walker/walker.html.

42. Stephen B. Oates, *The Fires of Jubilee: Nat Turner's Fierce Rebellion* (New York: Harper & Row, 1975), 125.

43. "Born in Slavery: Slave Narratives from the Federal Writers' Project, 1936–1938," http://memory .loc.gov/ammem/snhtml/snhome.html.

44. Genovese, *From Rebellion to Revolution,* 116.

45. William Lloyd Garrison, "No Compromise with Slavery: An Address Delivered in the Broadway Tabernacle, New York, February 14, 1854," http://memory.loc.gov/cgi-bin/query/r?ammem /rbaapc:@field(DOCID+@lit(rbaapc11000div2)).

46. John Stauffer, *The Black Hearts of Men: Radical Abolitionists and the Transformation of Race* (Cambridge: Harvard University Press, 2001), 212.

47. Sherwin, *Prophet of Liberty,* 100.

48. "Declaration of the Anti-Slavery Convention, Assembled in Philadelphia, Dec., 1833," http://hdl.loc .gov-loc.rbc.rbpe.15302500; John Demos, "The Antislavery Movement and the Problem of Violent 'Means,'" *New England Quarterly* 37, no. 4 (December 1964): 503.

49. Bartlett, *Wendell Phillips,* 195–96.

50. Sherwin, *Prophet of Liberty,* 166.

51. Ibid., 85.

52. Theodore Dwight Weld, *American Slavery as It Is: Testimony of a Thousand Witnesses* (New York: American Anti-Slavery Society, 1839), 62–63, http://docsouth.unc.edu/neh/weld/weld.html.

53. *The Anti-Slavery Alphabet* (Philadelphia: Merrihew & Thompson, 1847), www.gutenberg.org/files-16081-16081-h-16081-h.htm.

54. David Reynolds, *Mightier Than the Sword: "Uncle Tom's Cabin" and the Battle for America* (New York: W. W. Norton, 2011).

55. Michael Fellman, "Theodore Parker and the Abolitionist Role in the 1850s," *Journal of American History* 61, no. 3 (December 1974): 677–78, 680.

56. Douglass, *Autobiographies,* 663.

57. Ruchames, *A John Brown Reader,* 262, 263; Fellman, "Theodore Parker and the Abolitionist Role in the 1850s," 493–94; Otto Scott, *The Secret Six: John Brown and the Abolitionist Movement* (New York: Times Books, 1979), 285.

58. Litwack, *North of Slavery,* 22, 224, 225, 226; Litwack, "The Abolitionist Dilemma," 60; Renehan, *The Secret Six,* 43; Finkelman, *His Soul Goes Marching On,* 76.

59. William Lloyd Garrison, "Garrison's Defense of His Positions," 1854, http:// teachingamericanhistory.org/library/index.asp?document=1432.

60. Litwack, "The Abolitionist Dilemma," 64.

61. Litwack, *North of Slavery,* 229; Litwack, "The Abolitionist Dilemma," 64, note 37.

62. Litwack, *North of Slavery,* 227; Stewart, *Holy Warriors,* 129.

63. Page Smith, *The Nation Comes of Age* (New York: McGraw-Hill, 1981), 604; Henry Mayer, *All on Fire: William Lloyd Garrison and the Abolition of Slavery* (New York: St. Martin's Press, 1998), 122–23.

64. Goodheart, "A Capital under Slavery's Shadow," 66; John C. Calhoun, "Slavery a Positive Good" (speech to the U.S. Senate, 1837), http://caho-test.cc.columbia.edu/ps/10157.html.

IV. MIGHTY MAN OF VALOR

1. Sanborn, *The Life and Letters of John Brown,* 10–11.

2. Jonathan Edwards, *The Injustice and Impolicy of the Slave Trade, and of the Slavery of the Africans* (Thomas and Samuel Green, 1791), http://memory.loc.gov/cgi-bin/ampage?collId=ody_ rbcmisc&fileName=ody/ody0302/ody0.

3. Sanborn, *The Life and Letters of John Brown,* 10–11, 122.

4. Ibid.

5. Ibid., 14–15.

6. Ibid., 14–15, 116.

7. Ibid., 35, 37, 40–41.

8. Ibid., 37; Carton, *Patriotic Treason,* 79–80.

9. Boyer, *The Legend of John Brown,* 311.

10. Ibid., 314; Villard, *John Brown,* 45–46.

11. Steven H. Shiffrin, "The Rhetoric of Black Violence in the Antebellum Period: Henry Highland Garnet," *Journal of Black Studies* 2, no. 1 (September 1971): 48.

12. Sanborn, *The Life and Letters of John Brown,* 97; John Brown, letter to Owen Brown, January 10, 1849, in Ruchames, *A John Brown Reader,* 67.

13. Reynolds, *John Brown, Abolitionist,* 129; Stauffer, *The Black Hearts of Men,* 173–74.

14. Litwack, *North of Slavery,* 47.

15. J. C. Furnas, *The Road to Harpers Ferry* (New York: William Sloane, 1959), 305.

16. Ralph Korngold, *Two Friends of Man: The Story of William Lloyd Garrison and Wendell Phillips and Their Relationship with Abraham Lincoln* (Boston: Little, Brown, 1950), 164; Mayer, *All on Fire,* 319; Sherwin, *Prophet of Liberty,* 213.

17. William Lloyd Garrison, "The American Union," *Liberator,* January 10, 1845, http://fair-use.org/the-liberator/1845/01/10/the-american-union.

18. Frederick Douglass, *The Nature, Character, and History of the Anti-Slavery Movement: A Lecture Delivered Before the Rochester Ladies' Anti-Slavery Association* (Glasgow: G. Gallie, 1855), 22–23.

19. Craven, *The Coming of the Civil War,* 274–75.

20. Potter, *The Impending Crisis,* 132; Sherwin, *Prophet of Liberty,* 181, 217.

21. Orestes A. Brownson, "The Higher Law: Conscience and the Constitution, with Remarks on the Recent Speech of the Hon. Daniel Webster . . . ," *Brownson's Quarterly Review* (January 1851), www.orestesbrownson.com/106.html.

22. Craven, *The Coming of the Civil War,* 311.

23. Sherwin, *Prophet of Liberty,* 332; Reynolds, *John Brown, Abolitionist,* 218.

24. Korngold, *Two Friends of Man,* 239; Mayer, *All on Fire,* 443–444; Donald Yacavone, "A Covenant with Death and an Agreement with Hell," Massachusetts Historical Society, July 2005, www.masshist.org/objects/2005july.cfm.

25. Douglas R. Egerton, *Year of Meteors: Stephen Douglas, Abraham Lincoln, and the Election That Brought on the Civil War* (New York: Bloomsbury Press, 2010), 18.

26. Boyer, *The Legend of John Brown,* 470.

27. Sherwin, *Prophet of Liberty,* 318.

28. Ibid.

29. Boyer, *The Legend of John Brown,* 496; Egerton, *Year of Meteors,* 25.

30. Thomas Goodrich, *War to the Knife: Bleeding Kansas, 1854–1861* (Mechanicsburg, PA: Stackpole Books, 1998), 48–49.

31. Renehan, *The Secret Six,* 92; Korngold, *Two Friends of Man,* 244.

32. John Brown, letter to John Brown Jr., August 21, 1854, in Ruchames, *A John Brown Reader,* 68.

33. Villard, *John Brown,* 90.

34. Ibid., 83–84.

35. Ruchames, *A John Brown Reader,* 68.

36. William A. Phillips, "Three Interviews with Old John Brown," *Atlantic Monthly,* December 1879, www.theatlantic.com/past/docs/issues/1879dec/phillips.htm; Oates, *To Purge This Land with Blood,* 97; Ruchames, *A John Brown Reader,* 84.

37. Benjamin Quarles, *Allies for Freedom & Blacks on John Brown* (Boston: Da Capo Press, 2001), 13; William W. Freehling, *Secessionists Triumphant, 1854–1861,* vol. 1 of *The Road to Disunion* (New York: Oxford University Press, 2007), 208.

38. James Redpath, *The Public Life of Capt. John Brown* (Boston: Thayer and Eldridge, 1860), 105; Boyer, *The Legend of John Brown,* 242.

39. Quarles, *Allies for Freedom,* 25.

40. Hannah N. Geffert, "John Brown and His Black Allies: An Ignored Alliance," *Pennsylvania Magazine of History and Biography* 126, no. 4 (October 2002): 593; Renehan, *The Secret Six,* 63–64.

41. Trodd and Stauffer, *Meteor of War,* 77–79.

42. Ibid., 84.

43. Villard, *John Brown,* 78.

44. Ibid., 88.

45. Ibid., 88–89.

46. Oates, *To Purge This Land with Blood,* 106–7; Furnas, *The Road to Harpers Ferry,* 6.

47. Villard, *John Brown,* 123–24.

48. Ibid., 145; Goodrich, *War to the Knife,* 117.

49. Eric Foner, *Free Soil, Free Labor, Free Men: The Ideology of the Republican Party Before the Civil War* (New York: Oxford University Press, 1995), 114–15; Sherwin, *Prophet of Liberty,* 346.

50. Michael D. Pierson, "'All Southern Society Is Assailed by the Foulest Charges': Charles Sumner's 'The Crime against Kansas' and the Escalation of Republican Anti-Slavery Rhetoric," *New England Quarterly* 68, no. 4 (December 1995): 553–54; William E. Gienapp, "The Crime against Sumner: The Caning of Charles Sumner and the Rise of the Republican Party," *Civil War History* 25, no. 3 (September 1979): 218–45.

51. Manisha Sinha, "The Caning of Charles Sumner: Slavery, Race, and Ideology in the Age of the Civil War," *Journal of the Early Republic* 23, no. 2 (Summer 2003): 245–46.

52. Avery O. Craven, *The Growth of Southern Nationalism, 1848–1861,* vol. 6 of *A History of the South* (Baton Rouge: Louisiana State University Press, 1953), 234; Sherwin, *Prophet of Liberty,* 354.

53. Boyer, *The Legend of John Brown,* 101; Craven, *The Growth of Southern Nationalism,* 230.

54. Oates, *To Purge This Land with Blood,* 129; James Townsley, "The Pottawatomie Killings," *Republican Citizen,* December 20, 1879, http://kansashistory.us/pottamassacre.html.

55. Scott, *The Secret Six,* 6; Townsley, "The Pottawatomie Killings"; Villard, *John Brown,* 148–88; Reynolds, *John Brown, Abolitionist,* 138–78.

56. Sanborn, *The Life and Letters of John Brown,* 157; Walter Laqueur, *The Age of Terrorism* (Boston: Little, Brown, 1987), 144; Reynolds, *John Brown, Abolitionist,* 438.

57. Sanborn, *The Life and Letters of John Brown,* 270, 273; Villard, *John Brown,* 165–66, 167.

58. Sanborn, *The Life and Letters of John Brown,* 621.

59. Richard J. Hinton, *John Brown and His Men, with Some Account of the Roads They Traveled to Reach Harper's Ferry,* rev. ed. (New York: Funk & Wagnalls, 1894), 69; Sanborn, *The Life and Letters of John Brown,* 251.

60. Sanborn, *The Life and Letters of John Brown,* 259; Redpath, *The Public Life of Capt. John Brown,* 226.

61. Goodrich, *War to the Knife,* 128; Reynolds, *John Brown, Abolitionist,* 486.

62. Reynolds, *John Brown, Abolitionist,* 196–97.

63. Sanborn, *The Life and Letters of John Brown,* 299–300; Oates, *To Purge This Land with Blood,* 152–57.

64. Goodrich, *War to the Knife,* 160; Reynolds, *John Brown, Abolitionist,* 196–97.

65. Villard, *John Brown,* 255, 260.

66. Dale E. Watts, "How Bloody Was Bleeding Kansas? Political Killings in Kansas Territory, 1854–1861," *Kansas History: A Journal of the Central Plains* 18, no. 2 (Summer 1995): 116–29.

67. Villard, *John Brown,* 248.

V. INTO "AFRICA"

1. F. B. Sanborn, *Recollections of Seventy Years,* 2 vols. (Boston: Richard Badger, 1909), 1:83, 48.

2. Ernest Freeberg, *The Education of Laura Bridgman: First Deaf and Blind Person to Learn Language* (Cambridge, MA: Harvard University Press, 2001), 29–37.

3. Oates, *To Purge This Land with Blood,* 189; David Herbert Donald, *Charles Sumner and the Coming of the Civil War* (Naperville, IL: Sourcebooks, 2009), 293.

4. Boyer, *The Legend of John Brown,* 349; Villard, *John Brown,* 288.

5. Oates, *To Purge This Land with Blood,* 181–92; Villard, *John Brown,* 271–72, 398–400.

6. Sanborn, *The Life and Letters of John Brown,* 122.

7. Ibid.; Jules Abels, *Man on Fire: John Brown and the Cause of Liberty* (New York: Macmillan, 1971), 131.

8. Ruchames, *A John Brown Reader,* 94; James C. Malin, *John Brown and the Legend of Fifty-Six* (Philadelphia: American Philosophical Society, 1942), 349; Potter, *The Impending Crisis,* 222.

9. Dred Scott v. Sandford, 6 U.S. 393 (1856), http://hdl.loc.gov/loc.law/list./22.

10. Boyer, *The Legend of John Brown,* 269.

11. "Supreme Court vs. the Abolitionists," (VA) *Enquirer,* March 13, 1857, http://history.furman.edu/benson/docs/vareds57313a.htm.

12. Craven, *The Coming of the Civil War,* 386; Sherwin, *Prophet of Liberty,* 371.

13. Franklin, *From Slavery to Freedom,* 246; Renehan, *The Secret Six,* 55; Jeffery Rossbach, *Ambivalent Conspirators: John Brown, the Secret Six, and a Theory of Slave Violence* (Philadelphia: University of Pennsylvania Press, 1982), 136–37; Edwin W. Bowen, "Thomas Wentworth Higginson," *Sewanee Review* 23, vol. 4 (October 1915): 436.

14. James Redpath, *Echoes of Harper's Ferry* (Boston: Thayer and Eldridge, 1860), 81; *The Liberator,* February 4, 1859; Demos, "The Antislavery Movement and the Problem of Violent 'Means,'" 522.

15. Sherwin, *Prophet of Liberty,* 372; Renehan, *The Secret Six,* 54.

16. Gerrit Smith to John Thomas, "Letter on the 1859 Celebration of the Rescue of Jerry," August 27, 1859, New York History Net, http://nyhistory.com/gerritsmith/jerry59.htm.

17. Douglass, *Autobiographies,* 716–17.

18. Ibid., 717–18.

19. Ibid., 718.

20. Oates, *To Purge This Land with Blood,* 200.

21. Finkelman, *His Soul Goes Marching On,* 31; Reynolds, *John Brown, Abolitionist,* 113; Oates, *To Purge This Land with Blood,* 234.

22. Villard, *John Brown,* 56; Sanborn, *The Life and Letters of John Brown,* 269.

23. Villard, *John Brown,* 331–36.

24. Oates, *To Purge This Land with Blood,* 229–30; Hinton, *John Brown and His Men,* 673.

25. Sanborn, *The Life and Letters of John Brown,* 439.

26. Oates, *To Purge This Land with Blood,* 233–34; Renehan, *The Secret Six,* 170.

27. Reynolds, *John Brown, Abolitionist,* 262–63; Villard, *John Brown,* 331–35; Hinton, *John Brown and His Men,* 715–18.

28. Oates, *To Purge This Land with Blood,* 248.

29. Ibid., 250–51; Ralph Volney Harlow, "Gerrit Smith and the John Brown Raid," *American Historical Review* 38, no. 1 (October 1932): 42.

30. Allan Nevins, *The Emergence of Lincoln,* 2 vols. (New York: Charles Scribner's Sons, 1950), 2:25.

31. Quarles, *Allies for Freedom,* 54–56.

32. Redpath, *The Public Life of Capt. John Brown,* 239.

33. Robert E. McGlone, "Rescripting a Troubled Past: John Brown's Family and the Harpers Ferry Conspiracy," *Journal of American History* 75, no. 4 (March 1989): 1186, 1189–90.

34. Reynolds, *John Brown, Abolitionist,* 320; Geffert, "John Brown and His Black Allies," 600; Sanborn, *The Life and Letters of John Brown,* 544.

35. McGlone, "Rescripting a Troubled Past," 1189–90.

36. Sanborn, *The Life and Letters of John Brown,* 544.

37. Ibid., 541–42.

38. Nevins, *The Emergence of Lincoln,* 2:75–76; Furnas, *The Road to Harpers Ferry,* 29.

39. Reynolds, *John Brown, Abolitionist,* 303–4; Oates, *To Purge This Land with Blood,* 284–85.

40. Douglass, *Autobiographies,* 759.

41. Ibid., 760.

42. Redpath, *The Public Life of Capt. John Brown,* 244; Sanborn, *The Life and Letters of John Brown,* 554.

43. Villard, *John Brown,* 430; Sanborn, *The Life and Letters of John Brown,* 554.

44. Quarles, *Allies for Freedom,* 100; Reynolds, *John Brown, Abolitionist,* 313.

45. Villard, *John Brown,* 433; Reynolds, *John Brown, Abolitionist,* 315–16.

46. Goodrich, *War to the Knife,* 231, 245.

47. Osborne P. Anderson, *A Voice from Harper's Ferry . . .* (Boston: Printed for the Author, 1861), 36.

48. Geffert, "John Brown and His Black Allies," 600.

49. Hinton, *John Brown and His Men,* 312.

50. Ibid., 303.

51. Goodrich, *War to the Knife,* 237.

52. Villard, *John Brown,* 448.

53. Sanborn, *The Life and Letters of John Brown,* 559; Villard, *John Brown,* 449; Reynolds, *John Brown, Abolitionist,* 326.

54. Douglas Southall Freeman, *Robert E. Lee,* 4 vols. (New York: Charles Scribner's Sons, 1934–35), 1:398.

55. Ibid., 1:397.

56. Goodrich, *War to the Knife,* 241.

57. Hinton, *John Brown and His Men,* 301.

58. Robert E. McGlone, *John Brown's War against Slavery* (New York: Cambridge University Press, 2009), 299–300.

59. Israel Green, "The Capture of John Brown," *North American Review,* December 1885, www2.iath.virginia.edu/jbrown/igreen.html.

60. Ibid.

61. Cecil D. Eby, ed., "The Last Hours of the John Brown Raid: The Narrative of David H. Strother," *Virginia Magazine of History and Biography* 73, no. 2 (April 1965): 173.

62. Villard, *John Brown,* 455.

63. Green, "The Capture of John Brown."

VI. THE CAUSE HE LOVED SO MUCH

1. Sanborn, *The Life and Letters of John Brown,* 624.

2. Hinton, *John Brown and His Men,* 679.

3. *The Life, Trial and Execution of Captain John Brown, Known as "Old Brown of Ossawatomie," with a Full Account of the Attempted Insurrection at Harper's Ferry* (New York: Robert M. De Witt, 1859).

4. Ibid.

5. Ibid.

6. Finkelman, *His Soul Goes Marching On,* 41–66.

7. Trodd and Stauffer, *Meteor of War,* 135.

8. Villard, *John Brown,* 487.

9. Reynolds, *John Brown, Abolitionist,* 349; Villard, *John Brown,* 485.

10. Thomas Fleming, "Verdicts of History III: The Trial of John Brown," *American Heritage* 18, no. 5 (August 1967).

11. *The Life, Trial and Execution of Captain John Brown.*

12. "The Virginia Excitement," *New York Times,* November 30, 1859.

13. Fleming, "Verdicts of History III."

14. Robert E. McGlone, "The 'Madness' of John Brown," *Civil War Times* 48, no. 5 (October 2009); Renehan, *The Secret Six,* 273.

15. *The Life, Trial and Execution of Captain John Brown.*

16. Sanborn, *The Life and Letters of John Brown,* 576.

17. Redpath, *The Public Life of Capt. John Brown,* 372, 387.

18. Sanborn, *The Life and Letters of John Brown,* 613; Redpath, *The Public Life of Capt. John Brown,* 357, 364, 378; Trodd and Stauffer, *Meteor of War,* 102.

19. Villard, *John Brown,* 164.

20. Redpath, *The Public Life of Capt. John Brown,* 390; "The Interview between Brown and His Wife— Incidents of the Execution," *New York Times,* December 3, 1859.

21. "Execution of John Brown," *New York Times,* December 3, 1859; Villard, *John Brown,* 554.

22. Villard, *John Brown,* 555.

23. Reynolds, *John Brown, Abolitionist,* 397.

24. John Bowers, *Stonewall Jackson: Portrait of a Soldier* (New York: William Morrow, 1989), 92; Redpath, *The Public Life of Capt. John Brown,* 391–92.

25. Bowers, *Stonewall Jackson,* 92.

26. Villard, *John Brown,* 557.

27. Sherwin, *Prophet of Liberty,* 407–8.

28. Hinton, *John Brown and His Men,* 269; Freeman, *Robert E. Lee,* 1:401.

29. Harlow, "Gerrit Smith and the John Brown Raid," 50–52; "Gerrit Smith: Harper's Ferry and the Aftermath," New York History Net, http://nyhistory.com/gerritsmith/harpers.htm; Oates, *To Purge This Land with Blood,* 313; Reynolds, *John Brown, Abolitionist,* 341–42.

30. Villard, *John Brown,* 532.

31. Reynolds, *John Brown, Abolitionist,* 5.

32. Oates, *To Purge This Land with Blood,* 315.

33. Villard, *John Brown,* 533; Renehan, *The Secret Six,* 273–74.

34. Thoreau, *A Plea for Captain John Brown,* 1, 11, 18, 19; Finkelman, *His Soul Goes Marching On,* 324.

35. C. Vann Woodward, *The Burden of Southern History* (Baton Rouge: Louisiana State University Press, 1993), 56.

36. Finkelman, *His Soul Goes Marching On,* 305.

37. Potter, *The Impending Crisis,* 376; Redpath, *Echoes of Harper's Ferry,* 262; Renehan, *The Secret Six,* 38; Chowder, "The Father of American Terrorism," 144.

38. Stewart, *Holy Warriors,* 205; James Brewer Stewart, *Wendell Phillips: Liberty's Hero* (Baton Rouge: Louisiana State University Press, 1986), 218; John J. McDonald, "Emerson and John Brown," *New England Quarterly* 44, no. 3 (September 1971): 377–96, 386–87; Redpath, *Echoes of Harper's Ferry,* 177; Sherwin, *Prophet of Liberty,* 405; Finkelman, *His Soul Goes Marching On,* 215; Goldfield, *America Aflame,* 161.

39. William Lloyd Garrison, "John Brown and the Principle of Nonresistance," *Liberator,* December 16, 1859, http://teachingamericanhistory.org/library/index.asp?document–569.

40. Redpath, *Echoes of Harper's Ferry,* 81.

41. Ibid., 157; Richard O. Curry and Lawrence B. Goodheart, "Ambivalence, Ambiguity, and Contradiction: Garrisonian Abolitionists and Nonviolence," *Journal of Libertarian Studies* 6, no. 3 (Summer/Fall 1982): 221.

42. Finkelman, *His Soul Goes Marching on,* 50; Reynolds, *John Brown, Abolitionist,* 394; John Greenleaf Whittier, "Brown of Ossawatomie," *New York Independent,* December 22, 1859, http://chnm.gmu.edu/lostmuseum/lm/144.

43. Hazel Catherine Wolf, *On Freedom's Altar: The Martyr Complex in the Abolition Movement* (Madison: University of Wisconsin Press, 1952), 128–29.

44. Gary Alan Fine, "John Brown's Body: Elites, Heroic Embodiment, and the Legitimation of Political Violence," *Social Problems* 46, no. 2 (May 1999): 233; "Arrival of John Brown's Remains at Troy," *New York Times,* December 7, 1859; Mayer, *All on Fire,* 499; Abels, *Man on Fire,* 394–95.

45. "Address by J. Sella Martin," *Liberator,* December 9, 1859, http://chnm.gmu.edu/lostmuseum /lm/143.

VII. HIGH NOON FOR THE UNION

1. Villard, *John Brown,* 267.

2. Richard Wheeler, *A Rising Thunder: From Lincoln's Election to the Battle of Bull Run; An Eyewitness History* (New York: HarperCollins, 1994), 10–11.

3. Quarles, *Allies for Freedom,* 107, 160; Reynolds, *John Brown, Abolitionist,* 434.

4. Reynolds, *John Brown, Abolitionist,* 418.

5. Woodward, *The Burden of Southern History,* 65; Reynolds, *John Brown, Abolitionist,* 426–27.

6. Finkelman, *His Soul Goes Marching On,* 309.

7. James M. McPherson, *What They Fought For, 1861–1865* (New York: Anchor Books, 1995), 48.

8. Steven A. Channing, *Crisis of Fear: Secession in South Carolina* (New York: Simon & Schuster, 1970), 19, 22; Potter, *The Impending Crisis,* 382.

9. Egerton, *Year of Meteors,* 16.

10. Basler, *The Collected Works of Abraham Lincoln,* 7:281.

11. Louis Austin Warren, *The Slavery Atmosphere of Lincoln's Youth* (Fort Wayne, IN: Lincolniana Publishers, 1933).

12. Basler, *The Collected Works of Abraham Lincoln,* 1:260.

13. Ibid., 4:240.

14. Ibid., 1:75.

15. Allen C. Guelzo, "Lincoln and the Abolitionists," *Wilson Quarterly* 8, no. 4 (Autumn 2000): 70; Michael Burlingame, *Abraham Lincoln: A Life,* 2 vols. (Baltimore: Johns Hopkins University Press, 2008), 1:125; Basler, *The Collected Works of Abraham Lincoln,* 2:130.

16. Basler, *The Collected Works of Abraham Lincoln,* 3:541.

17. Ibid., 2:405.

18. William Lee Miller, *President Lincoln: The Duty of a Statesman* (New York: Alfred A. Knopf, 2008), 296; Lerone Bennett Jr., *Forced into Glory: Abraham Lincoln's White Dream* (Chicago: Johnson Publishing, 2000), 94, 107.

19. Burlingame, *Abraham Lincoln,* 1:250–52.

20. Sherwin, *Prophet of Liberty,* 312; Basler, *The Collected Works of Abraham Lincoln,* 3:235, 487.

21. Basler, *The Collected Works of Abraham Lincoln,* 3:276.

22. Hinton, *John Brown and His Men,* 681–82.

23. James M. McPherson, *Battle Cry of Freedom: The Civil War Era* (New York: Oxford University Press, 1988), 220; Fergus M. Bordewich, "John Brown's Day of Reckoning," *Smithsonian,* October 2009, 63.

24. Sherwin, *Prophet of Liberty,* 416–17; "Black Republican Argument," *Pennsylvania Statesman,* October 20, 1860, http://elections.harpweek.com/1860/cartoon-1860-Medium .asp?UniqueID=14&Year=1860.

25. James M. McPherson, *The Struggle for Equality: Abolitionists and the Negro in the Civil War and Reconstruction* (Princeton, NJ: Princeton University Press, 1964), 17, 25.

26. Basler, *The Collected Works of Abraham Lincoln,* 3:145–46.

27. Korngold, *Two Friends of Man,* 269–70; Guelzo, "Lincoln and the Abolitionists," 68.

28. McPherson, *Ordeal by Fire,* 125; McPherson, *Battle Cry of Freedom,* 223.

29. "The Terrors of Submission," *Charleston (SC) Mercury,* October 11, 1860, http://civilwarcauses.org /mercury.htm.

30. Burlingame, *Abraham Lincoln,* 1:631; Finkelman, *His Soul Goes Marching On,* 237; Vicki Smith, Associated Press, "John Brown's Legacy Hasn't Changed, but America Has, Some Historians Say," *Columbia Missourian,* June 17, 2009; Trodd and Stauffer, *Meteor of War,* 260; Channing, *Crisis of Fear,* 287.

31. Basler, *The Collected Works of Abraham Lincoln,* 4:183.

32. Goodheart, "A Capital under Slavery's Shadow."

33. Basler, *The Collected Works of Abraham Lincoln,* 4:262–71.

34. "The Declaration of War," *Richmond (VA) Enquirer,* March 5, 1861.

35. Korngold, *Two Friends of Man,* 272; McPherson, *The Struggle for Equality,* 33.

36. Bartlett, *Wendell Phillips,* 232; Carl Sandburg, *Abraham Lincoln: The Prairie Years,* 2 vols. (New York: Harcourt, Brace, 1926), 2:380; "The Unholy Alliance: The Abolitionists Giving the Right Hand of Fellowship to the Disunionists. Wendell Phillips on Secession. Wendell Phillips' Address," *New York Times,* January 22, 1861.

37. "The Unholy Alliance"; Korngold, *Two Friends of Man,* 279–80; Gordon, *Slavery in the Arab World,* 50–51.

38. McPherson, *The Struggle for Equality,* 46.

39. James M. McPherson, *For Cause and Comrades: Why Men Fought in the Civil War* (New York: Oxford University Press, 1997), 16; Allan Nevins, *The War for the Union,* 4 vols. (New York: Charles Scribner's Sons, 1959–1971), 1:88.

40. Quarles, *Allies for Freedom,* 166–68.

41. George Templeton Strong, *Diary of the Civil War, 1860–1865,* ed. Allan Nevins (New York: Macmillan, 1952), 120.

42. Abels, *Man on Fire,* 391.

43. Wendell Phillips, "The War and Our Leaders," *New York Times,* August 16, 1862.

44. Basler, *The Collected Works of Abraham Lincoln,* 4:426, 438.

45. Ibid., 6:410.

46. Ibid., 5:537.

47. James M. McPherson, "'For a Vast Future Also': Lincoln and the Millennium," (Jefferson Lecture, National Endowment for the Humanities, Washington, DC, March 27, 2000), www.neh.gov/about /awards/jefferson-lecture/james-mcpherson-lecture.

48. McPherson, *For Cause and Comrades,* 19, 111; McPherson, *What They Fought For,* 28.

49. McPherson, *What They Fought For,* 29, 30; McPherson, *For Cause and Comrades,* 113.

50. Goldfield, *America Aflame,* 213; Margaret E. Wagner, Gary W. Gallagher, and Paul Finkelman, eds., *The Library of Congress Civil War Desk Reference* (New York: Simon & Schuster, 2002), 666–67; E. B. Long, *The Civil War Day by Day: An Almanac, 1861–1865* (Garden City, NY: Doubleday, 1971), 702.

51. McPherson, *For Cause and Comrades,* 96–97.

52. Goldfield, *America Aflame,* 208; McPherson, *What They Fought For,* 48.

53. McPherson, *What They Fought For,* 50.

54. Fehrenbacher, *The Slaveholding Republic,* 306.

55. Alexander H. Stephens, "'Corner Stone' Speech," March 21, 1861, http://teachingamericanhistory .org/library/document/cornerstone-speech/.

VIII. WIPED OUT IN BLOOD

1. Sherwin, *Prophet of Liberty,* 259, 268.

2. Frederick Douglass, "Notes on the War," in *Frederick Douglass: Selected Speeches and Writings,* 455.

3. E. Merton Coulter, *The Confederate States of America, 1861–1865,* vol. 7 of *A History of the South* (Baton Rouge: Louisiana State University Press, 1950), 258–59.

4. Channing, *Crisis of Fear,* 39–40; Thomas Wentworth Higginson, *Army Life in a Black Regiment* (New York: Riverside Press, 1900; first published 1870), diary notations December 5 and 16, 1862.

5. Armstead L. Robinson, "In the Shadow of Old John Brown: Insurrection Anxiety and Confederate Mobilization, 1861–1863," *Journal of Negro History* 65, no. 4 (Autumn 1980): 286, 289.

6. Drew Gilpin Faust, "Altars of Sacrifice: Confederate Women and the Narratives of War," *Journal of American History* 76, no. 4 (March 1990): 1213; Robinson, "In the Shadow of Old John Brown," 283–84.

7. Chandra Manning, *What This Cruel War Was Over: Soldiers, Slavery, and the Civil War* (New York: Alfred A. Knopf, 2007), 48.

8. Bell Irvin Wiley, "Billy Yank and the Black Folk," *Journal of Negro History* 36, no. 1 (January 1951): 41–42.

9. Manning, *What This Cruel War Was Over,* 49; McPherson, *For Cause and Comrades,* 19.

10. McPherson, *What They Fought For,* 57.

11. Reynolds, *John Brown, Abolitionist,* 471; McPherson, *The Struggle for Equality,* 108–9.

12. Basler, *The Collected Works of Abraham Lincoln,* 7:282.

13. Burlingame, *Abraham Lincoln,* 2:397; Korngold, *Two Friends of Man,* 301.

14. Basler, *The Collected Works of Abraham Lincoln,* 6:428–29.

15. Margaret Sanborn, *Robert E. Lee,* 2 vols. (Philadelphia: J. B. Lippincott, 1966–1967), 1:302.

16. Goldfield, *America Aflame,* 253.

17. Allen C. Guelzo, *Lincoln's Emancipation Proclamation: The End of Slavery in America* (New York: Simon & Schuster, 2004), 112.

18. James Oakes, *The Radical and the Republican: Frederick Douglass, Abraham Lincoln, and the Triumph of Antislavery Politics* (New York: W. W. Norton, 2007), 193–94.

19. Basler, *The Collected Works of Abraham Lincoln,* 5:371, 372.

20. Frederick Douglass, "The President and His Speeches," *Douglass' Monthly,* September 1862, in *Frederick Douglass: Selected Speeches and Writings,* 510–13.

21. Basler, *The Collected Works of Abraham Lincoln,* 5:388–89.

22. Goldfield, *America Aflame,* 262.

23. Basler, *The Collected Works of Abraham Lincoln,* 5:336–37.

24. Guelzo, *Lincoln's Emancipation Proclamation,* 161.

25. Ibid., 182–83.

26. Stephen B. Oates, *With Malice Toward None: A Life of Abraham Lincoln* (New York: Harper Perennial, 2011), 333; Sherwin, *Prophet of Liberty* (Bookman Associates, 1958), 473.

27. Sherwin, *Prophet of Liberty,* 473.

28. Mayer, *All on Fire,* 546; "Grand Emancipation Jubilee," *New York Times,* January 1, 1863.

29. James M. McPherson, *Marching toward Freedom: Blacks in the Civil War, 1861–1865* (New York: Facts on File, 1991), 30.

30. Manning, *What This Cruel War Was Over,* 89.

31. Guelzo, *Lincoln's Emancipation Proclamation,* 214.

32. Jim Downs, *Sick from Freedom: African-American Illness and Suffering During the Civil War and Reconstruction* (New York: Oxford University Press, 2012), 22.

33. Ibid., 162, 27.

34. McPherson, *Marching toward Freedom,* 6.

35. Frederick Douglass, "Address for the Promotion of Colored Enlistments," *Douglass' Monthly,* August 1863, in *Frederick Douglass: Selected Speeches and Writings,* 536; James M. McPherson, *Abraham Lincoln and the Second American Revolution* (New York: Oxford University Press, 1991), 139.

36. Basler, *The Collected Works of Abraham Lincoln,* 5:423.

37. Douglass, *Autobiographies,* 786, 796–97.

38. McPherson, *Marching toward Freedom,* 42–43.

39. Guelzo, *Lincoln's Emancipation Proclamation,* 219.

40. "United States Colored Troops in the Civil War," Lest We Forget, www.coax.net/people/ewf/data .htm; Reynolds, *John Brown, Abolitionist,* 490.

41. Basler, *The Collected Works of Abraham Lincoln,* 6:357.

42. Drew Gilpin Faust, *This Republic of Suffering: Death and the American Civil War* (New York: Alfred A. Knopf, 2008), 45.

43. W. L. Miller, *President Lincoln,* 309–12; William Wells Brown, "The Massacre at Fort Pillow," in *The Negro in the American Rebellion: His Heroism and His Fidelity* (Boston: Lee & Shepard, 1867), www.coax.net/people/1wf/CW_FP.HTM; Andrew Ward, *River Run Red: The Fort Pillow Massacre in the American Civil War* (New York: Viking, 2005), 200–269.

44. W. L. Miller, *President Lincoln,* 310–11.

45. McPherson, *Marching toward Freedom,* 85.

46. Frederick Douglass, "How to End the War," *Douglass' Monthly,* May 1861, in *Frederick Douglass: Selected Speeches and Writings,* 448.

47. Ulysses S. Grant, *Memoirs and Selected Letters* (New York: Library of America, 1990), 18.

48. Joseph T. Glatthaar, *Forged in Battle: The Civil War Alliance of Black Soldiers and White Officers* (New York: Free Press, 1990), 135.

49. Reynolds, *John Brown, Abolitionist,* 490.

50. Robert W. Allen, "Say, Brother, Who Wrote This Melody?," www.trans-video.net/~rwillisa /SayBrother.htm.

51. McGlone, *John Brown's War against Slavery,* 328.

52. McPherson, *Marching toward Freedom,* 44–45.

53. Guelzo, *Lincoln's Emancipation Proclamation,* 217; Harvey Wish, "Slave Disloyalty under the Confederacy," *Journal of Negro History* 23, no. 4 (October 1938): 447.

54. Lloyd Lewis, *Sherman: Fighting Prophet* (New York: Harcourt, Brace, 1958), 439; Goldfield, *America Aflame,* 349.

55. Quarles, *Allies for Freedom,* 161–63; Bruce Levine, *Half Slave and Half Free: The Roots of Civil War* (New York: Hill & Wang, 1992), 103.

56. Fehrenbacher, *The Slaveholding Republic,* 321.

57. Basler, *The Collected Works of Abraham Lincoln,* 8:333.

58. Ibid., 333.

59. Strong, *Diary of the Civil War,* 529.

60. McPherson, *Battle Cry of Freedom,* 778.

61. Burke Davis, *To Appomattox: Nine April Days, 1865* (New York: Rinehart, 1959), 132–37; Philip Van Doren Stern, *An End to Valor: The Last Days of the Civil War* (New York: Bonanza Books, 1958), 187.

62. David Dixon Porter, *Incidents and Anecdotes of the Civil War* (New York: D. Appleton, 1885), 195.

63. Ibid., 195, 300–1.

64. Trodd and Stauffer, *Meteor of War,* 252.

65. Quarles, *Allies for Freedom,* 169.

66. Frederick Douglass, "Oration in Memory of Abraham Lincoln," in *Frederick Douglass: Selected Speeches and Writings,* 618.

67. Ibid., 621.

68. Frederick Douglass, "John Brown, Speech delivered . . . May 30, 1881," in *Frederick Douglass: Selected Speeches and Writings,* 636.

69. Ibid., 648.

IX. LEGACY

1. George Breitman, ed., *Malcolm X Speaks: Selected Speeches and Statements* (New York: Grove Press, 1965), 224–25.

2. Zoe Trodd, "Writ in Blood: John Brown's Charter of Humanity, the Tribunal of History, and the Thick Link of American Political Protest," *Journal for the Study of Radicalism* 1, no. 1 (2007): 16.

3. H. Rap Brown, *Die Nigger Die!* (New York: Dial, 1969), 116; Eldridge Cleaver, *Soul on Ice* (New York: McGraw Hill, 1968), 82–83.

4. Chowder, "The Father of American Terrorism," 91.

5. Trodd and Stauffer, *Meteor of War*, 269; Chowder, "Father of American Terrorism."

6. "Al Qaeda's Fatwa," http://www.pbs/org/newshour/terrorism/international/fatwa_1998.html; "Contemporary Islamist Ideology Authorizing Genocidal Murder," The Middle East Research Institute, Special Report No. 25, January 2, 2004, http://www.memri.org/bin/printerfriendly/pf.cgi.

7. Quarles, *Allies for Freedom,* 139.

Further Reading

BOOKS

Abels, Jules. *Man On Fire: John Brown and the Cause of Liberty.* New York: Macmillan, 1971.

Aptheker, Herbert. *Abolitionism: A Revolutionary Movement.* Boston: Twayne, 1989.

———, ed. *A Documentary History of the Negro People in the United States.* Vol. 1, *From Colonial Times through the Civil War.* New York: Citadel Press, 1951.

Blassingame, John W., ed. *Slave Testimony: Two Centuries of Letters, Speeches, Interviews, and Autobiographies.* Baton Rouge: Louisiana State University Press, 1977.

Boyer, Richard O. *The Legend of John Brown: A Biography and a History.* New York: Alfred A. Knopf, 1973.

Burlingame, Michael. *Abraham Lincoln: A Life.* 2 vols. Baltimore: Johns Hopkins University Press, 2008.

Carton, Evan. *Patriotic Treason: John Brown and the Soul of America.* New York: Free Press, 2006.

Davidson, Basil. *The African Slave Trade.* Boston: Little, Brown, 1980.

Davis, David Brion. *Inhuman Bondage: The Rise and Fall of Slavery in the New World.* New York: Oxford University Press, 2006.

———. *The Problem of Slavery in Western Culture.* Ithaca, NY: Cornell University Press, 1966.

Douglass, Frederick. *Autobiographies.* New York: Library of America, 1994. First published 1845, 1855, 1893.

———. *Frederick Douglass: Selected Speeches and Writings.* Edited by Philip S. Foner. Abridged and adapted by Yuval Taylor. Chicago: Lawrence Hill Books, 1999.

Equiano, Olaudah. *The Interesting Narrative of the Life of Olaudah Equiano, Written by Himself.* New York: St. Martin's Press, 1994. First published 1789 in London.

Fehrenbacher, Don E. *The Slaveholding Republic: An Account of the United States Government's Relations to Slavery.* New York: Oxford University Press, 2001.

Finkelman, Paul, ed. *His Soul Goes Marching On: Responses to John Brown and the Harpers Ferry Raid.* Charlottesville: University of Virginia Press, 1995.

Foner, Eric. *The Fiery Trial: Abraham Lincoln and American Slavery.* New York: W. W. Norton, 2010.

Franklin, John Hope, and Loren Schweninger. *Runaway Slaves: Rebels on the Plantation.* New York: Oxford University Press, 1999.

Fredrickson, George M. *The Black Image in the White Mind: The Debate on Afro-American Character and Destiny, 1817–1914.* Middletown, CT: Wesleyan University Press, 1987.

Goldfield, David. *America Aflame: How the Civil War Created a Nation.* New York: Bloomsbury Press, 2011.

Goldstone, Lawrence. *Dark Bargain: Slavery, Profits, and the Struggle for the Constitution.* New York: Walker, 2005.

Goodrich, Thomas. *War to the Knife: Bleeding Kansas, 1854–1861.* Mechanicsburg, PA: Stackpole Books, 1998.

Greene, Lorenzo Johnston. *The Negro in Colonial New England, 1620–1776.* New York: Columbia University Press, 1942.

Guelzo, Allen C. *Abraham Lincoln: Redeemer President.* Grand Rapids, MI: William B. Eerdmans, 1999.

———. *Lincoln's Emancipation Proclamation: The End of Slavery in America.* New York: Simon & Schuster, 2004.

Hinton, Richard J. *John Brown and His Men, with Some Account of the Roads They Traveled to Reach Harper's Ferry.* Rev. ed. New York: Funk & Wagnalls, 1894. books.google.com /books?id=uiaYWp66b-cC.

Jordan, Winthrop D. *White over Black: American Attitudes Toward the Negro, 1550–1812.* Chapel Hill: University of North Carolina Press, 1968.

Korngold, Ralph. *Two Friends of Man: The Story of William Lloyd Garrison and Wendell Phillips and Their Relationship with Abraham Lincoln.* Boston: Little, Brown, 1950.

Lester, Julius. *To Be a Slave.* New York: Dial Press, 1968.

The Life, Trial and Execution of Captain John Brown, Known as "Old Brown of Ossawatomie," with a Full Account of the Attempted Insurrection at Harper's Ferry. New York: Robert M. De Witt, 1859. avalon.law.yale.edu/19th_century/john_brown.asp.

Maier, Pauline. *American Scripture: Making the Declaration of Independence.* New York: Alfred A. Knopf, 1997.

Manning, Chandra. *What This Cruel War Was Over: Soldiers, Slavery, and the Civil War.* New York: Alfred A. Knopf, 2007.

Mayer, Henry. *All on Fire: William Lloyd Garrison and the Abolition of Slavery.* New York: St. Martin's Press, 1998.

McFeely, William S. *Frederick Douglass.* New York: W. W. Norton, 1991.

McGlone, Robert E. *John Brown's War against Slavery.* New York: Cambridge University Press, 2009.

McKitrick, Eric L., ed. *Slavery Defended: The Views of the Old South.* Englewood Cliffs, NJ: Prentice-Hall, 1963.

McPherson, James M. *Abraham Lincoln and the Second American Revolution.* New York: Oxford University Press, 1991.

———. *Battle Cry of Freedom: The Civil War Era.* New York: Oxford University Press, 1988.

———. *For Cause and Comrades: Why Men Fought in the Civil War.* New York: Oxford University Press, 1997.

———. *Marching toward Freedom: Blacks in the Civil War, 1861–1865.* New York: Facts on File, 1991.

———. *Ordeal by Fire: The Civil War and Reconstruction.* New York: Alfred A. Knopf, 1982.

———. *The Struggle for Equality: Abolitionists and the Negro in the Civil War and Reconstruction.* Princeton, NJ: Princeton University Press, 1964.

———. *What They Fought For, 1861–1865.* New York: Anchor Books, 1995.

Mellon, James, ed. *Bullwhip Days: The Slaves Remember.* New York: Weidenfeld & Nicolson, 1988.

Miller, William Lee. *President Lincoln: The Duty of a Statesman.* New York: Alfred A. Knopf, 2008.

Oates, Stephen B. *The Fires of Jubilee: Nat Turner's Fierce Rebellion.* New York: Harper & Row, 1975.

———. *To Purge This Land with Blood: A Biography of John Brown.* New York: Harper & Row, 1970.

Pope-Hennessy, James. *Sins of the Fathers: The Atlantic Slave Traders, 1441–1807.* Edison, NJ: Castle Books, 1967.

Quarles, Benjamin. *Allies for Freedom & Blacks on John Brown.* Boston: Da Capo Press, 2001.

———. *Lincoln and the Negro.* New York: Oxford University Press, 1962.

Rediker, Marcus. *The Slave Ship: A Human History.* New York: Viking, 1973.

Redpath, James. *The Public Life of Capt. John Brown.* Boston: Thayer and Eldridge, 1860. books.google.com/books?id=dO8DAAAAYAAJ.

Renehan, Edward J., Jr., *The Secret Six: The True Tale of the Men Who Conspired with John Brown.* New York: Crown Publishers, 1995.

Reynolds, David S. *John Brown, Abolitionist: The Man Who Killed Slavery, Sparked the Civil War, and Seeded Civil Rights.* New York: Alfred A. Knopf, 2005.

Rodriguez, Junius P., ed. *The Historical Encyclopedia of World Slavery.* 2 vols. Santa Barbara, CA: ABC-CLIO, 1997.

Ruchames, Louis, ed. *A John Brown Reader.* New York: Abelard-Schuman, 1959.

Sanborn, F. B., ed. *The Life and Letters of John Brown: Liberator of Kansas, and Martyr of Virginia.* 3rd ed. Concord, MA: F. B. Sanborn, 1910.

Segal, Ronald. *Islam's Black Slaves: The Other Black Diaspora.* New York: Farrar, Straus and Giroux, 2001.

Sherwin, Oscar. *Prophet of Liberty: The Life and Times of Wendell Phillips.* New York: Bookman Associates, 1958.

Stampp, Kenneth M. *The Peculiar Institution: Slavery in the Ante-bellum South.* New York: Alfred A. Knopf, 1956.

Stewart, James Brewer. *Holy Warriors: The Abolitionists and American Slavery.* New York: Hill & Wang, 1976.

Thomas, Hugh. *The Slave Trade: The Story of the Atlantic Slave Trade, 1440–1870.* New York: Simon & Schuster, 1997.

Trodd, Zoe, and John Stauffer, eds. *Meteor of War: The John Brown Story.* Maplecrest, NY: Brandywine Press, 2004.

Villard, Oswald Garrison. *John Brown, 1800–1859: A Biography Fifty Years After.* Gloucester, MA: Peter Smith, 1965. First published 1910.

Waldstreicher, David. *Slavery's Constitution: From Revolution to Ratification.* New York: Hill & Wang, 2009.

USEFUL INTERNET SITES

The Antislavery Literature Project. antislavery.eserver.org. Contains electronic versions of hundreds of antislavery writings, chiefly from the 1800s.

The Anti-Slavery Society. www.anti-slaverysociety.addr.com/index.htm. This original English society still fights slavery wherever it exists in the world.

The Atlantic Slave Trade and Slave Life in the Americas: A Visual Record. http://hitchcock.itc.virginia.edu/Slavery/index.php. A collection of pictures showing all aspects of the slave trade.

Born in Slavery: Slave Narratives from the Federal Writers' Project, 1936–1938. http://memory.loc.gov/ammem/snhtml/snhome.html. Firsthand accounts of slavery, from those who lived it.

Chronology on the History of Slavery and Racism. www.innercity.org/holt/slavechron.html. A year-by-year account relating key events in the history of American slavery.

Freedmen and Southern Society Project. www.history.umd.edu/Freedmen/. A major cache of documents hosted by the University of Maryland.

The *Liberator* Files. www.theliberatorfiles.com. Contains copies of articles from William Lloyd Garrison's newspaper.

National Underground Railroad Freedom Center. http://freedomcenter.org. A comprehensive site about people and places linked to the Underground Railroad.

North American Slave Narratives. http://docsouth.unc.edu/neh/index.html. A treasure trove of firsthand accounts by former slaves; also has hundreds of illustrations.

Schomburg Center for Research in Black Culture. www.nypl.org/locations/schomburg. A huge site dealing with all aspects of African American life, from slavery to today.

West Virginia Memory Project, John Brown/Boyd B. Stutler Collection Database. www.wvculture.org/history/wvmemory/imlsintro.html. An extensive collection of online copies of John Brown letters, photographs, and illustrations.

Image Credits

Index

Note: *Italic* page numbers refer to illustrations.